First World War
and Army of Occupation
War Diary
France, Belgium and Germany

16 DIVISION
Divisional Troops
Royal Army Medical Corps
113 Field Ambulance
1 February 1916 - 30 April 1919

WO95/1967/3

The Naval & Military Press Ltd
www.nmarchive.com
Published in association with The National Archives

Published by

The Naval & Military Press Ltd

Unit 10 Ridgewood Industrial Park,

Uckfield, East Sussex,

TN22 5QE England

Tel: +44 (0) 1825 749494

www.naval-military-press.com

www.nmarchive.com

This diary has been reprinted in facsimile from the original. Any imperfections are inevitably reproduced and the quality may fall short of modern type and cartographic standards.

© **Crown Copyright**
Images reproduced by permission of The National Archives, London, England, 2015.

Contents

Document type	Place/Title	Date From	Date To
Heading	WO95/1967. 16 Division Divisional Troops Feb 1916-Apr 1919 113 Field Ambulance		
Heading	16th Division 113th Fld Ambulance Feb 1916-1919 Apl		
Heading	113th Field Ambulance Vol I		
Heading	113th F.A. Vol I		
Heading	War Diary of 113th Field Ambulance from February 1st 1916 To February 29th 1916 (Volume I)		
War Diary	Haig Hutments	01/02/1916	16/02/1916
War Diary	Southampton	17/02/1916	17/02/1916
War Diary	Havre	18/02/1916	19/02/1916
War Diary	Rely	20/02/1916	25/02/1916
War Diary	Gonnehem	26/02/1916	29/02/1916
Heading	War Diary of 113th Field Ambulance from March 1st 1916 To March 31st 1916 (Volume 2)		
War Diary	Gonnehem	01/03/1916	08/03/1916
War Diary	Raimbert	09/03/1916	12/03/1916
War Diary	Auchel	13/03/1916	25/03/1916
War Diary	Noeux Les Mines	26/03/1916	31/03/1916
Heading	War Diary of 113th Field Ambulance from April 1st 1916 To April 30th 1916 (Volume 3)		
War Diary	Noeux Les Mines	01/04/1916	30/04/1916
Heading	War Diary of 113th Field Ambulance from May 1st 1916 To May 31st 1916 (Volume 4)		
War Diary	Noeux Les Mines	01/05/1916	31/05/1916
Heading	War Diary of 113th Field Ambulance from June 1st 1916 To June 30th 1916 (Volume 5)		
War Diary	Noeux Les Mines	01/06/1916	30/06/1916
Heading	16th Division 113th Field Ambulance July 1916		
Heading	War Diary 113th Field Amb. RAMC 1st. July 1916 to 31st. July 1916. Volume No. 8		
War Diary	Noeux Les Mines	01/07/1916	31/07/1916
Heading	War Diary. 113th Field Ambulance Month Of August, 1916 Volume. 7		
War Diary	Noeux Les Mines	01/08/1916	25/08/1916
War Diary	Auchel	26/08/1916	28/08/1916
War Diary	Fouqueruiel	29/08/1916	29/08/1916
War Diary	Sailly Le Sec	30/08/1916	30/08/1916
War Diary	Gibralter	31/08/1916	31/08/1916
Heading	War Diary 113th Field Ambulance. RAMC For Month Of September 1916. Volume 8		
War Diary	Gibralter	01/09/1916	05/09/1916
War Diary	Bronfay Farm	06/09/1916	08/09/1916
War Diary	Monteubam Choreh	24/09/1916	24/09/1916
War Diary	Happy Valley	10/09/1916	10/09/1916
War Diary	Sailly	11/09/1916	11/09/1916
War Diary	Sailly le Sec	12/09/1916	17/09/1916
War Diary	Doncq	18/09/1916	19/09/1916
War Diary	Pont. Remy	20/09/1916	20/09/1916
War Diary	Westoutre	21/09/1916	23/09/1916
War Diary	Locre	24/09/1916	30/09/1916

Heading	War Diary Month Of October, 1916. Volume 9 113th Field Ambulance R.A.M.C.		
War Diary	Locre	01/10/1916	31/10/1916
Heading	War Diary For Month Of November, 1916 Volume 10 113th. Field Ambulance R.A.M.C.		
War Diary	Locre	01/11/1916	30/11/1916
Heading	War Diary For Month Of December, 1916. Volume 11 RAMC 113th Field Ambulance		
War Diary	Locre	01/12/1916	31/12/1916
Heading	War Diary for month of January, 1917. Volume 12 RAMC 113th Field Ambulance		
War Diary	Locre	01/01/1917	31/01/1917
Heading	War Diary. For Month Of February, 1917. Volume 13. Unit. 113th Field Ambulance RAMC		
War Diary	Locri	01/02/1917	08/02/1917
War Diary	Locre	09/02/1917	28/02/1917
Heading	War Diary For Month Of March, 1917. Volume 14 Unit. 113th Field Ambulance RAMC		
War Diary	Locre	01/03/1917	31/03/1917
Heading	War Diary For Month Of April, 1917. Volume. 15 Unit. 113th Field Ambce RAMC		
War Diary	Locre	01/04/1917	30/04/1917
Heading	War Diary Volume 16 For Month Of May, 1917. Unit. RAMC 113th Fd Ambce		
War Diary	Locre	01/05/1917	31/05/1917
Heading	War Diary For Month Of June, 1917. Volume 17 Unit RAMC 113th Field Ambulance		
Miscellaneous	Summary Of Medical War Diaries Of 113th F.A. 16th Div.	22/06/1917	22/06/1917
Miscellaneous	113th F.A. 16th Div. 8th Corps. 5th Army.		
Miscellaneous	Summary Of Medical War Diaries Of 113th F.A. 16th Div.	22/06/1917	22/06/1917
Miscellaneous	113th F.A. 16th Div. 8th Corps. 5th Army.	22/06/1917	22/06/1917
War Diary	Locre	01/06/1917	12/06/1917
War Diary	Ref 27 W 27 d 6.8	13/06/1917	16/06/1917
War Diary	Woborn Camp	17/06/1917	18/06/1917
War Diary	1 W 27 d 6.8	19/06/1917	19/06/1917
War Diary	Q 19 C 26	20/06/1917	21/06/1917
War Diary	Broxele	22/06/1917	30/06/1917
Heading	War Diary For Month Of July, 1917. Volume. 18. Unit. 113th Field Ambulance RAMC		
Heading	War Diary of 113th Field Ambulance from July 1st 1917 To July 31st 1917 (Volume 18)		
Miscellaneous	Summary Of Medical War Diaries Of 113th F.A. 16th Div.	22/08/1917	22/08/1917
Miscellaneous	113th F.A. 16th Div. 8th Corps. 5th Army.	22/08/1917	22/08/1917
Miscellaneous	113th F.A. 16th Div. 19th Corps. 5th Army	22/08/1917	22/08/1917
Miscellaneous	113th F.A. 16th Div. 8th Corps. 5th Army.	22/08/1917	22/08/1917
Miscellaneous	113th F.A. 16th Div. 19th Corps. 5th Army.	22/08/1917	22/08/1917
War Diary	Broxeple	01/07/1917	08/07/1917
War Diary	Winnizeele	09/07/1917	24/07/1917
War Diary	Luna Park	25/07/1917	31/07/1917
Heading	War Diary. For Month Of August, 1917. Volume 19 Unit 113th Field Ambulance RAMC		
Heading	War Diary of 113th Field Ambulance From 1st August 1917 To 31st August 1917 (Volume 19)		

Type	Description	Start	End
Miscellaneous	Summary Of Medical War Diaries Of 113th F.A. 16th Div.	22/08/1917	22/08/1917
War Diary	Luna Park	01/08/1917	02/08/1917
War Diary	Brandhoek	03/08/1917	17/08/1917
War Diary	Watou	18/08/1917	22/08/1917
War Diary	Achiet le Garnd	23/08/1917	23/08/1917
War Diary	Lacouchie	26/08/1917	31/08/1917
Heading	War Diary. For Month Of September, 1917. Volume 20 Unit. RAMC 113th Field Ambulance		
Heading	War Diary of 113th Field Ambulance From Sept 1st 1917 To Sept 30th 1917 (Volume 20		
War Diary	La Couchie	01/09/1917	30/09/1917
Heading	War Diary For Month Of October, 1917. Unit 113th Fld Ambce RAMC Volume Number 21		
Heading	War Diary of 113th Field Ambulance From 1-10-17 To 31-10-17 (Volume 21)		
War Diary	La Couchie	01/10/1917	17/10/1917
War Diary	Sapignies	18/10/1917	31/10/1917
Heading	War Diary of 113th Field Ambulance from 1st November 1917 To 30th November 1917 (Volume 22)		
War Diary	Sapignies	01/11/1917	30/11/1917
Heading	War Diary For Month Of December, 1917. Volume 25 Unit. 113th Field Ambulance RAMC		
Heading	War Diary of 113th Field Ambulance from Dec 1st 1917 To Dec 1st 1917 (Volume 23)		
War Diary	Sapignies	01/12/1917	03/12/1917
War Diary	Barastre	04/12/1917	04/12/1917
War Diary	Tincourt	05/12/1917	06/12/1917
War Diary	V Faucon	07/12/1917	31/12/1917
Heading	War Diary For Month Of January 1918. Volume 24 Unit. 113th Fld Ambce RAMC		
Heading	War Diary of 113th Field Ambulance from Jan 1st 1918 To Jan 31st 1918 (Volume 24)		
War Diary	Villers Faucon	01/01/1918	14/01/1918
War Diary	V. Faucon	15/01/1918	31/01/1918
Heading	War Diary. For Month Of February, 1918. Volume. 25 Unit. 113th Field Ambulance RAMC		
Heading	War Diary of 113th Field Ambulance from Feby 1st 1918 To Feby 28th 1918 (Volume 25)		
War Diary	Villers Faucon	01/02/1918	13/02/1918
War Diary	V. Faucon	14/02/1918	28/02/1918
Heading	113th Field Ambulance March 1918		
Heading	War Diary of 113th Field Ambulance from 1st March 1918 To 31st March 1918 (Volume 26)		
War Diary	Villers Faucon	01/03/1918	20/03/1918
War Diary	Tincourt	21/03/1918	21/03/1918
War Diary	Doingt	22/03/1918	22/03/1918
War Diary	Near Biaches	23/03/1918	23/03/1918
War Diary	Near Cappy	24/03/1918	24/03/1918
War Diary	Querrieu	25/03/1918	25/03/1918
War Diary	X S.W. of Bois De Vaire	26/03/1918	26/03/1918
War Diary	Road Junction S. of Blangy Tronville	27/03/1918	27/03/1918
War Diary	S. of Blangy Tronville	28/03/1918	31/03/1918
Heading	War Diary of 113th Field Ambulance from April 1st 1918 To April 30th 1918 (Volume 27)		
War Diary	S.W. of Blangy Tronville	01/04/1918	02/04/1918

War Diary	Saleux	03/04/1918	04/04/1918
War Diary	Ercourt	05/04/1918	08/04/1918
War Diary	Meneslies	09/04/1918	10/04/1918
War Diary	Assinghem	11/04/1918	24/04/1918
War Diary	Blequin	25/04/1918	30/04/1918
Heading	War Diary of 113th Field Ambulance From 1/5/18 To 31/5/18 (Volume 28)		
War Diary	Blequin	01/05/1918	14/05/1918
War Diary	Menneville	15/05/1918	17/05/1918
War Diary	Niemburg	18/05/1918	31/05/1918
Heading	War Diary of 113 Field Ambulance. From 1st June 1918 To 30th June 1918 Volume 29		
War Diary	Niemburg	01/06/1918	30/06/1918
Heading	War Diary of 113 Field Ambulance. From 1st July 1918 To 31st July Volume 30		
War Diary	Niemburg	01/07/1918	05/07/1918
War Diary	Brevillers	06/07/1918	23/07/1918
War Diary	Saulty	24/07/1918	30/07/1918
War Diary	Warluzel	31/07/1918	31/07/1918
Heading	War Diary of 113 Field Ambulance. From 1st August 1918 To 31st August 1918 Volume 31		
War Diary	Warluzel	01/08/1918	17/08/1918
War Diary	Ligny-St. Flochel	18/08/1918	18/08/1918
War Diary	Ruitz	19/08/1918	31/08/1918
Heading	War Diary of 113 Field Ambulance from 1st September 1918 To 30th Sept 1918 Volume 32		
War Diary	Ruitz	01/09/1918	09/09/1918
War Diary	Barlin	10/09/1918	22/09/1918
War Diary	Vaudricourt	23/09/1918	30/09/1918
Miscellaneous	16th Division Medical Arrangements	09/09/1918	09/09/1918
Operation(al) Order(s)	16th. Division. R.A.M.C. Operation Order No. 28	22/09/1918	22/09/1918
Heading	113th F.A		
War Diary	Vaudricourt	01/10/1918	05/10/1918
War Diary	Cambrin	06/10/1918	16/10/1918
War Diary	Provin	17/10/1918	17/10/1918
War Diary	Camphin-En-Carembault	18/10/1918	18/10/1918
War Diary	Rumes	22/10/1918	31/10/1918
Heading	War Diary of 113 Field Ambulance 1 Nov. 1918-30 Nov. 1918 Volume 34		
War Diary	Rumes	01/11/1918	09/11/1918
War Diary	Antoing	10/11/1918	14/11/1918
War Diary	Elbail	15/11/1918	15/11/1918
War Diary	La Posterie	16/11/1918	16/11/1918
War Diary	Ardompretz	17/11/1918	18/11/1918
War Diary	Paradis	19/11/1918	30/11/1918
Operation(al) Order(s)	16th. Division R.A.M.C. Operation Order No. 32	09/11/1918	09/11/1918
Operation(al) Order(s) Miscellaneous	48th Infantry Brigade Order No. 44	14/11/1918	14/11/1918
Operation(al) Order(s) Miscellaneous	48th Infantry Brigade Order No. 45 Reference Brigade Order No. 45	15/11/1918	15/11/1918
Operation(al) Order(s) Miscellaneous	48th Infantry Brigade Order No. 46	16/11/1918	16/11/1918
Miscellaneous	No 113 Field Ambulance		
War Diary	Paradis	01/12/1918	11/12/1918
War Diary	Le Paradis	12/12/1918	31/12/1918

Miscellaneous	Amendment To 16th. Division Medical Arrangement No. S. 192/359	29/11/1918	29/11/1918
Miscellaneous	Amendment To 16th Division Medical Arrangements	22/11/1918	22/11/1918
Miscellaneous	A.D.M.S. 16th Div. No. S192/359/1	10/12/1918	10/12/1918
Heading	War Diary of 113th Field Ambulance from 1st January to 31st January 1919 Volume 36		
War Diary	Le Paradis	01/01/1919	31/01/1919
Miscellaneous	No. 113 Field Ambulance Feb. 1919		
War Diary	Le Paradis	01/02/1919	28/02/1919
Heading	War Diary 113 Field Ambulance From 1st March 1919 To 31st March 1919 Volume 38		
War Diary	Le Paradis	01/03/1919	31/03/1919
Heading	War Diary 113th Field Ambulance From 1st April 1919 To 30th April 1919 Volume 39		
War Diary	Le Paradis	01/04/1919	30/04/1919

(3)

WO 95/1964
16 Division
Headquarters Branches + Services
Divisional Troops.

Feb 1916 - Apr. 1919

113 FIELD AMBULANCE

16TH DIVISION

113TH FLD AMBULANCE
FEB 1916 - ~~DEC 1918~~
1919. APL

113th Field Ambulance
Vol I

February
March 1916
April 1916

Dec '18

113th F.A.
Vol: I

Confidential.

War Diary
of
113th Field Ambulance.

(Volume 1)

From February 1st 1916

To February 29th 1916

W.J. Bennett.
Major R.A.M.C
O/c 113th Field Ambulance

Army Form C. 2118.

WAR DIARY
or
INTELLIGENCE SUMMARY.
(Erase heading not required.)

Instructions regarding War Diaries and Intelligence Summaries are contained in F. S. Regs., Part II. and the Staff Manual respectively. Title pages will be prepared in manuscript.

Place	Date 1916	Hour	Summary of Events and Information	Remarks and references to Appendices
HAIG HUTMENTS	1st Oct	—	Mobilisation	
HAIG HUTMENTS	2nd "	—	Mobilisation proceeding. Instructions received to close accounts	G.T.V.
HAIG HUTMENTS	3rd "	—	Mobilisation proceeding	G.T.V.
HAIG HUTMENTS	4th "	—	Got work to be ready for preceding orders	G.T.V.
HAIG HUTMENTS	5th "	—	Mobilisation completed	G.T.V.
HAIG HUTMENTS	6th "	—	Section commanders drew gas Helmets & shrove parts of wagons from Q.M. Stores	B.T.V.
HAIG HUTMENTS	7th "	—	Corps Training	G.T.V.
HAIG HUTMENTS	2nd "	—		G.T.V.
HAIG HUTMENTS	9th "	—	Route March	G.T.V.
HAIG HUTMENTS	10th "	—	Field Day	G.T.V.
HAIG HUTMENTS	11th "	—	Field Ambulance Photograph taken	G.T.V.
HAIG HUTMENTS	12th "	—	About 30 MR. OS men receiving I.S.C. Meant Typhoid Vaccine	G.T.V.
HAIG HUTMENTS	13th "	—	Received orders for embarkation at Southampton. Final leave for personnel commenced	G.T.V.
HAIG HUTMENTS	14th "	—	Most of men on Final Leave	G.T.V.
HAIG HUTMENTS	15th "	—	Majority of personnel received 2nd I.S.C. Inns of Typhoid Vaccine	G.T.V.
HAIG HUTMENTS	16th "	—	8 wagon taken point preparation made for an departure on following morning	G.T.V.

Army Form C. 2118.

113th Field Ambulance WAR DIARY ~~of~~

INTELLIGENCE SUMMARY.

(Erase heading not required.)

Instructions regarding War Diaries and Intelligence Summaries are contained in F. S. Regs., Part II. and the Staff Manual respectively. Title pages will be prepared in manuscript.

Place	Date	Hour	Summary of Events and Information	Remarks and references to Appendices
	1916			
SOUTHAMPTON	19th Feb.	—	Departure from AlGHUTMENTS in two parties, 1st at 4.30 a.m, 2nd at 5.30 a.m	
			Entrained at FARNBOROUGH at 7.45 a.m. & 8.45 a.m. respectively	
			Arrived at SOUTHAMPTON at 9.30 a.m. & 10.30 a.m. respectively	
			Embarked ~~at immediately~~ on arrival on S.S. COURTFIELD	G.T.V.
HAVRE	16th "	—	Disembarked at 10.30 a.m. after a delay at the docks, we proceeded by march to Rest Camp No. 1	G.T.V.
~~BILLEY~~	19th "	—	Departs from Rest Camp at 7 a.m. Entrained at point No. 3 at 12 noon	G.T.V.
RELY	20th "	—	Detrained at LILLERS. Marches on from there to RELY, approximately a distance of 7 miles. Billets taken in barn	G.T.V.
RELY	21st "	23rd hr	Received some of our motor Transport & A.S.C. attached. Bent orders to be in readiness to move.	G.T.V.
RELY	22nd "	19th hr	More extra N.C.O.s men and attached units marched by mess Vehicles	G.T.V.
RELY	23rd "	18th hr	Fresh orders for moving – Previous cancelled – Later these cancelled too.	G.T.V.
RELY	24th "	19th hr	One or two more men inoculated. Weather – frosty. Roads slippy & dangerous	G.T.V.
RELY	25th "	29th	Fresh Orders to move. Weather – frosty & more snow	G.T.V.
GONNEHEM	26th "	16th hr	Departed from RELY at 15.15 hrs. & proceeded by road to GONNEHEM arriving there at we 16 hr & a half hour Route: COTTES–BOURECQ–LILLERS–BASRIEUX–BUSNETTES. Weather – cold & frosty	G.T.V.

Army Form C. 2118.

113th Field Ambulance

WAR DIARY
INTELLIGENCE SUMMARY.
(Erase heading not required.)

Instructions regarding War Diaries and Intelligence Summaries are contained in F.S. Regs., Part II. and the Staff Manual respectively. Title pages will be prepared in manuscript.

Place	Date	Hour	Summary of Events and Information	Remarks and references to Appendices
	1916 February			
GONNEHEM	27th	18th hr	Hosp Hospital opened; + nine patients admitted	E.T.V.
GONNEHEM	28th	12th "	Had a visit from our A.D.M.S. 4 more cases admitted to Hospital.	E.T.V.
GONNEHEM	29th	12th "	Another admission to Hospital. Weather - a good deal milder.	E.T.V.

113 F. Amb.
Vol 2

38th Div

Confidential.

War Diary.
of.
113th Field Ambulance

From March 1st 1916 to March 31st 1916.

(Volume 2.)

March 1916

COMMITTEE FOR THE
MEDICAL HISTORY OF THE WAR
Date 9 — JUN. 1916

Major Rawe
o/c 113 F.A.

#1 1/3rd Field Ambulance.

WAR DIARY
or
INTELLIGENCE SUMMARY.
(Erase heading not required.)

Army Form C. 2118.

Instructions regarding War Diaries and Intelligence Summaries are contained in F. S. Regs., Part II. and the Staff Manual respectively. Title pages will be prepared in manuscript.

Place	Date	Hour	Summary of Events and Information	Remarks and references to Appendices
	1916 March			
GONNEHEM	1st	19R	Collected sick from Brigade. Fatigue with duties as usual.	G.T.V.
GONNEHEM	2nd	19R	Collected sick from Brigade. Transferred some 8 patients to 51st Casualty Clearing Hospital	G.T.V.
GONNEHEM	3rd	19R	Collected sick from Brigade. In the afternoon the N.Z.O. Men were issued with waterproof coats; trousers off. Weather - windy, rainy.	G.T.V.
GONNEHEM	4th	19R	Two stretchers to be Hospital in the afternoon	G.T.V.
GONNEHEM	5th	15R	24 "B" Sector FR sent 10 clerks from "A" section, then duties starting at	G.T.V.
		9 a.m.	Church Parade at 9 a.m. Roads very wet.	G.T.V.
GONNEHEM	6th	15R	Waited having Roads very wet. Work in tropical epidemics as usual.	G.T.V.
GONNEHEM	7th	22ND	Orders received for preparing to move to the Back area. 3 C.O. along with	G.T.V.
			2 medls. & billetting approach to collect billets at AUCHELLE. Roads soft.	
GONNEHEM	8th	2WR.	Received orders to move at 2 a.m. next day to RAIMBERT. Final arrangements made in our billets.	G.T.V.
RAIMBERT	9th	2.0R	Had very our packs everything ready by twelve. We started for RAIMBERT at just under to approach Isbergues & proceeded	
			via LENGLET, ALLOUAGNE, & LOZINGHEM. Roads not for melting snow	G.T.V.
RAIMBERT	10th, 19R	Our move was a very temporary. No place suitable preferable for the Hospital	
			Child's hosp. HE KILLERS - RAIMBERT - PERNES was made to Rest & it was to be kept clear for march of a Division.	G.T.V. Apps no.71 No. 35-2 G.T.V.

T2134. Wt. W708-776. 500000. 4/15. Sir J. C. & S.

5/ 113th Field Ambulance

Army Form C. 2118.

WAR DIARY
INTELLIGENCE SUMMARY.
(Erase heading not required.)

Instructions regarding War Diaries and Intelligence Summaries are contained in F. S. Regs., Part II. and the Staff Manual respectively. Title pages will be prepared in manuscript.

Place	Date	Hour	Summary of Events and Information	Remarks and references to Appendices
	1916 March			
RAIMBERT	11th	9A	"A" Section took over the billets at AUCHEL - force over 500 men battle train with clean underclothing	G.T.V.
RAIMBERT	12th	2P	"A" Section got its bath. Thoroughly cleaned up. O.C. received message moving to AUCHEL next day. "C" Section to take over Hospital.	G.T.V
AUCHEL	13th	2.30P	"A" section continued its bath. "C" section left RAIMBERT before light to take over Hospital "B" section the remainder of "A" moved in here at 11am. We bath, now 1250 men at force area. Water gas trench mules	G.T.V.
AUCHEL	14th	21	Took over War Diary from Capt. Van DER VIJVER as A.D.M.S. wishes diary to be kept up by O.C. Ambulance. A young civilian was treated today for injury to R. hand due to explosion of a rifle cartridge which he was tampering with. He had lost three fingers & thumb. His left eye is also badly damaged. As there does not appear to be any local hospital for such cases, I have asked to A.D.M.S. 16th Division in hospital & bath continued today. D.A.D.M.S. 16th Division enquired was & pointed out to him how much more work could be got out of the baths, if the Ambulance had complete control of them. At present control divided with	

Army Form C. 2118.

WAR DIARY
or
INTELLIGENCE SUMMARY.
(Erase heading not required.)

Instructions regarding War Diaries and Intelligence Summaries are contained in F. S. Regs., Part II. and the Staff Manual respectively. Title pages will be prepared in manuscript.

Place	Date	Hour	Summary of Events and Information	Remarks and references to Appendices
AOEHEL			entrail divided with 48th Inf Brigade. Result today both working half time. One Motor Ambulance damaged last night & sent to workshop for repair this morning. Damage caused by driver running into a post when he was out after dark for a patient. Motor Ambulance damaged today due to having a runaway driver nervous good & under a less hanging branch of a tree. Present position of ambulans on 1/40,000 map 36.B¹ is about as last return. U4 B.a.5. at Jaynes R'acke OO 113 9 A.m.b.	36.B 1/40,000 O 27 & 7-6
"	15th	21	No 2.3 C.C Station took over ground yesterday. Hospital infected by A.D.M.S. Baths almost idle. St Sayeur M.T taken from Ambulance to-day as wanted in work-shop. Returned last month. Going to A.Ich S 16th Division C.C.S	
"	16th	22	Received 16 bars /E.S. 111 4/D. Also copies from 49th Inf Brigade clothing Stores. Booklet Daily. Appointed L.A.A.2. Histing Se Sgt, with pay to conduct any establishment funding sanitation from Record. He was messing as B Section needs a good Se Sgt, to keep it of to the mark.	
"	17th	21	St Patricks Day. Gave ½ holiday to men. Hospital infected D D.M.S 1st Army	1/13
"	18th	21	Workshop Horse Inspection, animals on the whole better than last week.	

T2134. Wt. W708-778. 500000. 4/15. Sir J. C. & S.

Army Form C. 2118.

WAR DIARY
or
INTELLIGENCE SUMMARY.
(Erase heading not required.)

Instructions regarding War Diaries and Intelligence Summaries are contained in F. S. Regs., Part II. and the Staff Manual respectively. Title pages will be prepared in manuscript.

Place	Date	Hour	Summary of Events and Information	Remarks and references to Appendices
AUCHEL	18.		(cont) attended office of A.D.M.S. at 10 o/c & received orders of next move. Case of cholera removed from 15th A.S.P. this 2 p.m. in that unit this week. Sanitary Squad notified etc. etc.	
"	19.	21.30	Proceeded to NOEUX-LES-MINES & talked over with A.F.A. our proposed change of station with that unit. Then went to advanced dressing station at PHILOSOPHE so as to get some idea of the work carried on there. Visited our ambulance M.A.C. of & saw about 3 pair of battles for stretchers. Going out. Then saw the A.D.M.S. called at the Hospital & left a message that I was to see him tomorrow evg.	
"	20. 21-18		Saw A.D.M.S. this morning at his office. Reported result of my journey of yesterday. Got permission to send forward tomorrow two officers & 20 men as an advance party to learn the geography of the trenches in our area. I was on the mat (for allowing officers commanding sections to tell off trivial offences in their sections, also for allowing my A.M. in command to act as president of a Board of Enquiry which occisant to an ambulance the A.D.M.S. would not have my explanation	

WAR DIARY or INTELLIGENCE SUMMARY

Army Form C. 2118.

Place	Date	Hour	Summary of Events and Information	Remarks and references to Appendices
AOREL	20'	(cont)	(my Explanation) that I was treating the goings to find their feet. In future I am to tell off all cases myself & the President of all Boards. M.O. & N.S. 16ᵗʰ Division inspected Hosp. & Transport & seemed pleased, the brightened an otherwise disappointing day, w's P.S. One of Harry D Horses which had been ill for some time died yesterday. Vet verified Enteritis w's	
"	21ˢᵗ	21	Sent off an advance party who one ready, one officer & one man to L O O S tonight, so as to get a knowledge of the trenches & injured at first. One must know as to the Ambulance this afternoon who looked like [illegible] it & thought it best to transfer him at once to 23 C.C. Station so as to stop two more will probably be sent, 1.245- men were bathed at FOSSE 3 today & clean earlier issued w's	
"	22ⁿᵈ	20·30	Lt Damen 9 Manchester attached from Army to 12ᵗʰ Division as a Tiernobeneylexpter asking to that effect having been received from 16 Division at 23·06 on 21ˢᵗ. 1962 men bathed today at Divisional Bath line (FOSSE 3). 2/Lt Cole, S / 16 R.W.F. visited trenches today / is also Lt Col. Keable 2/Y & F Ambulance who is to relieve us has the Ambulance are for 2 Y visit he states ambulances not received at 7 A.m. & can it. Soon to get	
"	23	20·45	Sent off this morning two Ambulances (horsed) to 4ᵗʰ F.Amb. soon to get	

WAR DIARY
or
INTELLIGENCE SUMMARY.
(Erase heading not required.)

Army Form C. 2118.

Place	Date	Hour	Summary of Events and Information	Remarks and references to Appendices
AUCHEL	23rd (cont)	(To get)	Hammerstones to the lines we have to take over. Gates over from 31 D.C.S. 16" Division for next move at 19.30 today. Driver a party in 25" Rescue in 26". O.C. Sanitary Section 9 & A.D.M.S. 16th Division visited ambulance today. Am sending with detachment from A.D.M.S. 11th Division two of my men to point to the. D.A.D.M.S. Both today 12 V.C. cases.	
"	24"	21.30	Sent off remainder of C Sect. to open section of Dressing Station (Samwell). When we move on to relieve 31st from that quoted. By me on the 3/11 Send aviation & relieve the one side for the future of entry shown. Have arranged for B Section to take over hospital from 249 F.A. at Divoille. Received marching orders for Division for the 26" cats.	L. 1223. R. 13859.
"	25"	9.0	Advance party from 47 3.A. arrived to take over hospital & Castle Shannon. Orders for 113 F.A. to move at 8 a.m. for entraining point at 9.26. Saw my advance party off at 9 o'clock. Evacuated to 23 C.C.S. at 11.30 o'c. cats	
NOEUX les MINES	26"	21	Marched at 8.15 from AUCHEL & arrived at LAPUGNOY at 9.15 & marched him at half-past ten. Reached their own hospital Dressing Station at 11 o'clock. Reported to A.D.M.S. 16" Division position of same on appended map by 11.25.	363. L13 a 4.9

Army Form C. 2118.

WAR DIARY
or
INTELLIGENCE SUMMARY.
(Erase heading not required.)

Instructions regarding War Diaries and Intelligence Summaries are contained in F. S. Regs., Part II. and the Staff Manual respectively. Title pages will be prepared in manuscript.

Place	Date	Hour	Summary of Events and Information	Remarks and references to Appendices
NOEUX les MINES	27	23	Day spent in getting things into running order. At 18.45 O'c. accompanied by my O. Divisr. I visited my dressing station at PHILOSOPHE & Advanced dressing station at LOOS. Also the R.A. Post from which we clear nightly. 1st & 2nd & 3rd S. 16th Division & Chateau 29.iii B/L Brigade accompanied as. A/P/C returned down to here questing at 23 o'clock a/s.	36.c G.20.a.3. G.35.b.2.8.
"	28th	21	Four wounded evacuated today, two of these were accidentals, one self-inflicted accidental, the fourth a flesh wound. The self inflicted was transferred to Special Hospital for such cases. There was a fine day but cold, the ground is drying up rapidly.	
"	29th	21	Day A.D.M.S. 16th Division today inspected my Field Ambulance here, also the afternoon my Dressing Station (at PHILOSOPHE) he seemed pleased. I have arranged for a reserve of 50 rations to be kept at my Dressing Station which in town will supply the Advance Dressing station. Today had to reprimand L/Sgt. Brocklerell W.R.A.M.C. for having a dirty kitchen. Softweresses prevented him to be permanent mess of Corporal. He has gone with his section to my Dressing station. One y.s.w. admitted today was marked PHILOSOPHE by dressing station w/s	
"	30th	21-30	attended meeting of Divisional dressing staff today.	

T2134. Wt. W708—776. 500000. 4/15. Sir J. C. & S.

Army Form C. 2118.

WAR DIARY
or
INTELLIGENCE SUMMARY.
(Erase heading not required.)

Instructions regarding War Diaries and Intelligence Summaries are contained in F. S. Regs., Part II. and the Staff Manual respectively. Title pages will be prepared in manuscript.

Place	Date	Hour	Summary of Events and Information	Remarks and references to Appendices
NOEUX les MINES	31st	21-30	Visited General Lawrey BETHUNE this afternoon to settle up about clothing drawn by me for the 8th at AUCHEL. Visited advanced depot Medical Store & saw about Dewars (anti gas) which they are refitting a supply of. Also found that no cases are furnished by them for the administration of Oxygen. The Ambulance Hosp. was inspected this afternoon by L/O.C. 16th Division, also by D.D.M.S. 1st Army. One case of accidental self wound was transferred this day to find Hosp. BUSNES. Sto. Venner & Paine who were attached from Ambulance as a Temporary measure to 12th Division returned this evening. With reference to entry on 16th Re. No. 1174 Sgt. Jones today unable to ascertain for confirmation of this W.O. Promotion to S.E.Sgt. at Base. Signal will reach us as my orderly of that date. W.J.Bennett Major RAMC	

T2134. Wt. W708—776. 500000. 4/15. Sir J. C. & S.

1st Div. | 113 F Amb
Vol 3

Confidential

War Diary

of

113th Field Ambulance

April 1916.

From April 1st 1916.

to April 30th 1916

(Volume 3.)

COMMITTEE FOR THE
MEDICAL HISTORY OF THE WAR
Date 3 — 9 – JUN 1916

Lt-Col Rank
O/C 113 L Field Amb.

Army Form C. 2118.

WAR DIARY
or
INTELLIGENCE SUMMARY.
(Erase heading not required.)

Instructions regarding War Diaries and Intelligence Summaries are contained in F. S. Regs., Part II. and the Staff Manual respectively. Title pages will be prepared in manuscript.

Place	Date	Hour	Summary of Events and Information	Remarks and references to Appendices
NOEUX les MINES.	1/11/15	21-15	Sent off last month's diary by morning post. Weather now appears settled fine, enemy flare is getting quite busy. Getting our patch rapidly into order now. G.O.C. Duncan (?CM) wandered this morning again in the afternoon he visited us. Seven wounded today from our line, 1 by German at LOOS. Last night were fired on & had many wild (rifle & machine fire). Asked O.C. Evacuating station for a report on capabilities of LOOS as regards wounded & evacuation of same CWS.	
"	2"	23-45	Just returned from LOOS. The ADMS wished for a report on the state of the road between PHILOSOPHE & that place. Also on QUALITY STREET, & how medical arrangements there are run. In reply to the above from the Capt & Adj. & O.O.S., for my Ambulance to draw up in Church Street LOOS, instead of MARE O.R.D., I have ordered a place to be cleared for it at the Brewery station on MARE O.R.D., as that interferes with transport arrangements, which its stopping on the Rd. as stated to have caused, will be divided & the Ambulance will at the same time be more sheltered from Maroun fire than in Church Street. Sick, wounded, &c. Enemy fire fine than. LOES 12	robt 1 — 293 sick wounds 12
			Admission 3 — 1 Evacuations — LOES 12 — robt 1 — 293	

T2134. Wt. W708—776. 500000. 4/15. Sir J. C. & S.

WAR DIARY or INTELLIGENCE SUMMARY

Army Form C. 2118.

Place	Date	Hour	Summary of Events and Information	Remarks and references to Appendices
NOEUX les MINES	3	22.20	St Dunman with the remainder of C Section returned today from the missing Station at PHILOSOPHE, having been relieved by 22 Cavanagh & Stewart of A Section. Was informed that we will be inspected tomorrow at 10-15 by Lt/Col A. e. Cm. Sick Wounded Evacuation Received e.e.S Admissions 12 4 6 1 17 6	
"	4	21	Received report of straying of two of our Horses (O. Robert) from PHILOSOPHE. They were sighted by Cpl. J. Sky & recaught by (Lt. —) Brigade. Hughes. I sent 2 as there but found they had again broken bounds. Our infantry line to Lorraine in seen as he got their number. Cpl. Garnet looking in today to our hospital & since Received. Pt Davis ret. for duty. Received 3 horses from C.e. System. Admissions Sick 5 Wounded 1 Subg. Alarm. e.e.S Rest Camp Sub 5 Wounded 1 us Admitted 11. 1. 10 Evacuated Subg. Alarm 1	
"	5	21.10	Got No. 2 of Horses which were sent from PHILOSOPHE & reported same to Divisional Office. Pte would Saunders ear & drew a Lift Section in its pew arranged for a gun alarm for Ambulance. Wrestler again turned out at S. 25. B. nan turned. to Dutis 30 e.e.S No Ad Evak Admitted 3. 2 — cwp	
"	6th	21.20	Subsistence of orders Stores, gone Care of Charles today transferred to MALASSISE	

WAR DIARY
or
INTELLIGENCE SUMMARY.

(Erase heading not required.)

Army Form C. 2118.

Place	Date	Hour	Summary of Events and Information	Remarks and references to Appendices
NOEUX LES MINES	6th		The Hansard Car and Pte Bell of this Ambulance. Pte C.S. Eave and 8 R.A.M.C. sections constantly have been working. Received pair of "Dug Outs" at LOOS from St Pancras in addition to those we now have these comparative shelter for thirty one or so stretcher cases, & as many more sitters. We need a bar one put in order as the water question is solved. I have got the promise of a telephone for FORT GLATZ from Divisional Signalling Officer, this is now welcome as S always but equally amongst my commands to CRUCIFIX CORNER. Ambulance is S 9 b 3 to C 2 S w; & 7 yards WOH E. 3 hampton to 11 9 a 9 0 . S 9 b 3 to C 2 S w, to Ypres Hoof S	
"	7	21.30	Our two at N.G.S. have turned out one of grandeur. Brought back any contacts whom I had transferred to No 14 F A at VAUDRICORE. Black & S Corn now saw our Hospital today, was not pleased. Received the two names which we had referred immediately. Sir R. A. Luis Genl Can Division sent word to me today that I might extend 30/- on the Hospital from ests, etc he said admitted 14 6 evac. 1 13 2	
"	8"	21.10	Heavy bombardment of this place today, but little damage done about to BETHUNE this afternoon to look at something for the Hospital	

WAR DIARY or INTELLIGENCE SUMMARY

Army Form C. 2118.

Place	Date	Hour	Summary of Events and Information	Remarks and references to Appendices
NOEUX les MINES	8th (Sun)		Arranged today for Iron Plates 2'×3'×¼"-¼" to be fitted to the front of our cars for protection of drivers. Shall F/Lier Harness for that [illegible] in [illegible].	W3
"	9th	23	Sunday. Inspected my two cars in a Dressing Station, & found men washing well in both. Plates are much larger than any that we felt uncertain [illegible] R.Ste eeS HospFirst wounded No 44 Admitted to Hosp 8" sick w 19; Evacuated 5; young SW Rifles 8; SeeS Admitted 9" sick 2; Wounded 4; 1; 6. 2; 6.	W3
"	10th	21	This morning A.D.S. Instructed by G.O.C Division, I.D.M.S. Army G.A.S & Any Army G.A.D.S. By General satisfied with what anyone here done. Showed men the field. I.S. ? Army inspected the hospital beds. I was almost in I was getting the Curé estes what the General brought. One word in the Hospital. Admitted 9" 5; W4 3; Y Eva 21; W4 5; 3; W-Y; =	W3
"	11th	21	Two officers today attended lectures on gas at Army School. Day not [illegible] for work. Brought the Iron [illegible] in for Armour plates. See S Admitted 3; Y. Evacuated W-1, sick-8; wounded-10.	W3
"	12th	21-45	A wet day, & had to get much work done. Continued planing much more [illegible]. Admitted S; Y; Y, Evacuated to Rest Camp 1; - SeeS 3; Y.	

WAR DIARY
or
INTELLIGENCE SUMMARY.
(Erase heading not required.)

Army Form C. 2118.

Place	Date	Hour	Summary of Events and Information	Remarks and references to Appendices
NOEUX les MINES	13	21-16	This was a quiet day here, but my advanced dressing station PHILOSOPHE had a bad time. We had our first casualty today. Sgt Bedford A.S.C. was wounded slightly by a falling fragment of Anti Air craft shell (wounds of mouth at Duty). Divisional general inspected our Hospital agun today. I got a list from D.M.S. 1 Army. Admitted Sick 18; Wounded, Ernee, Duty 3; S-2; W4, S-4, W-4. Sg. Bomb.	
"	14	22-50	Another wet day. Admitted one officer for observation by order of A.D.M.S. This was a quiet day in my out station. Today the answering of ans. Paris was completed & sent it out on the "LOOS" man Phi O.G. being returned today from have seabacx Church for Staff Infw. e e s Admitted Sick 14; Wounded 9. Encanate S, W, 2 S.6 W.5. To Div. Y.pperettast disorder 1.	
"	15	21	Our A.D.M.S. was out to e.e.S. sick this day. A fine day & free of any noising. Yesterday had to send one of my officers (Lt Price) to take the place of quart Bomb School. Have also Pte St Benoit under observation. We are doing 20 German in place of St Paul to above duty & good his name in, but he was in LOOS, so had to get an above as meter even argent. Admitted 12 - 5 Evacuated to duty 3 - 1 Sealed 3. e.e.S 2,2 S.W. m, en Hos officer 1, Reese S, W, W.B	

WAR DIARY or INTELLIGENCE SUMMARY

Army Form C. 2118.

Place	Date	Hour	Summary of Events and Information	Remarks and references to Appendices
NOEUX les MINES	16	23.45	Made my weekly inspection of LOOS. Things there were quiet, but shelling had been bad. Evacuation Officer (Lt Banks) 2/3 C.C.S. sent report in car with Lieut. S. also reported on him to Headquarters	
"	17	21.20	Was afterwards asking A.D.M.S. for the Division thirty cars given rank of & Steve. I am glad to say I am still to take charge of Ambulance. Went to PHILOSOPHE this afternoon to see about fitting up shelter flats over our wards at the Dressing Station there & at LOOS. Shelling however is too severe to do anything. Have arranged however for plates which is possible to handle thus. Admissions 3 - VI 3 - A - 4 - Evac. today 2 - 4, 20 C.C.S. S. W. 1 - A, ORB	
"	18	22.05	This was another wet cold day, this was unfortunate as Army Commander had selected it for his inspection. He found the ground that we were at White Sepulchre also said something about Eye Dash. At the same time he said he was pleased & wish he had looked for the Ivy Bowes. I have decided to enlarge my depot at FORT GLATZ, LOOS. I have sent out tonight to plan it out. At present Station is not safe. We are also trying to enlarge our place at PHILOSOPHE. I wrote to Divisional A.P.M. today, that I was not satisfied with the behaviour	

T2134. Wt. W708—776. 500000. 4/15. Sir J. C. & S.

WAR DIARY
INTELLIGENCE SUMMARY

Place	Date	Hour	Summary of Events and Information	Remarks and references to Appendices
NOEUX les MINES	18th	Cont	of a civilian at PHILOSOPHE. He on investigation proved that the man was all right. Admitted H.2. Evacuated to duty S.W. 3. Pet Sergt. S.6. W.1. OR's	
"	19	21	A quiet day. Weather still very wet. Wrote a report on the Officers Ward & Bath for Potmin. Admitted 3, 3. Evacuated to duty 5-1-3. 30 O.R.s S/W Sealers 4-3. OR's	
"	20	93:45	This morning the D.A.D.M.S. (Capt, came in with intention of inspecting LOOS through. We went up at 90 o'clock & got there in about an hour. Fort GLATZ was broken & a much good work had been done by my officers & men there since last Sunday. Then the infantry officer posted to #1/B.A. Advance Dressing station guided him to it as he has never seen it posted on the map. We came round & went fine an easy thing & had a look, but I am thankful to say no one got OP OPC & OP O.S. chan S/W 8-2 Evac. 1-30 duty 5-17 Sealers 1. 30 ORs S/W 5-2	
"	21	21-20	Sent ambulance today with officers to ARQUES. Started creation of both Officers Ward today. Stopped Rum issue for the present. Inspected Bhg R.A. Aid Post at QUALITY ST. As reported unsafe, and unsafe it was, everyone to get it right. Admitted 1-7. Evacuated duty - 30 O.R.s S/W 6-3 OR's	

WAR DIARY
or
INTELLIGENCE SUMMARY.
(Erase heading not required.)

Army Form C. 2118.

Place	Date	Hour	Summary of Events and Information	Remarks and references to Appendices
NOEUX les MINES	22	21-30	Again a wet day, Nothing much doing. We are having what I call a "coffin Stretcher" fitted up instead of the 2 wheeled. Only not our stretcher got outfit from the C.R.E. to draw more shoes/leather for R.O. 1 officer & advance dressing station. Have arranged to go on with the work for the R.A. 12 Our post tomorrow night. Work in progress at own O.P. Station. Admitted 5; W. Evacuated to C.C.S. 7. Q. OWB	
"	23rd	28-25	Showers & fine day. Ordinary routine work carried out at dusk. Sent to artillery Aid post, & with half of party from 111 F.A. started work on the aid post. Admitted 4. I; Evacuated to duty 1-2. to C.C.S. 7-2.	
"	24th	21	Work was carried out on aid post all night, party returning at daybreak. Our fine trench stretcher became a finished article today, as at least today it was accepted by the I Corps. The D.M.S. ordering one to be sent to each of the Divisions in the Corps. The Divisional General also has taken it up. He felt that the fine Tuesday are so narrow nowdays, it necessary Prince of a single a flat board with a movable funnel outfit to which the footrest is strapped in nightly & so get set as a board or bank. W. Evacuated to duty 3 = 30 R.S. 7 Y. C.C.S. 3. 2. Admitted 9 2 = W	

WAR DIARY or INTELLIGENCE SUMMARY

Army Form C. 2118.

Place	Date	Hour	Summary of Events and Information	Remarks and references to Appendices
NOEUX les MINES	25	28.45	Just returned from QUALITY St. The shelter is rapidly becoming an established fact & I expect it to be completed in about 3 more nights. This morning we had our French Stretcher out to the reserve first under it. I must say it was a success. The usual amount of shelling today but nothing very frightful. Weather fine & summer like. Admitted S. 9. 3. Evacuated Duty 1, Sections 2, Rest Stations & & S 6. One Officer acute Appendicitis admitted & evacuated.	
"	26	20.30	Had Stretchers in trenches today & they did very well, we instructed the Regimental Bearers in their use. It was a good day today & we got on well with our work at the Hospital. R.O.E. Inspection manual. Admitted 9-3. Evacuated S.K. Sections 1. ⊙ Section 1. To Rest Sta 3 To C.C.S. 3-3 rms	
"	27	24.-	This was our most strenuous day so far. St started with a gas attack at 3-30. Warning reached us at 6.a.m & when it arrived have about 3/4 of an hour later we were ready for it. It was not however here & I have not heard of any the cause for it in NOEUX. There was another wave an hour later but this was negligble. Our alarm gave us station had enough time & during the	

WAR DIARY or INTELLIGENCE SUMMARY

Army Form C. 2118.

Place	Date	Hour	Summary of Events and Information	Remarks and references to Appendices
NOEUX les MINES	27	a.m.	day. Two gas cases died at PHILOSOPHE with symptoms of chlorine poisoning. They were almost dead on admission. Two other cases of severe gassing were evacuated from here to 33 C.C.S. Sections carried at dressing station. Inspiration of ammonia & Oxygen. Sent off 7/50 a.m. Hypodermic injections of the morning of 43 fell their cases evacuated off 27 7 R.A. an list as under 33 gas 957 wounded cases [illegible]... Sunday I had cleared my ambulance of cases so as to be ready for the rush. A gas shower came up in the evening but [illegible] to factory.	
"	28th	2.2	Yu.A.g. S.E. cases have been very heavy all day 9 by 3 a.m. 169 cases had passed through the A.D.S. we started the evacuation. At 9 o'clock there was another gas alarm as I return cleared my ambulance sending on 14 cases to Phil over returning empty 2/1 ... [illegible] (Pekin Farm.) Our own A.D.S. as it takes the gas casualties [illegible] up for men wounds.	
"	29	21-30	This has been a hard day. It was decided to yain admin at 5-30. At 5.30 we began to get in cases. From 6 am to 12 am we admitted 94 men & 1 officer from 12 am to 3/1 o'clock in a little 124 men & 1 officer, one officer Lt. Wharton 7 S.M. Fordson & an other [illegible] died. All other cases were	

Army Form C. 2118.

WAR DIARY
or
INTELLIGENCE SUMMARY.
(Erase heading not required.)

Instructions regarding War Diaries and Intelligence Summaries are contained in F. S. Regs., Part II. and the Staff Manual respectively. Title pages will be prepared in manuscript.

Place	Date	Hour	Summary of Events and Information	Remarks and references to Appendices
NOEUX MINES	24th	cont	Evacuated to C.C.S. at 2:58 p.m. ambulances were v.[?] trying for motor and more. Practically all cases were general Artillery who had to get it A cart or more were general before they got the gas H[?] on, any of them slightly thin helmets were fairly tard to cheap [?] amongst them stated they were gassed through their [?]. The future of the men [?] to [?] any officer "(e a D station was awful). I gave instructions on his opinion, that the said Smoke Helmet (P.H.) has been refused as much for the past few days that they [?] the strong I instructs only for a limited period while the [?] men was [?] of this [?]. had had no food for 24 hours, or at any rate since breakfast the previous day. There was a conference of A.D.M.S, DDS, OC's FAmb, OC's ambulances at BETHUNE which I was even unable to attend owing to being on Noeux Stretcher.	
	30	28 Ap	A quiet day. Yesterday my A D Station in the evening also the Artillery [?] put up at QUALITY ST. Things were going well, with all sent in my refund on the few cases to A D.H.S admitted 5 [?] 9 SW 6 1/3 (13 of the gun 2 in.) Shot two gun cm evacuated to C.C.S. 4 [?] 9 SW going [?] 8	

A. W. Bennett
Lt. Col. R.A.M.C.

Confidential

War Diary
of
113th Field Ambulance.

From May 1st 1916.
To May 31st 1916.

(Volume 4.)

Vol. 4

Lt-Col-Name
O/C 113th Field Amb.

Army Form C. 2118.

WAR DIARY
or
INTELLIGENCE SUMMARY.
(Erase heading not required.)

Instructions regarding War Diaries and Intelligence Summaries are contained in F. S. Regs., Part II. and the Staff Manual respectively. Title pages will be prepared in manuscript.

Place	Date	Hour	Summary of Events and Information	Remarks and references to Appendices
NOEUX les MINES	1/12/15	21	Another month has gone & 29 of III has been sent off. There has been a quiet day. We have been getting on with our work at the Hospital. Our tramway staff is going strong. Admitted 18 - W. Evacuated to 8. C.S. 1 K 13.	
"	2/12/15	21	This has been a lovely showery day. Things generally quiet. At 12-30 got news of a badly wounded man in LOOS who required immediate evacuation. LOOS promised to get him as far as junction of 10th Avenue & Up of S. & would take him on from there. S. and St Emdeigh & Lty. LOOS did not carry out their part of the bargain, result was any men had to go down to Emden corner before they got the patient. They took him over stretcher. He had nearly of his men carried away by a bit of a shell. He was in with from in the trench, that they carried him in the open night through from the junction of Railway alley & 10th Avenue to Quality Street. They were heavily shelled but escaped unengaged. The patient was w BETHUNE by ambulance. Admitted 18-W. Evacuated 18-W. To C.C.S. 7-2.	
"	3	20.45	Showery during today. Got on with my first shelters etc now.	S&EES 8-3 Sommet S&
"	4	20.40	A quiet day. We got on with our work in the Ambulance Bathing & Evacuation Station. 12 S&EES 1-b. aw3 =	

Army Form C. 2118.

WAR DIARY
or
INTELLIGENCE SUMMARY.
(Erase heading not required.)

Instructions regarding War Diaries and Intelligence Summaries are contained in F. S. Regs., Part II. and the Staff Manual respectively. Title pages will be prepared in manuscript.

Place	Date	Hour	Summary of Events and Information	Remarks and references to Appendices
NOEUX LES MINES	5-	20-10	Again a glorious day. There was considerable shelling at our advanced posts but no casualties to speak of. The gas Shield of the 1st Corps drew heavy enemy enquiry into the last attack. Admitted. Casualties to e.e.S. $W. 6 S.W.H. Sea/on 1. So Rest Station 5. Evacuated 3.	
"	6"	21-15	Today there was a full parade of the Ambulance when the A.D.M.S. 16th Division went out a letter from the G.O.C. Division in which he expressed his satisfaction for the way in which the Ambulances had served out these men in the recent gas attack. Three men R.A admitted to hospital today suffering from severe burns, which the received from the evening syntony flyer etc. Been admitted to Hosp yesterday 1st. Evacuated July S.W. Rest 5. &.e.S. S.W. cas. Admitted in 2. Evacuated to July 11 S.W. G.e.e.S. W. 3. Seaton 1.	
"	7	24	Sorry. A quiet one at that Accompanied by the A.D.M.S. 16" Division S visited PHILOSOPHES LOOS this evening. We made return our extended tour as we also called on the 141 F.A. & De Pature & the R Riel Post /4 Br. Sector. in cells at Fort gently. We also investigated Ruitistant tunnel a view to the evacuation of wounded during the day. Admitted to Y. Evac July/ Seaton/ Rest Station 7 to e.e.S. y. S.	

Place	Date	Hour	Summary of Events and Information	Remarks and references to Appendices
NOEUX ses MINES	8th	23	The day has been spent with some men. Working party on well, but a matériel S. will have to give up some of the implements I proposed as labour need be so difficult. I have sent I men and 4 horses to find a river transport officer 1 NCO & 15 men. The rest together but the land but there are only enough men.	
"	9	23-16	Wet ever day. Sent a fatigue party of one 1 NCO, 9 4 15-men off this morning with heavier rations on a Decauville fatigue. They are not back yet. General work in trenches much as usual. Got a further amount of aluminium out of LOOS today by daylight by means of our Branch Stretchers dumies yesterday (8.h.) S.W.B. Evacuation Dug 1. Seulincs, Rest Stat 2, EES S.W. Dumps	
"	10	9.20	A Fine day. Fatigue party again at the trenches draining sewage. Pillary continued to infect the trenches. Ambulance journey Seli 17. Wounded 3 Evac Party 3-4 Rest Sta 3, EES S.W.	
"	11	23-13	Got S. 1st Champagne at the Ambulance today. S. may come to his own shine this evening. Set him one of our trench stretchers through the canal channel. Second shelling of PHILOSOPHE today. Attacks in our area. Ambulance journey 19. L. Evacuated duty/S.W. Rest Stat 3, EES S.W. Seulin 1.	

Army Form C. 2118.

WAR DIARY
or
INTELLIGENCE SUMMARY.
(Erase heading not required.)

Instructions regarding War Diaries and Intelligence Summaries are contained in F.S. Regs., Part II. and the Staff Manual respectively. Title pages will be prepared in manuscript.

Place	Date	Hour	Summary of Events and Information	Remarks and references to Appendices
NOEUX MINES	16"	21-10	Today a Parade of the Ambulance at which the A.D.C.M.S. presented Divisional certificates to one Officer & 3 Bearers for bravery carrying a patient through the open under shell fire. Today made arrangements for the taking over of their A.D.S. LOOS from the 141 F. Amb., the transfer to take place tomorrow. The A.D.C.M.S. today inspected the Field Ambulance. Admit S.W. Evac. Sedan/ cluring 3 to E.C.S. 2 B.	
"	17	21-"	This was a quiet day. We got on with the transfer. We made arrangements for taking over the A.D.S. LOOS from 141 F.A. tonight.	
"	18	21.30	Advanced dressing station taken over successfully last night. It is called the Chateau (CHATEAU. 4 is the 1st horse on the Right entering LOOS by HOSPITAL Rd. Another Salvage & Fatigue Party ordered for tomorrow. Ordinary work at hospital today. Received a reinforcement of 4 men today. Admitt. jaterway 10-3. Evac. duty 3. Sedans 2. E.C.S. 9.	
"	19	22	Fatigue Party returned from Fosse 8 number without casualty. They report there was very little first there. to Convoy in. However a fine day & general work at the hospitals Admits 5 W. = 1 Hellsmah 5 W. A.S.G. Road accidents 1 = 1 counter fatigue 1 = 3 G. Evac. duty 1 = 3. Pass 3, 3, 2. E.C.S. 4 G. ER3	

Army Form C. 2118.

WAR DIARY
or
INTELLIGENCE SUMMARY.
(Erase heading not required.)

Instructions regarding War Diaries and Intelligence Summaries are contained in F. S. Regs., Part II. and the Staff Manual respectively. Title pages will be, prepared in manuscript.

Place	Date	Hour	Summary of Events and Information	Remarks and references to Appendices
NOEUX LES MINES	12	22.30	A quiet day. As instructed by the D.C.M.S I am to send one of our French S. W to 1st Division Sanitary Admitted S. W Evac. Duty 2 ees 8-S- Section 3	
"	13	20.30	Had to send a fatigue, officer, N.C.O. 14 men to clean fine French today. Idealike there very much as there is always great risk of getting the men hit. We are good, as the regiments have over enough for the work, but I am sure that is not my department to complain. Gave them to-day the work I am doing. Cleaning up the area etc to furnish such parties who just bring down old rifles equipment etc. It was lucky that the day was wet, so no Observation balloon aeroplane were up, I may have awaited the stuffing they would at mined from here first. Would in hospital as usual. S. W. Evacuated Duty 1. B. Evacuated Duty 2 & K Section 2. ees S. W Section 2. ees 1.2.3.	
"	14	23.45	Sunday. Made my usual weekly round of PHILOSOPHE & LOOS. Things were looking well in both places. No fatigue party for salvage in trenches to-day Admitted yesterday 21- S.W Evacuated Duty 3-3. To ees. 12 S. W sirs.	
"	15	21.15	Went to BETHUNE this morning to get some things for the Officers Mess. Fatigue Party again testing gas-hood for transmission class. Admitted yesterday S. W (Evacuated Duty S.W Punt S.W sees S.W. 4.4 Punt 2.5 sees 2.5 sirs.	

2353 Wt. W25144/1454 700,000 5/15 D. D. & L.   A.D.S.S./Forms/C. 2118.

WAR DIARY
or
INTELLIGENCE SUMMARY.
(Erase heading not required.)

Army Form C. 2118.

Instructions regarding War Diaries and Intelligence Summaries are contained in F. S. Regs., Part II. and the Staff Manual respectively. Title pages will be prepared in manuscript.

Place	Date	Hour	Summary of Events and Information	Remarks and references to Appendices
NŒUX les MINES	20	9:32	About an hour before sunset CHATEAU St PATRICK LOOS from my party. I have taken it over. They report enemy quiet. Work progressing without interference. We are endeavouring to get it cleaned up. Work progressing well. 4 offrs & 9 & 14 OR's offrd. Signal CoS G Sec 2. Days	
"	21	23:45	Yesterday Occupied 4 officers 9:00 hrs B. & 4 mrs. E.C.S. offrd. Signal Cos G Sec 3 Days. 3 Pl. This was our initial 8 of the enemy. They had constructed for a while 3 visited our Customer Dressing Station this evening. We are getting the men and cleaned up. But it was very costy. Contacted perhaps.	
"	22	22:15	14 days now getting into the war as general The Personal uncommon mints feeder & fainter today, Sent in N.C.O. & 6 men endeavouring to clear out the trail town with Dressing Station out in house in nothing dangerous. Admitted Yesterday 11 OR wounded 3 R.A.S.T. 7 C.E.S. 8 C/	
"	23	21	Enemy had to evacuate Cap't Van der Vyver way 3 commands with the Hostage to-day. A quiet somewhat day. Things going well with the Hostage Society letters 5 offrs & 1 offrs for Enna Duty. R.A.S.T. 6 E.C.S. 2 & 2 offrd B.W.R.	
"	24	21-15	A wet day. 10 Sully has all day. Had further interviews & visits in the from of a central head trenches & a platoon of another Coy dreaded Yesterday 14 O.R. & W. Enna E.C.S. a 3 R.A.S.C. 2 duty 7 offrs. 3 Sec	

WAR DIARY
or
INTELLIGENCE SUMMARY.
(Erase heading not required.)

Army Form C. 2118.

Place	Date	Hour	Summary of Events and Information	Remarks and references to Appendices
NOEUX LES MINES	25	21	Again a wet day but not too bad. The Stanhren came again forward with about 12 loads. They are known as huns & are from 69 to 90 act late night I had our orderly & stretcher bearers at Loos rather heavy. Two through both thighs by a bullet, one rather back with a load of wounded. This & one of another went to long in his aid to have a station. We have arranged that in future such an our party of carriers will be closer up on Road. Admitted gateway 15. K.E. men ees 11 B. Roust 5 B duty 2. ors	
"	26	21	Shower of rain again today. Enemy got out Hospital but do not no casualties, etyh in the afternoon after a reinforcement of 10 min arty. evacuated 23.29 officer & 54 o/rs. Evacuatees 30 25 Rest, duty 5. Seabra 3 ors 5 E	
"	27	22	This was a quiet day & no shelling. New officers went in in many. Both my carpenters have gone on leave. Sgt. N.C.D. arrived as up that ene admitted to studied. Admitted gateway 13 B. One ees 13 " 30 duty 2 ors or Shair 9 Evac ees 5 21 10 Seabra, ebraco	
"	28	24	Suffered O.A station to night, things never in good order. Burnt any here. Commttee 5 w officer 7 14 officer. Evac Budre, Duty 7 1. ees 5 & 17 ors	

Chas. Buchan.

WAR DIARY
or
INTELLIGENCE SUMMARY.

(Erase heading not required.)

Army Form C. 2118.

Place	Date	Hour	Summary of Events and Information	Remarks and references to Appendices
NOEUX les MINES	29th	21-30	A Quiet day today only two killed came in. Officers arrived. Previous very useful. Two bad days. Started a Motuary today. Senots omens to St Venant out to relieve St Eunuery at the A.D.S. Arranged for Officers men to apued one coach in. 100's casualty of 30 up or at present 20 entry from today cps	
	30	21-15	Again a quiet day expt 2 Gasman Oyner returned from Hospital today + was sent back to the Divi'n'l. Sent Sl Sherman out to look after a refreshment today where there is on Caserne Sgt Handerson left today for 1st Gas Ching with SgtJ Smith. Admit Yesterday, 10½ Evac. 9es Sit Runst Sit 30 Duty 5 at Officer 8 A.D.S Evacuatu at once to 33 C.C.S.	
"	31.	23	A quiet day nothing of note. Rut SEnt. 8 Admitted 15-13 Evac. 0 at c/p 8/10. Rut SEnt. 8 atherewett	

Confidential

War Diary
of
113th Field Ambulance

from June 1st 1916 to June 30th 1916

Volume 5

Army Form C. 2118.

WAR DIARY
or
INTELLIGENCE SUMMARY.
(Erase heading not required.)

Instructions regarding War Diaries and Intelligence Summaries are contained in F. S. Regs., Part II. and the Staff Manual respectively. Title pages will be prepared in manuscript.

Place	Date	Hour	Summary of Events and Information	Remarks and references to Appendices
NOEUX les MINES	1/6/16	21/6/15	Quiet day. Dressed wound at stretcher today & return getting the evacuants the trenches to manage with them. Sent diary off yesterday. Admitted yesterday S.W. Evac. EES & 16; Rest, S. Duty 1 up 3	
"	2	21	This was a quiet day, things going well without station. Sent up 8 Sergeant & men stretcher to my advance posts. Had the reserve receivers in the trenches today learning their work. Admitted yesterday 10/12 Evac. EES. S.W. Rest 1-J. Duty 8. Sew officer adv Coques	
"	3	21-30	Pay day for the Ambulance. Received some heavy for patients from St John Amb. Drive on with the diary. Admitted 10 24 officer! Evac EES Sw & M. Seven 2. Rest 8 & Duty 1 Off.	
"	4	23-15	Made my weekly inspection of the Advance Dressing Station in the evening. Things are much improved & the station has been made fairly safe. Admitted 8 - 15 Evac EES 10/16. Duty 12.	
"	5	22	Another quiet day. This evening a dead man was sent to the Ambulance from a unit (RE stationed here) I declined to take over the body, as it had just been sent casually & sent on a Sick Report signed by a Sergeant, & under the	

Army Form C. 2118.

WAR DIARY
or
INTELLIGENCE SUMMARY.
(Erase heading not required.)

Instructions regarding War Diaries and Intelligence Summaries are contained in F. S. Regs., Part II. and the Staff Manual respectively. Title pages will be prepared in manuscript.

Place	Date	Hour	Summary of Events and Information	Remarks and references to Appendices
NOEUX les MINES	5	22	Existing orders for dealing with dead bodies. I considered it was wiser not to push it over in view of a proper Authority. S.W. at Officers 2 Evac, eeS, 12 Duty 2.2 Officers eeS 12 Admitted 12. 21 Officers 2 Evac, eeS.	
"	6	21	A.D.M.S. has gone on leave & I have to sign all his papers rather busy. Things are going well there time. One WEO9 three men attached from ¾ Can F.A. for instruction. Have sent him to the A.D.S. Admitted 13. 15— Evac 15 N. eeS 5 W Duty 3 Officers as 2 Evac eeS 1.	
"	7	22	A Quiet day in my quarters of the line. Started to build workshops for my tailor & barber. As acting D.A.D.S. I went round with the D.A.D.S. of infantry the three ambulances.	
"	8	21	A Wet day. Things still quiet on our front. As A.D.D.S. went round the billets of the 4 R.E. Rifles, Infantry and A.D.S. PHILOSOPHE. 5 W Officers eeS. 5 H 3 Officers 5 H. 3 Rest Camp 3 2 Duty § 2, UPS Admitted 12. 8.	
"	9	21	Quiet day. nothing doing. Day wet & unsettled. S.W. 5 H. S. Officers 2, Evac Hilton RWNF 1 Duty § 2. Rest 1 eeS St S W S W Admitted 14 5 Officers 5 W Evac eeS 11 6. Rest St 2. Sidier, Duty § 1, UPS	
"	10	21	Admitted 11 6. Evac eeS 11 6. Sir J.C. & S.	

Army Form C. 2118.

WAR DIARY
or
INTELLIGENCE SUMMARY.
(Erase heading not required.)

Instructions regarding War Diaries and Intelligence Summaries are contained in F. S. Regs., Part II. and the Staff Manual respectively. Title pages will be prepared in manuscript.

Place	Date	Hour	Summary of Events and Information	Remarks and references to Appendices
NOEUX LES MINES	11	23.25	Today the A/C O. & 3 men from 7 Cav. F.A. who had been attached left for their unit, having completed their week's training. One section of 134 F.A. arrived for 10 days training today. Sent 30 of them to A.D.S. as preliminary measure tonight. Accompanied by Staff Surgeon Bell R.N. Sunday Duty W. A.D. Station. OCS. admitted 14. W.Off. 1. S W. 9. Off. Evac. ees 3.6 Seal. 1. Rest Camp 2. Duty 3.	
"	12	22	A wet day. Quiet. Admitted 16-11. Officer 2. Evac. ees 2/10. Rest St 2/1. Sealed Duty 1/1.	
"	13	23	A wet cold day nothing much doing. Parade at 11 am Representation Service for Sanctuary for Wars, so not much work done outside the ambulance.	
"	14	23.15	Bets on the show time tonight. Again a quiet day. Nothing doing. Admission ggt. Acting 21. 9. Evac. ees S/8. Rest St. S. Duty 4 2. Admission today 21. 11. Evac. Sealed. ees 3.9. Charles 3 Rest Camp 2 Duty S.	
"	15	21-30	This was a surprise day. An Officer & 30 of Co 9 Arrived from 9 F.A. arrived here today for a week's training. I have sent them on to Philosophe & then to be evacuated with the section of 134 F. for training. Still things quieter on our front, & consequently few casualties. Admitted 23.4 Evac. ees 2/2 Rest Stat. 1 Duty 1 cws	

T2134. Wt. W708-776. 500000. 4/15. Sir J. C. & S.

Army Form C. 2118.

4.

Instructions regarding War Diaries and Intelligence
Summaries are contained in F. S. Regs., Part II.
and the Staff Manual respectively. Title pages
will be prepared in manuscript.

WAR DIARY
or
INTELLIGENCE SUMMARY.
(Erase heading not required.)

Place	Date	Hour	Summary of Events and Information	Remarks and references to Appendices
NIEUX and MINES	16	23	Weather has changed once more & flares are dripping of again. Bro A.D.M.S. returns from leave tonight so far left by tomorrow. Smith to be able to give my full time to the Ambulance again. Work there is however going on well. Admitted 21-14. Evac. e.e.S 16 14. Sedno 1. Ret St. 2. Duty 3.	
"	17	23.45	Fine day, but quiet on our front. Last night some shelling of motor parties. Advanced Out station the enemy. A.D.M.S. has returned. Admitted 22. 13. Evac e.e.S 22. 13. Sedno 2 Ret St. 2. Duty 3.	
"	18	22	Another fine day. Sent off party this evening to take over my A.D.S. from sections in training, as they are required to rejoin their units. Admitted 19-10. Evac. e.e.S 13. 9 Ret St. 5 Sed'n S1. C.I.B.	
"	19	21	Got all attached men in from my A.D.S. & my own men up to their various posts again. We are ready but nothing doing. Admitted 11. 12. 0.fficer 4. Evac. e.e.S 8.13. 3 Ret St. S.W. Sed'n 3/1. Duty 3. e.e.S Officer 2.	
"	20	22	Very dull attacked men returned to their units. Had section goes to 112 F.A. Admitted 13-33. Evac. e.e.S 12 23. Off S W. Duty 2 1.	
"	21	22	Admitted 26 11. 4 Officer. Evac. e.e.g off S W 1 S.A. Sedno, 1 Ret St 3 Duty 3 2. C.I.B.	

Army Form C. 2118.

WAR DIARY
or
INTELLIGENCE SUMMARY.
(Erase heading not required.)

Instructions regarding War Diaries and Intelligence Summaries are contained in F.S. Regs., Part II. and the Staff Manual respectively. Title pages will be prepared in manuscript.

Place	Date	Hour	Summary of Events and Information	Remarks and references to Appendices
NOEUX ês MINES	22.	23	A quiet day. Was informed of the plan of advance by D.d.S. 1st Army & others. Admitted 23. 21. Officers 2. Evac. eeS. 11. 23. Rest Camp. 1. Duty 3. 3. Offrs. 1. Sick 2. W	
"	23.	22	A very hot day. Turned to rain. Nothing much doing as things very quiet on our section of the front just now. W Admitted 25. 16. Admit OS. 2-1. Evac. eeS. 5-11. Rest Camp. 1. Duty 2. Offrs. 2. Offrs 1 Rest 1	
"	24.	21	A wet day. Things quieter than usual during	
"	25.	23	Was informed by the a.D.M.S. & this evening inspected my advance D. Station & the Reg. Aid Posts. We learn from all areas in quite good order. W Admitted 13. Offrs 1. Evac eeS. 9-11 Officers 1 Sedice 1. Rest St 5-2. Duty 4. 1. Offr W	
"	26.	22.	Acting on information I sent 18 extra bearers up to forward a.D.S. Admitted 8 -13. Offrs S. Evac eeS. 26. 14. Offr 1. Rest St. 2. Duty 4. 1. Officer W at	
"	27.	23	Ordered in my extra bearers tonight, as attack passed successfully. Admitted S. W. Evac eeS. 9. g. Sedice 2. Rest Camp 1. Duty 13-1.	
"	28.	23.10	We evacuated 40 wounded from the R.A.P on the night of 26. 27" & got them out of LOOS last night. Evacuation was very difficult on account of shell fire often died well on dead on road all night.	

T2134. Wt. W708—776. 500000. 4/15. Sir J. C. & B.

WAR DIARY or INTELLIGENCE SUMMARY

Army Form C. 2118.

Place	Date	Hour	Summary of Events and Information	Remarks and references to Appendices
NOEUX LES MINES	29th	22	Last night had to send up 1 Off, R.C. & 6 Bomrs to hold part of A.2.S. Line as on the night of 27/28th there had been considerable bombardt & also a few slightly wounded came back in from the previous nights raid by us. 93 other ranks in L.O.S. have practically 46 hours continuous work. We cleared 46 wounded last night from L.O.S. besides sick. Little bombardt of RE so evacuation was comparatively easy w/.	
	30	21	Things a bit quieter this day. Started having 2 wind frames made for stretchers. Such in the Division are lighter than that now last distributed & to the fact that 2 orderlies & W/Proof capes were withdrawn from the men just before the weather broke, & through cold. Casualties 26/7 to 30/7 Officers 2, Evac. to CCS 13-46 Rest up; Seatres Sick, S.w. CCS 60; A 3 Off. Duty Rest Camp A 930 omtts.	

T2134. Wt. W708—776. 500000. 4/15. Sir J. C. & S.

July 1916

16th Division

113th Field Ambulance

WAR DIARY

113th Field Amb
RAMC

1st. July 1916 to 31st. July 1916.

VOLUME No. 8.

Army Form C. 2118.

WAR DIARY
or
INTELLIGENCE SUMMARY.
(Erase heading not required.)

Instructions regarding War Diaries and Intelligence Summaries are contained in F. S. Regs., Part II. and the Staff Manual respectively. Title pages will be prepared in manuscript.

Place	Date	Hour	Summary of Events and Information	Remarks and references to Appendices
NOEUX les MINES	1/4/16		Fine weather again. Quiet 24 hours on our front. Today for first time got our everything except of LOOS by daylight. Sent off last month's return this morning. Admitted 18.30. Officers 2. Evac C.C.S 21.20. Rest Camp 2. Duty 1. Dead 3. Staff off	
"	2	23.45	Inspected A.D.S. this evening. They have suffered somewhat during the past week from the bombardment, but none the worse for it. Wonderful careful. Casualties 32-25 officer 1 Evac C.C.S. 19.14 (4 gen Host) 1. Rest Camp 3.1. Officer 3 w Duty 5. 3-Officer —	
"	3	22	This has been a quiet day. Have decided that it is not necessary to move force C.C.S if necessary. Also motor car for some future —	
"	4	21"	Wet day once more. Things still quiet in our area. We have been suffering very much lately from P.C.O. & extra mental conditions. These were caused mainly, I think, by knocks in the weather, which unfortunately coincided with date on which old unites were withdrawn from the men, show that days are getting correspondingly are entering. Admitted 12.16 Evac C.C.S.20. Officers admit 3 Rain 2 w 3 S w Duty 5 w	
"	-	21.30	Again a wet day, but things are not as it did not hinder work. Admitted 23. 10. Evac. C.C.S w. Rest 1.6 Duty 4.7 Officer Adm. 5 Evac 2 w 3	

WAR DIARY or INTELLIGENCE SUMMARY

Army Form C. 2118.

(Erase heading not required.)

Place	Date	Hour	Summary of Events and Information	Remarks and references to Appendices
NOEUX les MINES	6	22	Quiet again on our section, but went to our get it rather heavy. One of my men Pt Whittaker was today granted the Military Medal for digging out a burried gunner under fire etc. Evac o/S 10. Evac o.e.S 21. 11 Sendia 2 Officers Admit o/S 5. o.e.S 1 sick admitted 25. 10.	
"	7	22	Again a quiet wet day. Medal was presented to Pt Whittaker by Brigadier commander today.	WB
"	8	21	A good day, but still quiet on the front observed by us. I have to report that one of my men was hit by a bit of shell, at my A.D.S. LOOS last night. The wound does not appear to be severe & the fragment has been extracted. One of my Ford Cars is out of action for the present. Part of the engine gave way while in my absent east & has had many hard work ever worst of the carburettor. Evacuating from LOOS in all weather every night. Things in Hosp. Breviary admitted 15/ o/S Evac o.e.S 5. o/S Post St 3. Officers Evac. Run from yest.S. was 2 sick o/S	
"	9	23.45	Visited my A.D.S stations this evening. Things are quiet, only occasional shelling. Telephone has broken down between any station in LOOS probably cut by the shelling. The station went going very well. If we had only one casualty in the week. Admitted o/S (-- Evac o.e.S o/S Post Stat. S o/S Evac o/S 8.13.11 Sir I.C. & 8.13.11 Post Stat. 3. 2. Sedan, Duty 7. 1.	WB

Army Form C. 2118.

WAR DIARY
or
INTELLIGENCE SUMMARY.
(Erase heading not required.)

Instructions regarding War Diaries and Intelligence Summaries are contained in F. S. Regs., Part II. and the Staff Manual respectively. Title pages will be prepared in manuscript.

Place	Date	Hour	Summary of Events and Information	Remarks and references to Appendices
NOEUX LES MINES	10	21	Yesterday my A.D.S PHILOSOPHE & headquarters were visited by a party from Headquarters Army (Divisional). This was a lovely day & drived over the work of my own in the ambulance which have been very bad lately. Then morning had a patient sent down from Reg. Aid Post L.O.S to the 1st staff & Lns. W. Strachan. He was suffering from Shock Shell W. for the time he was widely excited & at every gas alarm which he could he rushed outside. SW CCS 11-21. BUSNES 2 (Staff Rifle) Rest Camp S. W. 1 July 2 Offrs. aud 5 (Corporls.) 1 NCO	
"	11	21.h5	These days there have been a bombardment of this place, but so far as I am aware of our batteries. They were firing & nothing of head doing in the hospital.	
"	12.	22	Again a quiet day, but some shelling of town. Some of shelling over the way has been 12 to 12.40 o'clock previously it was usually 16 o'clock. Another car 2.30 this time he gone wrong. Sent to evacuate it to the Ford Lorrymor. Saw changing the Staff at L.O.D. Some a week as I think some days at any rate for any one there at one time. all etc. of men & women besides the General there 2 Lieut: as I am arranging for leave. CWB	
"	13.	23	An Ordinary day. Started work on a Crown for Warrant Officers CWB	

T2134. Wt. W708—776. 500000. 4/15. Sir J. C. & S.

WAR DIARY
or
INTELLIGENCE SUMMARY.

(Erase heading not required.)

Army Form C. 2118.

Place	Date	Hour	Summary of Events and Information	Remarks and references to Appendices
NOEUX les MINES	14	22	Shelling of town again today. Interested drawings of Latrines at PHILOSOPHE to Dr. S who arrived for them. Arranging by Lt Cavanagh to get w/bearer equipment of one section together for men to practise loading. Adm⁴ 20 10. Evac Seater 1. C & S.10. S. Rest St. 85. W. Duty 5.	PHILOSOPHE
"	15	23	Again a good day, also a quiet on our own front, but tonight shrapnel shells are coming over the Reserve as I expect a little crest now. I have inspected all carts in turn today, as those on the side at Les Brebis are successful and well Adm⁴ 20 10. Evac Seater 1. C & S.10. S. Rest St. 3-4. Duty 3.	
"	16	23	Emptied my out station this evening. They had been rather busy last night in consequence of a raid by us, we had 37 wounded to clear. They were all got out before daylight. This morning which I arrived good as the move which we arranged for the front did not get it until 10 oc. Last night. Tonight I exfort to be busy, also as I hear there are about 30 C.O. Lys. easier to get out, also one wounded gunner.	
"	17	21	Showed a quiet day. We got out our cases by 1 am. One of my bearers was hit though both thighs (Irwin) as he returned with stretcher from loading ambulance. German Prisoners also in loft (Wounded) carried stretcher for me. Adm⁴ts 23-35. Evac. Sealer 3. Rest S. S. C & S. 15-17. Duty 4-5. C & S	

T2134. Wt. W708—770. 500000. 4/15. Sir J. C. & S.

Army Form C. 2118.

WAR DIARY
or
INTELLIGENCE SUMMARY.
(Erase heading not required.)

Place	Date	Hour	Summary of Events and Information	Remarks and references to Appendices
NOEUX les MINES	18	22	Town shelled again today, but the quiet. See have German Pr̃s on hands shale were fewer today. I am glad to say. Had my new factory waggons today. Admitted 7S 6. Evac Scabies 2. C.C.S. 23. Rest St. 3. Duty S.	
"	19	21	Had to detail a M.O today to a Regiment (on loan from O.C 1/S Dewsbury). Settled on Capt Chaufty, as seem relieved his departure would interfere least with the working of the Ambulance, as he only been with us for about 2½ months. This was a quiet day as enemy resting went. Admitted 22 B. Evac. Duty 5-5, Rest St. 3, C.C.S. 13. Aff̃rs Admi. Enclosed 21 uus 3.	
"	20	22	A fine day & as usual on such we were shelled. Today we had two searches to bring an enemy at the R.E. stationed here. I have got all my unit of Bilots now & in tents. They are so glad to say fit. Admtt'd 14 is. Evac. C.C.S.y 10, Scabies 2. Rest St. 3 Duty 2. S.W. 1. Shr.wdun?	
"	21	23.45	Received orders today from A.D.M.S. 16 Division to hand over A.D. Station LOOS tonight to 137 F.A. The A.D.M.S. went off with the A.D.M.S of the relieving division, & I accompanied them. Things were quiet & we handed over as ordered, only Surgery Panny & all investigation equipment.	

WAR DIARY
or
INTELLIGENCE SUMMARY.
(Erase heading not required.)

Army Form C. 2118.

Place	Date	Hour	Summary of Events and Information	Remarks and references to Appendices
NOEUX les MINES	22	29	Today handed over A.D.S. Brewery PHILOSOPHE to 137 F Amb. & took over my section thus relieved the CHATEAU VERNELLES A.D.S. together with the various Dug Outs in that section which had been held by 13" Division. A quiet day at Head Quarters. Sent off cars & various A.S.C. for Field & gen Countinio Draink in Active Service. Duties. 10" shew I have to send off Admitted 23 B. Evac C.C.S. 11.9. Post Section 3 Duty 5. S of Officers Aunt ? C.C.S. 3 An	
"	23	24	Visited this evening all my new A.D.S. at old Posts. The trenches in the area are neither straight or even single. There is no front of area of evacuation Better there who are how overtired batterly. Our new A.D.S. in the CHATEAU at VERMELLES. Our road we are in and in the colour scale down has been shot away. The other Stations are dugouts in connection with the trenches which are clear. The chain are St Mary's is well situated with one opening on HULUCH R^d & one in trench. Is Residency which we are all using by whether abundant night is much afraid to shew a rifle fine, I am looking out for some after route of evacuation.	

Army Form C. 2118.

WAR DIARY
or
INTELLIGENCE SUMMARY.
(Erase heading not required.)

Instructions regarding War Diaries and Intelligence Summaries are contained in F.S. Regs., Part II. and the Staff Manual respectively. Title pages will be prepared in manuscript.

Place	Date	Hour	Summary of Events and Information	Remarks and references to Appendices
NOEUX les MINES	24	22	This has been a quiet day, a number of wounded dealt with in this section are less than on last 2 nights, remarks as to dangerous road for evacuation seem to be upheld, as one case started down last night Shell slightly from St Denys, on arrival at the Château he was found also to be shot through the hose, a fact not yet dead. Evacuation by trench taken about 3 hrs, but artillery our men unaffected. Similar Admits 11, 12. Evac e.e.S. 5, St. 2, 6. Rd St. 2, Into 4 B.	
"	25–27		Again a quiet day. Went up to new A.D.S & found things going well. there on enquiry I found that the man whom I mentioned yesterday as having been killed during evacuation (who had received his wound earlier) & he had been injured by a shell in both legs also chest & the head received & seems to have been cured by a splinter. St. B. 9 J.N.S. Corps was around my A.D.S. today & I met him at the CHATEAU on his return to normal outposts ecs	
"	26	22	A fine day, but nothing much doing. This section rejoin quieter than our last / Admitted 14, 14. Evac. e.e.S. 5, G.R. Rei evng 5, 9, Rei evng 3, Into 5. Officers 3 Evac ees 1.	

Army Form C. 2118.

WAR DIARY
or
INTELLIGENCE SUMMARY.
(Erase heading not required.)

Place	Date	Hour	Summary of Events and Information	Remarks and references to Appendices
NOEUX les MINES	27	21	Went around the ADS. this afternoon. My chaps have got them fairly going now but they want flyproof latrines, as those at present in use are no good. S.t. Sgt Jones of the Ambulance today received orders out for good work done.	
"	28	2	Shelley of the Lincs again today. I got in the lines some from it. I returned with features of uneven 2 Patrolling with Flavine sockets and found they will prove useful but I got them off early to get down a Reserve. It Smith was over, we also took leg work with those today was	
			I had to sene in one of my S.A.O. (Stevensorian) sent over a bus. My day staff of nothing between out for a month. This afternoon full marching order, as some of mine they are getting out the night duty now. We do the same in the morning. I have arranged three Levenworth Oscietta to 11. Enos, EES 9 & 10, Sudlen 1, Pvts 5 & Duty 3 at 4 at Afton. Oam at Wan & at	
"	29	23	0. Quiet day with nothing special to report. Cpt. Ebock 2 ADS was posted to this ambulance from yesterday damit. 15 at Enos EES 5 w 513 Duty 2 & 2 Seaton, Post 5 & 7 EES 2 Officers Allwd'd 5 & One EES 2	
	30	03-11	Satisfactory news of ADS a full Posts. Work of improvement was going on	

Army Form C. 2118.

WAR DIARY
or
INTELLIGENCE SUMMARY.
(Erase heading not required.)

Place	Date	Hour	Summary of Events and Information	Remarks and references to Appendices
NOEUX les MINES	31	22	The month has gone out quietly; work throughout it has been fairly satisfactory & the New drainage men of others my divisions is enforced & rendering its their work well, a feeling from all that we matter. A.W. Bennett Lt Colnl. R.A.M.C. O.C. No 113 Field Ambulance.	

Aug 1916

WAR DIARY.

113th Field Ambulance.

140/734 16th Divn

MONTH OF AUGUST, 1916.

VOLUME:— 7.

COMMITTEE FOR THE MEDICAL HISTORY OF THE WAR
Date 30 OCT. 1916

Army Form C. 2118.

WAR DIARY
or
INTELLIGENCE SUMMARY.
(Erase heading not required.)

Instructions regarding War Diaries and Intelligence Summaries are contained in F. S. Regs., Part II. and the Staff Manual respectively. Title pages will be prepared in manuscript.

Place	Date	Hour	Summary of Events and Information	Remarks and references to Appendices
NOEUX les MINES	1	22	Sent on last month's diary to O. &. C. S. as ordered this morning. This was again a quiet day. It is very hot & today f. sawa a typical case of Prickly Heat, it was sent in of y.d. chambers.	
"	2	93	Last night a Ambfious droffed bombe within 50 yards of our hospital & a died no harm, but I have ordered no lights distinguishing for the neuf on the inhabitants are nervous. This was a quiet day. Sent up returns forms for our trenches. L. Bennett	
"	3	23	Again a quiet day. Visited A.D.S. & Aid Post. Work at former was going well, at the latter there was little improvement. Am sending a faint tomorrow to get it going.	
"	4	22	A quiet day. Rain has been threatening & it is much cooler. Held my man for a practice march again this afternoon. Diminutes 2h. 9 Ensen. E.S.S.S. to R. & S. Ferdus 2 Sert. 3. or 1.	
"	5	23	Rumours of handing over my A.D.S. & Sto. a It Eli called today & said he was taking over tomorrow, but I which he is no to good a hurry. A.F.B.	
"	6	22	Received orders today that this Ambulance is to become the reserve	

WAR DIARY
or
INTELLIGENCE SUMMARY.

(Erase heading not required.)

Army Form C. 2118.

Place	Date	Hour	Summary of Events and Information	Remarks and references to Appendices
NOEUX les MINES	6	22	(cont) the reserve Ambulance for the Division. I have sent it orders as to the handing over of any A.S.C. & the taking over of both in the back area. I am not away for a rest for the men as they have been in the line since 22/3/16. Today I had a parade for the promulgation of the sentence on Gun Eff. Walls of the 14th Roy A.S.C. attached to Ambulance. (To be reduced to the ranks & fined 10/-	W.O. Rame No 113 S.A.
"	7	23	Have arranged for starting work at the Bath Tomorrow. We are being relieved tonight from our A.D. Station. Town was shelled twice today one in the morning & again this afternoon though it seems we are not to be forgotten here even although we have become an Ambulance in Reserve	
"	8	22	Handing over & taking over our new duties was completed this morning without hitch. As is only to be expected in our new quiet duties Lt W. V. Cross & S.S.J.B. Rest St. S & Officers Brea Rest S.S & S.S. were	
"	9	22	Most very quiet. Only 23 sick admitted, no wounded cases this afternoon other an one of another sound civilian produced fours, only one of which was	

WAR DIARY
or
INTELLIGENCE SUMMARY.

Army Form C. 2118.

Place	Date	Hour	Summary of Events and Information	Remarks and references to Appendices
NOEUX ds MINES	10	21.45	A quiet day & nothing unusual to report. We have completed one of the Dry Rooms (see Appendix) & today it was handed over by Div: General.	
"	11	22	Got a start made today on Shower Baths have in addition to the two which are at present in use I intend my new A.D.S. MAZINGARB & the baths there which we are running. On arriving at some of my own tenderers to build a decent innovator where there do not seem to me to be of to their work. I am trying to get a clash hit of them at the baths for down & dirty clothing. Hospital quiet an clothing to report today, just worth on our new area being carried on.	
"	12	22	Baths have closed for two days to give us a chance. We are getting on however & generally trying to get a lot of amateurs into the correspon. Hospital quiet ag.	
"	14	21	Some rain today. Getting on with work generally. Hospital quiet at B	
"	15	22	Visited my A.D.S. today. Things are going fairly there, but require some looking after, as the work being done requires more supervision. Hospital very quiet (—) St Waast visited hostel to Ourdenvie today.	
"	16	21	St Nemours was sent back from the trenches with fever & is one of	

Army Form C. 2118.

WAR DIARY
or
INTELLIGENCE SUMMARY.
(Erase heading not required.)

Instructions regarding War Diaries and Intelligence Summaries are contained in F. S. Regs., Part II. and the Staff Manual respectively. Title pages will be prepared in manuscript.

Place	Date	Hour	Summary of Events and Information	Remarks and references to Appendices
NOEUX les MINES	16	21	(cont) my officers who went to our Sanitary Duty 4 days ago, got his attack seems like Trench Fever. He goes into the Division today. What we had elected for two days to nowhere (Chocques) Hospital. That	
"	17	22	Weather has broken. After the last few days we have had heavy showers which seem to diminish the the fly hatch Our fly trap was only a partial success, 1000 was about our biggest 24 hrs catch. I am modifying it somewhat. Baths going strong. Hospital quiet. CWB	
"	18	21.30	Again a wet day. Visited my ADS 4 arr't baths. the Sanitary arrangements there are getting into good order, but Shoes for clothing at baths are still required. Things here are going well now. CWB	
"	19	22	Nothing of interest to report today CWB	
"	20	21	Wrote to base today asking to have four cases which were reported as 2/S.W. Bombs an admission, 9 which 8 afterwards discharged were accidental wounds, reclassified. Things in Hosp. quiet. CWB	
"	21	21.30	Visited ADS. & Baths there this afternoon, things were going well. Paid the servers for over 1st fortnight. Things in Hosp. going well. CWB	

T2134. Wt. W708—776. 500000. 4/15. Sir J. C. & S.

Army Form C. 2118.

WAR DIARY
or
INTELLIGENCE SUMMARY.
(Erase heading not required.)

Place	Date	Hour	Summary of Events and Information	Remarks and references to Appendices
NOEUX les MINES	22	23	This was again a fine day, which was good after the last few days. Work getting on well. Some shelling of town this afternoon 3) in all casualties nil. cwp3	
"	23	22	Just received R.A.L.E. Open envelop NO 4, which I put to an equipment. Today all clothing was taken in from the Divisional Bath. We are feeling our wounded them so as to leave our improvements completed by the time we move. cwp3	
"	24	22	Ordinary received. We kept open here until the 26th. On that morning we march for our new Station. Things quiet today. cwp3	
"	26	23	This morning closed A.D.S. & Baths at MAZINGARBE. And chosen BERTON for the baths. Then went to AUCHEL & saw about a site for us tomorrow when we move. Returned here & prepared to close the Hosp. Several orders for our march from here tomorrow 6 a.m. cwp3	
AUCHEL	26	22	Marched as arranged this morning with ambulance to AUCHEL & opened with one section. St Pierre man regained the ind. from extra this station this afternoon. St aley during turkway duty with ambulance cwp3	36 R E 25 ax 2

Army Form C. 2118.

WAR DIARY
or
INTELLIGENCE SUMMARY.
(Erase heading not required.)

Instructions regarding War Diaries and Intelligence Summaries are contained in F. S. Regs., Part II. and the Staff Manual respectively. Title pages will be prepared in manuscript.

Place	Date	Hour	Summary of Events and Information	Remarks and references to Appendices
AUCHEL	27	22	A good day. Sent Ambulance 9 M.O. arrived today & collected sick from 4 & 5 of Brig. Sent two sections out this afternoon for 1½ hours march with full packs, as when we were working the line it was hard to keep the men in marching trim. Received orders re entraining 29/3	
"	28	21/45	Start trying again getting ready, then had two marches one in the morning with full kit, in the afternoon weaving Smoke Helmets. Sent on our advance party tonight. Have arranged for bath for men tomorrow morning	
FOUQUEREUIL	29	21-10	Have just entrained my Ambulance for LONGUEAU. As we marched to the entraining point we were caught by a severe thunderstorm & the whole party got wet through. We were unfortunate as we had no change of clothing for the men. We had to let the fellows & give them their tea before starting. Handed in remainder of all Transport this day to the N.S. Brown MINX.	W of BETHUNE one mile
SAILLY SEC	30	22	Detrained & ordered & marched to this place. The distance was about 16 miles & it rained steadily all day, it was a great trial on the men, but they got through wonderfully. We made one long stop on the way, whilst we sorted breakfast. We went of a Travelling Cooker in Ambulance Transport was felt this day very much	FRANCE ALBERT J 28 d 9-8

WAR DIARY
or
INTELLIGENCE SUMMARY.
(Erase heading not required.)

Army Form C. 2118.

Place	Date	Hour	Summary of Events and Information	Remarks and references to Appendices
GIBRALTER	31st	23	This morning received orders from 49th Brigade at 2.a.m. Again got these orders amplified from the A.D.S. at 5-30 A.M. The A.D.M.S. had told me the previous day what to expect, so I was ready for the radical change which these orders made in the running of the Ambulance & was able to have them carried out in time. The next visits were that at 8.45 A.M. the three bearer Subdivisions under my 2ic in command marched with the Brigade in quest, at least the remainder of the Ambulance, having outfitted two parties (consisting of 1 Officer & half R.O.s, 4 men to what is called the Corps Walking Wounded Collecting Post, & 1 N.C.O. & 12 of R.O.s & men to Entertainm Dressing Station) came on to this place where we have become the Divisional Reserve of R.A.M.C. Since arrival I have had to send one of my best remaining officers to the 7 London C/S as their M.O. had gone sick. So ends the diary of the Month	FRANCE ALBERT. (continued) L.3.E.3.0.

O.C. No 118 F.A.

Lt. Col. R^{ame}
F.A.

Sept. 1916

WAR DIARY

113th Field Ambulance. R.A.M.C.

FOR MONTH OF SEPTEMBER, 1916.

VOLUME 8

Army Form C. 2118.

WAR DIARY
or
INTELLIGENCE SUMMARY.
(Erase heading not required.)

Instructions regarding War Diaries and Intelligence Summaries are contained in F. S. Regs., Part II. and the Staff Manual respectively. Title pages will be prepared in manuscript.

Place	Date	Hour	Summary of Events and Information	Remarks and references to Appendices
GIBRALTER.	19/6/17		Sent off last month's Diary to A.D.M.S. This has been a fine day & one of my nursing men are looking themselves again. The officer I sent out last night to 4 L'inshen was St Watham	FRANCE ALBERT England Sheet 23.e.3.0
"	2	16	a fine quiet day & we all rested & ready for next move & went over today & inspected my Bearer Sub Divisions saw them nearly for their work which I believe starts soon. I today sent them St Michaels leave of St Ouenon who has gone sick P.U.O. orb.	
"	3	22	Bearer S. Divisional this morning to F.22 a.3.6. This afternoon received orders to send out another M.O. to 8" Munster S. sent Capt Black. Received copy of Secret orders A corps	
"	4	9¹	Received orders to pack up & to be prepared to move in ½ hour. This was followed by orders to be ready to move at 5 a.m., so tonight we are bivouacing.	
"	5	2²	Received orders this morning to march at 9 a.m to BRONFAY FARM Ambulance to march under orders of left Division which I went round the A.D. station which we were to take over with A.D.M.S. This day 1 officer O.R.Y.2 & my Bearer S.D. were attached to 3 Division	F29d.S.S.

T2134. Wt W708—776. 500000. 4/16. Sir J. C. & S.

WAR DIARY or INTELLIGENCE SUMMARY

Army Form C. 2118.

Place	Date	Hour	Summary of Events and Information	Remarks and references to Appendices
BRONFAY FARM	6"	23	This day saw appointed O.C. Bearer S.Bs. of the Division with orders to carry on the relief & evacuation from our A.D. Stations. There are two number one at BRIEFIELDS A.C.A.A. 9 & 13 ERNEFAY WOOD F26 d.5.5. 2 and really collecting stations, as this Corps no cases are admitted to Hosp. by Ambulance (A.-9.) (bearers) until they reach the Corps Dressing Station J.2d B. 2 in day. Hospital Casualties have 111.F.A. as follows Officers sk. O.R. 1 evac 2 (Wounded 2) The afternoon a reinforcement of 1 Officer & 30 O.R. from 61 F.A. was posted to me, until the return of my own bearers.	
"	7	2 2	Casualties today reported as follows 119 F.A. Officers sk. O.R. Killed 1 Driver 1. Wounded 8. Wounded on duty 2. Visited my A.D.S's this morning, with reliefs, all seemed going well, but there had been difficulty in front of ground to be cleared was very difficult, afterwards visited an A.D.S. (so called) at SAPPERS CORNER, which is staffed by no. 5. It is merely an Advance Dressed Stores. I then called on the A.D.M.S. who had just been asked for reinforcement to clear my left front. Shed informed this as being almost cleared, arrangements completed	

WAR DIARY or INTELLIGENCE SUMMARY

Army Form C. 2118.

Place	Date	Hour	Summary of Events and Information	Remarks and references to Appendices
BRONFAY FARM	7	22	(cont) for reinforcements to clear this point at S. remainder to reinforce the A.D.S. in question & the Brigade Head Quarters from which the report came, no enquiry with the A.D.n.S. we found things had quieted on that side & mental rases in question was cleared. This day my officer & 7 O.R's who had been sent to the S. Div returned, seemingly verbal orders, for the rating free of the party from 61/FA. which to be completed by 7 A.M. on the 8th, from which hour I am sending them off my strength. Yesterday had to detail St Cavanagh for duty with 5 Aust. Garrison whose M.O. was wounded.	
"	8	23	Received orders regarding a push in which great preparations to be gone. As the strenuous day from our infantry was further resisted (A.D.S) to all that had no bearing on. the M.O. of Py. The A.D.S. informed the forming of a new A.D.S. Col. Post, at GUILLEMONT. Shrinkage of its work was no longer in danger but I have sent out an Officer party to observe the best spot possible to locate at dressing stay for the day, I have chosen the south of MONTEUBAN as my headquarters for tomorrow I have which is about a mile long, no other for my reason beaven.	

Army Form C. 2118.

WAR DIARY
or
INTELLIGENCE SUMMARY.
(Erase heading not required.)

Instructions regarding War Diaries and Intelligence Summaries are contained in F. S. Regs., Part II. and the Staff Manual respectively. Title pages will be prepared in manuscript.

Place	Date	Hour	Summary of Events and Information	Remarks and references to Appendices
MONTAUBAN	MARCH 24		This has been a full day. This morning I got in touch with my new A.D.M.S. & sent there a reserve of dressings & water. At 6.35 am our artillery barrage started & at 6.45 am advance started. By 7 — hour wounded began to come in. There were large numbers of walking wounded at first but these at about 9 o'clock gave place to severe cases. By 21 o'clock I had to send on 50 severe bearer Squads on instructions from of the two near CCS. on the roads in their neighbourhood & as a result just put an Officer /SP 09.6 on duty diverting & helping wounded. I also got the Motor Ambulances to come to one half to a mile of my Post in the wood which was getting most cases. Stand expected these had taken to bearers from the put at the Creek files to augment their strength. At 1 gave a sentry well received & getting all wounded urgently as the same can expedited with them.	
HAPPY VALLEY	10.25		Have just arrived here as we were relieved this morning at 12 noon by the French. At 12.30 last night I had a message from the A.D.M.S. as he had had a report from 4.D.S. Brigade that we were being ascended with wounded. I was able to inform him and by 2 am we were actually away.	

WAR DIARY or INTELLIGENCE SUMMARY.

Army Form C. 2118.

(Erase heading not required.)

Place	Date	Hour	Summary of Events and Information	Remarks and references to Appendices
HAPPY VALLEY	1/10	23	(cont) Came however continued to come in and 6 am Stretcher parties left Bourges as I had been informed that the Germans would take over by 10 a.m. at the same time Stretchers & 30 Bearers who were sent on 4 sept down for a rest, but 4 out of my men were up. At 10 a.m my Adm. Car Post sent word that there were still some wounded out. By this the Germans had taken over our line & 9 their emitters were beginning to come in, as we had orders from O.C. our own wounded. I sent off a relief at 12.30. The Germans & ambulances came up & took over they at once sent out relief. Six hundred, on clearing all our own wounded. German having found one some after when there were still wounded to them, which could not be reached until night, without permission. We got orders to return & the German troops their wounded. Brigade accordingly I am ......O.C. of my own ambulance. I with the last Stretcher have on 3 our casualties amounting the wants were light Killed 9 Wounded 7 O.R.M. duty 2 O.R. wounded glass of adrift in the German own very slight.	
SAILLY-SEC	11	22	Sailly S. moved him with the ambulance having formed about my learned	

T2134. Wt. W708—776. 500000. 4/15. Sir J. C. & S.

Army Form C. 2118.

WAR DIARY
or
INTELLIGENCE SUMMARY.
(Erase heading not required.)

Instructions regarding War Diaries and Intelligence Summaries are contained in F.S. Regs., Part II. and the Staff Manual respectively. Title pages will be prepared in manuscript.

Place	Date	Hour	Summary of Events and Information	Remarks and references to Appendices
SAILLY e Sec	12	23	Spent today in cleaning up things after our late work.	
,,	13	22	A quiet day, sent the men for a march through a wood, & bathed in the afternoon. At the parade the remainder of the days events were to-morrow. He had evidently had some personal matter. Sergeant-Major & Sergeant.	
,,	14	20	Still have sent them for a march again today. Had to detail a party for duty with g.m.g. 2 C.S.N. Officer & 9.H.E.O. 6 others. To recently the officer. Sent was St. Peter's. The Body of the drowned man is still on my hands, but to be removed soon.	
,,	15-21		Being preserved from river taken over by 3 Major's Dep. & Corneal.	
,,	16	22	Some form of dianthoea has appeared amongst the men. It looks like Bacillary dysentery & must be looked to by Doctors.	
,,	17	20	Just ordinary work & cleaning of our surroundings or place is very dirty & flies abound everywhere. Sent off all our wheeled transport today.	
DONEQ	18	24	This has been a hard day. We closed at 4 marched 6 miles in the rain. After a three hours wait clear in the wet we were loaded in M. Busses which got as

Army Form C. 2118.

WAR DIARY
or
INTELLIGENCE SUMMARY.
(Erase heading not required.)

Instructions regarding War Diaries and Intelligence Summaries are contained in F.S. Regs., Part II. and the Staff Manual respectively. Title pages will be prepared in manuscript.

Place	Date	Hour	Summary of Events and Information	Remarks and references to Appendices
DONEGIE			(cont) got on here by 22-30. On arrival as there was no sign of our transport, which had come on the previous day, I got the men into huts. Later in the night I found our transport at the chateau.	
"	19"	22	This morning got my men together at the chateau, spent the day in getting things cleared up. There are still some cases of Diarrhoea amongst them	
PONT RENY	20	21	Have come on here with the Ambulance to entrain for an unknown destination. There are only moveable rompes for loading from, so the work is proceeding very slowly.	
WESTOUTRE	21"	92	Detrained this morning at BAILLEUL & after the men had breakfast marched here where we have orders to open up our position in an institute of Sort.	Sheet 28 M 9 C 4.
"	22 "	21	Have orders to hand over here to 112 F.A. & had myself in readiness to move	
"	23	20	Orders to move Ambulance on 24" to LOERE. Sent on an advance party today to take over the A.D.S. at KEMMEL from the Canadian F.A. I visited this line yesterday with our A.D.M.S. It seems a good one & the evacuation of wounded ought to be simple, as roads everywhere with good cover in most cases.	

Army Form C. 2118.

WAR DIARY
or
INTELLIGENCE SUMMARY.
(Erase heading not required.)

Instructions regarding War Diaries and Intelligence Summaries are contained in F.S. Regs., Part II. and the Staff Manual respectively. Title pages will be prepared in manuscript.

Place	Date	Hour	Summary of Events and Information	Remarks and references to Appendices
LOCRE	24	20	Horses here this morning & took over the building extant in rear of an out-house. The Hospital consists of two large wards capable of taking 150 cases & will take a considerable amount of work to make this place as it should be.	M27 26.8
"	25	21	This morning visited my advance line, & arranged for the drainage of the A.D.S. at KEMMEL which is waterlogged. Have arranged every 10 open a Rest Station in connection with my Dressing Station.	
"	26	20.	Today took over Baths at this place. The baths are showing a fairly good but the road to them is very bad, have reported on this to A, D. M. S.	
"	27	21	This morning had a parade at which the General Officer commanding the Division thanked the men for their services during our recent operations to the south. He presented three Military Medals which had been granted to the men (S. Sgt. James, Sgt. Hallewell & Pte Brumley. (by name). Pte Hill had also been granted one but he has been evacuated wounded, as has also Pte Pine (Siah), to whom another has been allotted.	
"	28	22	Visited the A.D.S. stations today, also went up the trenches to find some of the Reg: Aid. Posts which had been reported to me as recently constructed.	

Army Form C. 2118.

WAR DIARY
or
INTELLIGENCE SUMMARY.
(Erase heading not required.)

Instructions regarding War Diaries and Intelligence Summaries are contained in F. S. Regs., Part II. and the Staff Manual respectively. Title pages will be prepared in manuscript.

Place	Date	Hour	Summary of Events and Information	Remarks and references to Appendices
LOeRE	29	21	Accompanied by A.D.M.S. Division S again visited the trenches as there is to be a readjustment of Reg. Aid Posts. Any interest in these lies in the fact that I have four Dressers attached to each of them.	
"	30	22	Spent this day in seeing to the chain Dressing Station as there is a considerable amount of work which requires to be done there, before it will be up to the mark. Soon taking on the Kitchens, a Sergeant Ward of the House Lives first.	

W Barnett Lt Col RAMC
O. C. 113 Field Ambulance

Oct. 1916

WAR DIARY

MONTH OF OCTOBER, 1916.

VOLUME 9

113th Field Ambulance
R.A.M.C.

16th Div.

140/1819

Army Form C. 2118.

WAR DIARY
or
INTELLIGENCE SUMMARY.
(Erase heading not required.)

Instructions regarding War Diaries and Intelligence Summaries are contained in F. S. Regs., Part II. and the Staff Manual respectively. Title pages will be prepared in manuscript.

Place	Date	Hour	Summary of Events and Information	Remarks and references to Appendices
LOCRE	Sept 1	22	Borrowed lorry for September the day to A.D.M.S. 16 Division. Visited my A.D.S. & inspected the drainage which we are carrying out, in order to any the follow.	
"	2	21	Went this morning to the A.D.M.S. then to the D.R.E. & got sanction for the making of a Surgical Ward out of a Store Room here. Gave Capt Roswell the Personal Certificate which had been handed to me for him by G.O. Stevens.	
"	3	22	The weather has broken & this was a wet day. We made a start on the Surgical Ward.	
"	4	21	Another wet day. The A.D.M.S. was here this afternoon, he is transferring the Rest Camp to another site (M.F.A.). A few cases of Diarrhoea are coming in still, but none from the Ambulances.	
"	5	22	This was a fine day, & things look a great deal better even after the one day any. Wards going on well, but nothing special to report. CWS	
"	6	21	Today with A.D.M.S. I went to the line we at last were shown the Reg. A.P. We have been looking for, it was off the trench we had been given & that was the difficulty about it. Things quiet today CWS	

Army Form C. 2118.

WAR DIARY
or
INTELLIGENCE SUMMARY.
(Erase heading not required.)

Instructions regarding War Diaries and Intelligence Summaries are contained in F.S. Regs., Part II. and the Staff Manual respectively. Title pages will be prepared in manuscript.

Place	Date	Hour	Summary of Events and Information	Remarks and references to Appendices
LOERE	7	22	A showery unsettled day & hard to get on with outdoor work. Things in the line quiet.	
"	8	21	Visited A.D.S. today. The party there are getting on well with their work of drainage & making our nissen huts.	
"	9	22	A fine day. We carried on work on the Horse Lines & Surgeons Ward.	
"	10	21	Again a fine day, & we are getting on with our work at the Hospital. Our A.D.C.H.S. goes on leave tomorrow so I will have to be at headquarters only for a few days. Things in Hosp. quiet. Capt. J. van de Vijver returned from leave this morning.	
"	11	21	A fair day, rain threatening but not falling. General work in Hosp.	
"	12	22	Visited the A.D.S. & some of the R.A. Posts this afternoon. This morning after seeing work started at the Hosp. I went to A.D.i.S. office.	
"	13	21	Visited my A.D.S. again this afternoon as a report that it was not sufficiently manned. I found it in good order, & men arrive quite distinct.	
"	14	22	This was a showery day but work is going on well. A good day, ordinary work. Nothing of moment.	

WAR DIARY
or
INTELLIGENCE SUMMARY.
(Erase heading not required.)

Place	Date	Hour	Summary of Events and Information	Remarks and references to Appendices
LOREE	15	21	Sunday. Church Parade. Work carried on during morning at various works in progress as far as possible without alarm a Sunday.	
"	16	22	I have found that the Ambulance is to run the supply of water to the Garrison every man in the trenches to get a clean dry pair daily. Every 2 owned a stove for them & will start another same as soon as possible. They aim to be washed & moved at 10 am to the . General work here going on well. CWB	
"	17	22	Today I received notice that a case which I transferred to club 1 (Inpat.) No52 on 13" has been diagnosed "Scarlet Fever". The case was anyhow to Stranford. It was as a precautionary measure as I clued NYD with Posterior Eruption. As stated above they took three days to diagnose it. We had however disinfected the Hut & sent the immediate contact to Hospt. with the other as he also had fever. Today I went at 3 pm to vaccinate any in the Bry. who had not been recently vaccinated (6 years). They are on the firing Side & will be there for another 4 days, as wash, and inclets than we are not withdrawing them but having them inoculated daily. CWB	

Army Form C. 2118.

WAR DIARY
or
INTELLIGENCE SUMMARY.
(Erase heading not required.)

Instructions regarding War Diaries and Intelligence Summaries are contained in F. S. Regs., Part II. and the Staff Manual respectively. Title pages will be prepared in manuscript.

Place	Date	Hour	Summary of Events and Information	Remarks and references to Appendices
LOERE	18	21	Today I went to No 7 Gen Hosp to see my man, or rather the men I sent in who has been diagnosed Small Pox. They do not consider the case as such there neither indeed do I, but some one made the diagnosis which I suppose must now stand. Wink however progressing well up	
"	19	22	A very wet day. The D.D.M.S. Corps inspected the Hospital in the morning a series of fever reports from amongst the servants of the nobless Sandipon case. I went off somewhat from his house but could find no sign of that disease & however detained him for observation.	
"	20	23	A first day but cold. Spondlent illness as wind NE. As I went a fairly heavy Bombardment has started. One case admitted today The Smoke Rod (?.?) contrast of dite with today. Sgt Major See of the Ambulance went on Special leave today. CMB	
"	21	22	Went last night, nothing of much importance today.	
"	22	21	Again a good day. A.D.M.S. returned last night, as I am at my own work again. Nothing to report hence today. CMB	
"	23	22	Went the line today with D.D.M.S. Corps A.D.M.S. seeing a place where he	

WAR DIARY
or
INTELLIGENCE SUMMARY.
(Erase heading not required.)

Army Form C. 2118.

Place	Date	Hour	Summary of Events and Information	Remarks and references to Appendices
LOERE	23	22	(cont) wishes me to make an A.D.S. we went round the Lincolns. Today we entered on our Winter campaign against trench foot. We started the issue of a dry pair of socks daily to every man in the trenches. The ambulance is running the baths. Work here as usual. ACB	
"	24	21	A wet day, still we made good progress with our New Horse Lines and Sergeant Ward, Clothing Store &c to report.	
"	25--	20	Wet day. Went around A.D.S.'s. Have been granted 10 days Special Leave. Capt. G.S. van der Byl ver PACHE will be in command during my absence. A.W.Bennett	
"	26	19	Good weather. Lieut. Col. Bennett proceeds on 10 days Special leave this morning. Army handed over temporary command of 1st Ambulance to me. Wind safe. We has a short visit from the G.O.C. Division, Brigadier — , & Lt. Col. A.H. + 2nd # M.G. -This morning Lieut Vernon returned to-day from 10 days Special leave. G.T.van derByl was away owing to injury to ribs, reported for duty. A	
"	27	21	Miserably wet weather. Lieut Nicholls reported for duty. I visited the Batteries. Gave a course of gas lectures. I visited the 70 men on Sunday as messenger. Was short leaving to 70 men on Sunday as messenger. ward dangerous. G.T.V.	

Army Form C. 2118.

WAR DIARY
or
INTELLIGENCE SUMMARY.
(Erase heading not required.)

Place	Date	Hour	Summary of Events and Information	Remarks and references to Appendices
LOCRE	Oct. 1916 28	21	Weather - dull showery. Wind safe. I had a horse harness inspection at 10 a.m. Good progress being made with the Surgical ward projector. Shortage of material for processing with the enclosure of the Shelter.	2, T.V.
"	29	19	Dull showery weather. Wind dangerous. I visited the A.D.M.S. in the forenoon. In the afternoon I arranged for a Court of Inquiry to be held on the Injury sustained by Driver Walton W. on Friday evening.	2.T.V.
"	30	20	Showery weather in the forenoon. Wind safe. In the afternoon I held a Court of Inquiry as above stated.	2.T.V.
"	31	19	Windy showery weather. In the forenoon Sappers inspected our A.D.S. The two new dug-outs in connection with it. Work at the two new dug-outs at Spij Farm & Watling Street is progressing quite favourably. Wind safe. All other monthly returns rendered.	

E. T. Van Any ???
Capt. R.A.M.C

WAR DIARY.

FOR

MONTH OF NOVEMBER, 1916.

VOLUME 10

113th Field Ambulance.
R.A.M.C.

Army Form C. 2118.

WAR DIARY
or
INTELLIGENCE SUMMARY.
(Erase heading not required.)

Instructions regarding War Diaries and Intelligence Summaries are contained in F.S. Regs., Part II. and the Staff Manual respectively. Title pages will be prepared in manuscript.

Place	Date	Hour	Summary of Events and Information	Remarks and references to Appendices
LOCRE	Nov. 1916 1	19	Weather - windy not so cold. All the work of the surged was practically finished. Frame work of rack etc's finished. Had a visit from the D.D.M.S. + A.D.M.S. in the afternoon. The former especially went into the drainage question. G.T.V.	
"	2	19½	Showery weather. Work on rack etc. + surged wards progressing all night. Owing to shortage of material, there is only slow progress being made with the state. Paid off the ambulance in the afternoon. G.T.V.	
"	3	19	Very wet weather. Wind dangerous. Went up to the A.D.S. at ten in the forenoon. Paid three N.C.O.s, then up there. In the afternoon we had a visit from the A.D.M.S.; + at five p.m. Lieut. Nicholls gave us a "Gas" lecture. G.T.V.	
"	4	20	Devils good weather. Wind still dangerous. The manual work + jobs were continued with. I got them clothes on ready in the area of ground not in use. So as to avoid "puddling". There was a gas respirator drill for officers + senior N.C.O.C. in the afternoon. I saw that all weekly returns were rendered. G.T.V.	

Army Form C. 2118.

WAR DIARY
or
INTELLIGENCE SUMMARY.
(Erase heading not required.)

Instructions regarding War Diaries and Intelligence Summaries are contained in F.S. Regs., Part II. and the Staff Manual respectively. Title pages will be prepared in manuscript.

Place	Date	Hour	Summary of Events and Information	Remarks and references to Appendices
LOCRE	Nov. 1916 5	20	Very windy boisterous weather. Nothing unusual to report. In the afternoon I had a visit from the D.A.D.M.S. & watched the men working at some of the new drains. At 6 p.m. we had a death in the medical wards - a man who has been they were on D.A.H. G.T.V.	
"	6	19	Weather quite decent. Got the main drain in excess incinerator. In the forenoon we had a visit from our A.D.V.S. In the afternoon we had a gas respirator drill to the men. Govt Hygiene keep made with the new Sackettes; & we also got some of the "duck" boards laid down along the paths. G.T.V.	
"	7	19	Very windy quiet weather. Surgical wards practically finishes. Slow progress made with other jobs, on account of the bad weather. & we got more "duck" boards laid. Further progress made with the drainage. G.T.V.	
"	8	23	Miserably wet weather. Much the same as usual. Had a visit from our A.D.M.S. in the afternoon. More duck boards laid to drainage done. G.T.V.	

Army Form C. 2118.

WAR DIARY
or
INTELLIGENCE SUMMARY.
(Erase heading not required.)

Place	Date	Hour	Summary of Events and Information	Remarks and references to Appendices
LOERE	9	22	Returned last night from 5 days leave to England. I have again taken over the Diary. Went round today to ADS where they have made great improvements in the housing of the men since my departure. We have three horses over the drains to the Infantry and temporary measures. Work here at the drain DSStation also going well.	
"	10	21	A good day & cold. Warm breezy fighting much.	
"	11	22	A wet day. We managed however to get on with our work on Horse Shoe, Park etc. Nothing special to report.	CWB
"	12	22	Sunday & Church Parades, as want except that the Hospital was rather alight, as I sent in as many men as possible. Things went up the line. Capt Lyagone has today been posted to RA Buoy, was left who came to the Ambulance for relief. Stretchers have been sent from Auds to negro or temporary measures.	CWB
"	13	21	This was a good day & we got well on with our work of preparing for the Winter. Visited the ADS.	CWB
"	14	22	Weather still fine. This day evacuated Capt Lyagone to 2 CCS as he had Bronchitis & was not fit to take up duty with RA.	CWB

Army Form C. 2118.

WAR DIARY
or
INTELLIGENCE SUMMARY.
(Erase heading not required.)

Instructions regarding War Diaries and Intelligence Summaries are contained in F. S. Regs, Part II. and the Staff Manual respectively. Title pages will be prepared in manuscript.

Place	Date	Hour	Summary of Events and Information	Remarks and references to Appendices
LORHRE	15	21	Went around all of the ADS this morning & found things getting on very well.	
"	16	21	A rainy day but fine. The Surgeon general was around today & informed himself with our arrangements.	
"	17	21	Last night it snowed & today we have more snow. General an awful business as men not having cover.	
"	18	22	Quiet day.	
"	19	21	Snowing. Went around an dressing morning except for church parades. In the afternoon went for duty men. no special work.	
"	20	22	Rather wet day. Work as usual. Pale Stone & Surgeon Werner almost finished.	
"	21	21	Went around some of the ADS today & stretchers were very wet & getting about bad.	
"	22	23	A good day but nothing special to report except that Capt Roamer today left the Ambulance for duty with R.A. in relief of Capt Burch who has been posted to the Ambulance. ADS	

Army Form C. 2118.

WAR DIARY
or
INTELLIGENCE SUMMARY.
(Erase heading not required.)

Instructions regarding War Diaries and Intelligence Summaries are contained in F. S. Regs., Part II. and the Staff Manual respectively. Title pages will be prepared in manuscript.

Place	Date	Hour	Summary of Events and Information	Remarks and references to Appendices
LOCRE	23	22	A good day & we made good progress in our fight with mud.	
"	24	21	Ordinary work. The last few days there appears to be an increase in P.W.O. as yet I have no explanation for this, but it may have something to do with blankets, as I have noticed that blankets are treated as trench stores & handed over infested with lice.	
"	25	23	A wet day. Ambulance was inspected by D.D.M.S. Corps who expressed himself pleased with work done.	
"	26	21	A.D.M.S. Division inspected Amb. today. cups	
"	27	22	Ordinary Ambulance work	
"	28	21	Inspected A.D.S. today, nothing special to report	
"	29	22	A good day but very cold, ordinary work at Ambulance. We were to have taken over new billets today, but it has been postponed, as we have	
"	30	21	On 24th we lose our 1st case of Trench Foot for the year, & today we have had over 2 mt. Matter of the men has had the clean dry socks daily etc.	

WAR DIARY FOR MONTH OF DECEMBER, 1916.

VOLUME 11

R.A.M.C. 113th Field Ambulance

Army Form C. 2118.

WAR DIARY
or
INTELLIGENCE SUMMARY.
(Erase heading not required.)

Instructions regarding War Diaries and Intelligence Summaries are contained in F. S. Regs., Part II. and the Staff Manual respectively. Title pages will be prepared in manuscript.

Place	Date	Hour	Summary of Events and Information	Remarks and references to Appendices
LOERE	1/12	21	Journeyed three day last month down to A.D.M.S. today accompanied by A.D.M.S. Dinenen Savont round my O.D.S.a. also went to R aid Post in the area cleared by this Ambulance	
"	2/12/16	21	A very cold day. Two cases of trench foot admitted today both severe. On the 30th/11/16 Capt. Series also posted to this ambulance. Capt Beale was detailed for temp duty with a Regt. W3	
"	3	22	Sunday. Ordinary routine work nothing special	
"	4	21	Had a turn of Influenza today so could not get around, made arrangements however for the taking over of our new piece of line	
"	5	22	St Omer took over our new section of line this morning, he was accompanied by the A.D.M.S. Capt Van der Wyver Rache of this Ambulance came sick today	
"	6th	21	Today I am again at duty, but Capt V. de Wyver has still fever (Influenza) We are rather short handed just now, as we have three officers on temp duty with Regts, one sick, two at A.D.S. & tive here (main dressing station) Our section is working without a hitch, cys.	
"	7	22	Hosp inspected today by D.D.M.S. Corps, nothing to report.	

Army Form C. 2118.

WAR DIARY
or
INTELLIGENCE SUMMARY.
(Erase heading not required.)

Instructions regarding War Diaries and Intelligence Summaries are contained in F.S. Regs., Part II. and the Staff Manual respectively. Title pages will be prepared in manuscript.

Place	Date	Hour	Summary of Events and Information	Remarks and references to Appendices
LoRE	8	23	A wet day. Went around my A.D.S. inclining the new line today & have a considerable amount of work to be done there on dugouts etc. which have been started by the last holders.	
"	9	21	Again wet. Accompanied by A.D.M.S. again visited our new line. Ordinary ambulance work.	
"	10	23	Sunday. Today sent 23 cases direct to 112 F.Amb. was to relieve this one, as our numbers were mounting & we wished to avoid clearing single cases to C.C.S.	
"	11	22	A good day. Sent some more cases to 112 F.A. today, so as to get room for work in large wood which we are altering.	
"	12	21	Snowing all day & no outside work possible. Dot in hut progressing. Screen to divide big theatre ward now almost complete, when there are finished it will provide room to 3 wards each of which will be as a divey hall, large enough to suit the convenience.	
"	13	23	A good day, but nothing special to report.	
"	14	23	Accompanied by A.D.M.S. visited my A.D.S taken today.	

T2134. Wt. W708—776. 500000. 4/15. Sir J. C. & S.

WAR DIARY
or
INTELLIGENCE SUMMARY.
(Erase heading not required.)

Army Form C. 2118.

Place	Date	Hour	Summary of Events and Information	Remarks and references to Appendices
LOERE	15-22		A good day. Amb. was inspected by the 2 I/c O.C. Division in the morning & the D.D.M.S. Corps in the afternoon etc.	
"	16	23	This has been rather a hard day on the Ambulance, we had four men wounded. Dugout which was hit 3 times by 5-9" a piece of the men were badly damaged & the french entered. I often think it would be well if an intelligence could be made between F.E.S & Ambulances, as their staffs of their to me to be interchangable. If this could be carried out I think that an Ambulance would have 3 months as a F.E.S. & vice versa in the trenches. I am driven to this view by seeing my men, good men all, as they have proved again & again, knocked out daily, crushed in fact by almost gunner fire. This course also being about a better understanding between these units.	
"	17	22	Went around the line today to see how the men were after our effort of yesterday, at all our out stations they were doing their work well etc	
"	18	21	Nothing to report etc.	

Army Form C. 2118.

WAR DIARY
or
INTELLIGENCE SUMMARY.
(Erase heading not required.)

Instructions regarding War Diaries and Intelligence Summaries are contained in F. S. Regs., Part II. and the Staff Manual respectively. Title pages will be prepared in manuscript.

Place	Date	Hour	Summary of Events and Information	Remarks and references to Appendices
LOERE	19	23	A good clear frosty day turning to snow in the afternoon. The ambulance was inspected this afternoon by the Corps commander whose remarks on leaving was that "S Shades be pleased with my amb."	
"	20	23	A fine frosty Day. The Q & men have today but did not inspect the Hospital. We are getting on well in our duce fight & the fleas will soon be in fair water as regards receipts. Capt Varnon of the Amb left today on fortnight leave. WB	
"	21	23	We had service as thursday. St Ann Davies went on leave.	
"	22	22	Went around the area held by the Brigade with the Brigadier today nothing offered to inspect	
"	23	22	This was a fine day but very wild. The O.C. Brigade in whose area we were to put of a Brig. But has given us one near the place chosen as he does not wish anything put of there the position being too exposed. WB	
"	24	21	Christmas Eve. St has been a fine day. clothing & issue to infant	
"	25	21	Went around all my Bearer posts this morning. Say prayers well in Amb	

WAR DIARY
or
INTELLIGENCE SUMMARY.
(Erase heading not required.)

Army Form C. 2118.

Place	Date	Hour	Summary of Events and Information	Remarks and references to Appendices
LOERE	26	22	A quiet day. Christmas passes off all right. Sent relief up for my Bearers at A.D.S. but orders believed to remain at A.D.S. until ordered to return, so seems likely they may be wanted	
"	27	23	Went around the A.D.S. and the B.A.S.	
"	28	22	The bearers were not required as our divisn (Londonderry?) went off quite successfully, only two casualties, as I withdrew the entire bearers today. Cpt Cavenagh who has left us on the Somme wounded, rejoined us yesterday evg	
"	29	21	A wet day but work going on satisfactorily evg	
"	30	21	A good day, nothing special to report evg	
"	31	20	This has been a good day. The Divn General was around here today	

W Bennett

WAR DIARY for month of JANUARY, 1917.

VOLUME 12

R.A.M.C. 113th Field Ambulance

COMMITTEE FOR THE
MEDICAL HISTORY OF THE WAR
Date 13 MAR. 1917

Army Form C. 2118.

Instructions regarding War Diaries and Intelligence Summaries are contained in F. S. Regs., Part II. and the Staff Manual respectively. Title pages will be prepared in manuscript.

WAR DIARY
or
INTELLIGENCE SUMMARY.
(Erase heading not required.)

Place	Date	Hour	Summary of Events and Information	Remarks and references to Appendices
LOCRE	1-11-14	24	This was a good day. I visited my A.D.S. in the Left Sector was	
"	2"	23	Some shells dropped this side of the Trolley this afternoon. Shots they do not shell the Hospital. Observer returned from Scene.	
"	3	24	Quiet day nothing to report	
"	4	21	This was a stormy day as regards one of my A.D.S. 200 5.9 fell near it, all my men escaped & I have had a good report on their work during the bombardment. Our Journey yesterday turned out 45 k. point of order. 4,600 towels ans	
"	5	22	a good day & quiet up the line. Germans went nothing as well	
"	6	21	Went around our A.D.S. this morning our own Left Sector things were looking well, but they have been shelled somewhat heavily during the last few days.	
"	7	22	Went around the remainder of my line today with the A.D.M.S. who was looking into the work of some of the R.A.P's. There have been some heavy shelling during the night but out front escaped us	
"	8	21	This was a very cold day. Shelling still on increase	

Army Form C. 2118.

WAR DIARY
or
INTELLIGENCE SUMMARY.
(Erase heading not required.)

Instructions regarding War Diaries and Intelligence Summaries are contained in F.S. Regs., Part II. and the Staff Manual respectively. Title pages will be prepared in manuscript.

Place	Date	Hour	Summary of Events and Information	Remarks and references to Appendices
LORE	9	21	A good day, not much to report of interest, but things here are decidedly getting livelier	
"	10	22	This has been a fine day. Went around the left of my line WB	
"	11	22	Snow & sleet all day. Had to reinforce two of my A.D.S (Beavers) this evening but nothing happened. WB	
"	12	21	Again a wet wet day snow & sleet. Am getting on with a new Dug. I went down at our A.D.S on I/y 5 next & shall soon be finish. They reached it a yard WB	
"	13	21	Snow & sleet all day. WB	
"	14	22	Accompanied by A.D.M.S. Dereham, I went around all the A.D.S. & R.A.P.s of the Divisional Front today. Trenches were rather bad from frost & Snow. WB	
"	15-23		A cold day. We were inspected today by the Army Commander he seemed pleased with things. WB	
"	16	22	This was a fine day but cold, & the country Snow clad. Have in two days felt today. One an abrasion which had gone away in the frost the other french foot.	

Army Form C. 2118.

WAR DIARY
or
INTELLIGENCE SUMMARY.
(Erase heading not required.)

Instructions regarding War Diaries and Intelligence
Summaries are contained in F. S. Regs., Part II.
and the Staff Manual respectively. Title pages
will be prepared in manuscript.

Place	Date	Hour	Summary of Events and Information	Remarks and references to Appendices
LOCRE	17	21	Snowing all day. A number of cases of frost bite still coming in from one section of the line where the trenches were full of mush since last Staff. Rest of line few cases. cw3	
"	18	21	Snow a sleet, bad for work of all kinds. One man seen in the Amb. last night. Alcohol Poisoning, he apparently got hold of a Rum Jar cwg	
"	19	21	Still Snow. Went around DS. today. One case of frost bite admitted in person of a man whose vitality was lowered by PUO cw3	
"	20	22	This was a good day. Frost has event. The ADMS went on leave today & appointed me to act for him, an I will leave to rearrange work for the next few days. One case of frostbite admitted. He had PUO also which may account for the frost bite cw3	
"	21	21	Nothing special except indeed, that a soldier was found dead today & S. had to send the body to ADS ICCS. cw	
"	22	22	Went around ADs. today and visited the RAP. areas construction & dressing	
"	23	21	Hard frost. Both battalions of taken from frozen fit clothing of sent to rest	

Army Form C. 2118.

WAR DIARY
or
INTELLIGENCE SUMMARY.
(Erase heading not required.)

Instructions regarding War Diaries and Intelligence
Summaries are contained in F. S. Regs., Part II.
and the Staff Manual respectively. Title pages
will be prepared in manuscript.

Place	Date	Hour	Summary of Events and Information	Remarks and references to Appendices
LOCRE	24	23	Frost still holds, but men seem better than in summer weather & rain which we have had so far.	
"	25	23	Frost holds still. Went round the A.D.S. Put in cement at our Main A.D.S. a fragment of shell have been blown in to the gear. Have started work on the New Post near Sky Farm, & am fitting it for men & holding two beds, &	
	26	22	Still frost it touched 15°F last night. So far only two cases all like Frost Bite. Snowed with water pipe, A/S	
"	27	21	Two of my lorries were hit today their dug out being blown in. Should not ought to remove as wounds are not very severe, just flesh.	
	28	21	Watermans my O.D. Si the morning with D.D.M.S. Corps. Saw events done & settled on another post to be prepared as	
	29	22	Nothing to report.	
	30	23	Snow again today. Sent out carpenters from A.in.R to A.D.S.	
"	31	21	To start work on a new dug out for W. Barnett Nothing special to report	

WAR DIARY.

FOR MONTH OF FEBRUARY, 1917.

VOLUME 13

UNIT:- 113th Field Ambulance R.A.M.C.

Army Form C. 2118.

WAR DIARY
or
INTELLIGENCE SUMMARY.
(Erase heading not required.)

Place	Date	Hour	Summary of Events and Information	Remarks and references to Appendices
LOERI	1/My/91		Most obvious sign of trekking car ambush. Bernie transferred to Infts. Most of 1st E thought turns out to be Prisoner escort. One case of German measles today. CJB	
"	2	21	Frost again. Forwarded last month's Diary to ADMS on the 1st inst. CJB	
"	3	21	Nothing to report. CJB	
"	4	21	Went around ADS in the morning, work proceeding satisfactorily.	
"	5	22	Cases of sickness have attained, I think its first area on near 24 hrs up from the base. CJB	
"	6	21	Still hard frost. Went around some of the RAPs today. Work on some of the new ones is longing the amount of the frost as it is impossible to lay concrete just now.	
"	7	21	Frost still holds. We have given it trying to revet the back for the present but are trying to get them dried. one Hesl two lines below today 4 two men wounded by a dud shell, which exploded as they drove past. CJB	
"	8	22	Visited a RAP today which was damaged yesterday by shell fire. H as two men on repair work and had today by aerial. CJB	

Army Form C. 2118.

WAR DIARY
or
INTELLIGENCE SUMMARY.
(Erase heading not required.)

Instructions regarding War Diaries and Intelligence Summaries are contained in F. S. Regs., Part II. and the Staff Manual respectively. Title pages will be prepared in manuscript.

Place	Date	Hour	Summary of Events and Information	Remarks and references to Appendices
LOERE	9"	23	A quiet day & not much shelling	
"	10	21	Some shelling today near two of my A.D.S, but no casualties to my men. Frost shows signs of giving. Sent night patient admitted to Hosp., very dubious Temp. 105° Collected Papers, transferred to Sup. Hosp. at once as suspect today diagnosed Cer. Sp. Meningitis. (One of chumps admitted today (Officer) 12 days ago, he received a letter from his sister telling him she had another case)	
"	11	21	She A@cts returned from leave today. Have been granted 21 days Headquarters leave & Capt. J. Van de Veyver will take over the Ambulance & diary during my absence	
"	12	21	On Kemt. Col. W. Bennett being granted this week someone leave to the United Kingdom Have this day taken over Temporary Command of the Ambulance. Capt Connagh proceeds up to the A.D.S. in this afternoon to take over command of there. Work progressing satisfactorily. E T van den Vyver. (Capt R.a.m.c. (PR)	
"	13	21		
"	14	21	Clear Sunny weather. A case of N.Y.D was passed thro' the ambulance on ext 12 th. & diagnosed later at the C.C.S as a case of Cerebro-spinal meningitis.	

3.

Army Form C. 2118.

WAR DIARY
or
INTELLIGENCE SUMMARY.
(Erase heading not required.)

Instructions regarding War Diaries and Intelligence Summaries are contained in F. S. Regs., Part II. and the Staff Manual respectively. Title pages will be prepared in manuscript.

Place	Date	Hour	Summary of Events and Information	Remarks and references to Appendices
	1917 July.			
LOCRE.	14th	21	We received official intimation about Lieut Etemate. Every thing going on satisfactorily.	G.T.V.
"	15th	22	Fine sunny day. Our Brigadier visits the ambulance in the forenoon went round the wards & kitchens. Lieut. Nicholls was detailed to take temporary medical charge of the 9th R. Royal Irish Fusiliers; Capt Lewis returns to his Ching duty and the 11th Hants.	G.T.V.
"	16th	21	In the forenoon I paid the ambulance a visit the A.D.S. call normal. All work progressing satisfactorily. In the afternoon the A.D.M.S. call normal.	G.T.V.
"	17th	21	Good weather. Evacuates a case of mumps to-day. Lieut Dann & myself over to WIPPEN HOEK in the forenoon. On the way I called in to see the A.D.M.S. at WESTOUTRE. Work going on well.	G.T.V.
"	18th	21	Evacuates another case of mumps to-day. Work kept here & A.D.S. progressing satisfactorily. Capt Saxon now details to take temporary medical charge of the 9th R. Royal Inniskilling Fusiliers. Also Capt Vernon of the 10th Entrenching Battalion.	G.T.V.
"	19th	21	Foggy weather. An injection were we evacuants on the 17th K. was diagnosed as Scarlet fever. Also a case of the suspects enteric-proved	

T2134. Wt. W708–776. 500000. 4/15. Sir J.C. & S.

Army Form C. 2118.

WAR DIARY
or
INTELLIGENCE SUMMARY.
(Erase heading not required.)

Place	Date	Hour	Summary of Events and Information	Remarks and references to Appendices
LOCRE	1917 Feb. 19th	21	Strength evacuated to-day. Work progressing satisfactorily.	G.T.V.
"	(contd) 20th	21.	Dull showery. Capt Miller was posted to us to-day & taken on the strength accordingly. Very busy at the Baths. One man granted special leave to U.K.	G.T.V.
"	21st	21	Cloudy raw. Baths kept going from 8 a.m. until past 6 h.m. Capt Parsons returns from doing temporary duty with the 2/R.R. Royal Something Fusiliers. Was a meal from our A.D.M.S. in the afternoon.	G.T.V.
"	2nd	21.	Foggy damp. Two cases of infection were evacuated on the 21st were dangerous on measles. Work progressing satisfactorily.	G.T.V.
"	23rd	21	Foggy weather. In the forenoon went up to the A.D.S. Dug-outs work up at A.D.S. progressing very satisfactorily. Three cases of measles & suspected case of Cerebro spinal meningitis were evacuated to its isolation H.P.	G.T.V.
"	24th	21	Foggy damp. Our heavy guns were very active during the early part of the morning. Work progressing satisfactorily. 9 visits to dtn on the afternoon.	G.T.V.

Army Form C. 2118.

WAR DIARY
or
INTELLIGENCE SUMMARY.
(Erase heading not required.)

Place	Date	Hour	Summary of Events and Information	Remarks and references to Appendices
LOCRE	Feb. 1917 25th	21.	Fine weather. In the forenoon went up to the A.D.S. with our A.D.M.S. + D.A.D.M.S.. We visited PARRAIN FARM the dug-outs at REGENT ST. THUNDERHOEK. Work progressing satisfactorily. B.T.V.	
"	26th	21.	Fine weather. Engine of laundry broke down, delaying the output of works by some thousands. Evacuated a case of measles. Every thing else as usual. B.T.V.	
"	27th	21.	Fine weather. One of the children new on the Hospice here diagnosed as Diphtheria, him + self immediately taken to have inoculats to POPERINGHE. We had a visit from our A.D.M.S. in the afternoon. Daily Return shows 132 patients in Hospital. B.T.V.	
"	28th	21.	Good weather. We had four cases of alcoholic poisoning – two here + two at the A.D.S.. One of these died. Work progressing satisfactorily. B.T.V.	

B. van Anfyre
(ahl Name (S.R.))

Mar. 1917

WAR DIARY
FOR MONTH OF MARCH, 1917.

VOLUME 14

UNIT :- 113ᶠ Field Ambulance R.A.M.C.

16th Div.

140/2042

Vol. 14

Army Form C. 2118.

WAR DIARY
or
INTELLIGENCE SUMMARY.
(Erase heading not required.)

Instructions regarding War Diaries and Intelligence Summaries are contained in F.S. Regs., Part II. and the Staff Manual respectively. Title pages will be prepared in manuscript.

Place	Date	Hour	Summary of Events and Information	Remarks and references to Appendices
LOCRE	1917 March 1	21	Fine sunny day. Had one case of suspects Cerebro Spinal Mening. In from the 1st. Inniskilling Battalion. 119 Patients in Hospital. We had a visit from the D.D.M.S. in the forenoon. G.T.V.	
"	2	20	Fine day except for a shower or two in the forenoon. I paid the ambulance a visit in the morning then went up to the A.D.S. I visited all the dug-outs & Capt. Cavanagh. We received two new Trolleys for evacuating wounded. Work up there progressing splendidly. Had a case of Meningitis 1st- In Inniskilling Battalion. Number of patients in Hospital one hundred & twelve. G.T.V.	
"	3	21	Quite good weather. All much by return rendered. Trains up & numbers to the batth. Work progressing satisfactorily. G.T.V.	
"	4	21	Fine day, but colder. The ambulance was supplied from new for extra numbers. Number of patients in Hospitals one hundred & thirty five. The Divisionelle to-day. 15 fon. in in the afternoon. G.T.V.	
"	5	21	An inch & a half of snow. Twelve men were sent up to the A.D.S. to relieve the men there. The R.A.M.C. drivers were injured in the rescue of the battery slightly in their belief during enemy. G.T.V.	

Army Form C. 2118.

WAR DIARY
or
INTELLIGENCE SUMMARY.
(Erase heading not required.)

Instructions regarding War Diaries and Intelligence Summaries are contained in F. S. Regs, Part II. and the Staff Manual respectively. Title pages will be prepared in manuscript.

Place	Date	Hour	Summary of Events and Information	Remarks and references to Appendices
LOCRE	March 1917 6	20	Good weather. During the forenoon the work at the stables was inspected & order to allow our men to clean up. In green bi-day & medals. Work progressing satisfactorily. G.T.S.	
"	7	20	Cloudy rainy sleet wind snowy. Passed on from authority Capt A.A. Miller seems when to report for duty to the A.D.M.S. 25th Division. Lieut. Col. W. Bennett having returned from leave I gave up my duties as second in command, handing over to command to him. Number & details in Hospital 132. 2 Van de Vijver	
"	8	24	Good over gutering on return from leave. Fought in one lorry as our have been needed this afternoon. Wounded are coming in steadily. & the Ambulance is working steadily. Lt/Bennett	
"	9	25	Yesterday med cases were 25, P.U.O. were 5. We had 115 wounded. Last was attended to at about 3·30 a.m. We need the trailer in getting them in. AYB	
"	10	22	Things quiet again today. Loss of my bearers party was known in during that last attack, but the boys were away at the R.A.P. AYB	
"	11	22	Did not around some of my advance area today, nothing special to report AYB	

T2134. Wt. W708—776. 500000. 4/15. Sir J. C. & S.

Army Form C. 2118.

WAR DIARY
or
INTELLIGENCE SUMMARY.
(Erase heading not required.)

Instructions regarding War Diaries and Intelligence Summaries are contained in F. S. Regs., Part II. and the Staff Manual respectively. Title pages will be prepared in manuscript.

Place	Date	Hour	Summary of Events and Information	Remarks and references to Appendices
LOERE/2	12	21	Today completed the record of my A.D.S. One of them was badly damaged by a direct hit yesterday. Had one of my M. Ambulances put out of action today by a shell at my main A.D.S. Issued orders to my Advance line today for a readjustment of line observed by us, as ordered by A.D.M.S. Always to be completed by midday tomorrow. cup3	
"	13	22	Quiet day. Nothing of note to report. cup3	
"	14	22	Clearing to report.	
"	15	21	A Strong day. We are getting on with the Hoof generous cups	
"	16	22	Went of the line with A.D.S's today. Some staff officer have been around the Ambulances quarters today, and a new shelter to there be allotted to some other purpose. This seems a pity as we have accommodation for some 150 sick & wounded within 3 miles of firing line. Possibly sleeping the whole concern in in full warning orders & afraid of exposure to any capacity required. In fact as a M.O. I have never seen a better form for aid & wounded in an advanced a situation, it goes against the grain to give it up.	

Army Form C. 2118.

WAR DIARY
or
INTELLIGENCE SUMMARY.
(Erase heading not required.)

Place	Date	Hour	Summary of Events and Information	Remarks and references to Appendices
LOERE	17	21	Went around part of our line today with A.D.M.S. with a view to further reconnaissance. Nothing special to report. AWB	
"	18	21	Shining day. Sick in Hosp. becoming less. Am starting clearing out, as it looks as if we would have to shift from this spot soon & we have had on at average of 150 cases in Hosp all the winter.	
"	19	22	Again a quiet day. My Divt went in scrap by country in & relief	
"	20	21	Nothing special	
"	21	21	Snow again today AWB	
"	22	21	This afternoon for the first time since we came in our village was shelled, about 20 shells in all. There were few casualties & nothing fell near Ambulance. Nothing special to report AWB	
"	23	21	Went around my line today & found things going well. They are now shelled daily at my A.D.S. but so far only one of the men hit there	
"	24	21	Nothing to report AWB	
"	25	21	Nothing special. AWB	

WAR DIARY
or
INTELLIGENCE SUMMARY.
(Erase heading not required.)

Army Form C. 2118.

Place	Date	Hour	Summary of Events and Information	Remarks and references to Appendices
LOeRE	26	21	Snowing again today. Nothing special to report on	
"	27	21	Snow again last night. Am hoping to leave my officers mess as the building is wanted for an office etc. Besides both common & German is necessary translate. It seems to have come at from the line camps.	
"	28	21	Snow tonight but a good day. A Belgian interpreter to the hopital today still El Duston distant to interpret.	
"	29	24		
"	30	21	Went around our A.D.S.s today. The new shelter for my heavenly at end of the R.A.Ps is nearer finished & we have taken it over 24.75.	
"	31	21	Nothing special to report. WBennett	

WAR DIARY FOR MONTH OF APRIL, 1917.

VOLUME:- 15

UNIT:- 113th Field Ambce R.A.M.C.

Army Form C. 2118.

WAR DIARY
or
INTELLIGENCE SUMMARY.
(Erase heading not required.)

Instructions regarding War Diaries and Intelligence Summaries are contained in F. S. Regs., Part II. and the Staff Manual respectively. Title pages will be prepared in manuscript.

Place	Date	Hour	Summary of Events and Information	Remarks and references to Appendices
LOCRE	26	21	A quiet day again. Went up to A.D.S. and visited some of my posts was	
"	27	21	clothing to report.	
"	28	23	" "	
"	29	21	Went around my A.D.Ss today. There was some shelling of my main A.D.S. but nothing happened, as we are well sandbagged, etc. Left Swan downstairs amongst twenty + was wounded as it came from the Line today in a motor ambulance. Two men from a body of men we were leading put their feet under the wheels. I have referred the occurrence to the O.C. concerned etc. etc.	
"	30	24	There has been some shelling today near my A.D.S. but our forward central casualties also brought forty eight about 1000 at night but two men + three killed. Lt. Bennett.	

Lt. Col. R.A.M.C.
O.C. 113 F. Ambulance

WAR DIARY:
---------oOo---------

VOLUME:- 16

FOR MONTH OF MAY, 1917.

UNIT:- R.A.M.C. 113th Fd Amb.

Army Form C. 2118.

WAR DIARY
or
INTELLIGENCE SUMMARY.
(Erase heading not required.)

Instructions regarding War Diaries and Intelligence Summaries are contained in F. S. Regs., Part II. and the Staff Manual respectively. Title pages will be prepared in manuscript.

Place	Date	Hour	Summary of Events and Information	Remarks and references to Appendices
LOERE	1	22	Got news last month. Drawing to a close	
"	2	21	Nothing to report	
"	3	24	Went to ADS today to see about some extra sandbagging. One row of scarlet runners also a row of cabbage & knotweed	
"	4	21	Sent the leaves of our casement into our dear Lines yesterday also put the lemons in tents as the weather is becoming very warm again	
"	5	21	Nothing to report	
"	6	21	Went round ADS today as everest was	
"	7	21	Nothing to report.	
"	8	21	Some men today, which we wanted so things very, very quiet. Has three men wounded at ADS last night. They were hit after shell burst in house & fragments came through roof. One wounded through R chest, two other, one slight & a out pn.	
"	9	21	Nothing to report.	
"	10	21	One man who was hit through chest has had fragment removed last night & is still holding his own	
"	11	21	Nothing to report	

Army Form C. 2118.

WAR DIARY
or
INTELLIGENCE SUMMARY.
(Erase heading not required.)

Instructions regarding War Diaries and Intelligence Summaries are contained in F. S. Regs., Part II. and the Staff Manual respectively. Title pages will be prepared in manuscript.

Place	Date	Hour	Summary of Events and Information	Remarks and references to Appendices
LOERE	12	21	Nothing to report. arB	
"	13	23	Survey work around our ADS with the ADchS	
"	14	21	Some rain today what was badly wanted as water as bath etc hard to get about.	
"	15	21	Drew some extras from B.R.T. today with the object of further equipping our ADS. in ADS was lit by shell today but not much damaged, no casualties.	
"	16	21	Visited my ADS today & arranged for some more burrowing as now that the shells are coming in amidst our hourly huts from where they come, a shelter one wants to protect against them. arB	
"	17	23	Nothing to report.	
"	18	23	Went at line with ADchS & ADMS. Shelling at ADS still brisk.	
"	19	22	Our stretchers are getting on well, more & more are not now arriving now. Nothing to report. arB	
"	20	21	Went around the line today with the ADchS. Work progressing well arB	
"	21	21	Nothing to report	
"	22	21	Some rain today arB	

Army Form C. 2118.

WAR DIARY
or
INTELLIGENCE SUMMARY.
(Erase heading not required.)

Instructions regarding War Diaries and Intelligence Summaries are contained in F. S. Regs., Part II. and the Staff Manual respectively. Title pages will be prepared in manuscript.

Place	Date	Hour	Summary of Events and Information	Remarks and references to Appendices
LOERE	23	21	Am adapting an old French Shower apparatus to supply hot water to our men of firing trenches	
"	24	21	Visited A.D.S. alterations are being carried out rapidly	
"	25	21	Last night sent 4 G.S.W's. to our most advanced A.D.S. with stoves, they delivered their loads & returned empty carts	
"	26	21	Nothing to report in particular	
"	27	22	Went round my A.D.S. today	
"	28	21	Last night we had a lively time as there was a move on of which we received no notice. All arrived over got ly 4 am how when attempting there was smart shelling by the enemy. We had about 12 shells in the main A.D.S. but no casualties	
"	29	21	Shelling of Bush area again last night. Nothing else to report	
"	30	23	Heavy bombardment of Bush area as well as front no casualties amongst staff of Ambulance	
"	31	22	Things have considerably simmered down as we continue sandbagging the c.p's.	11 P.M. O.P. 113 F.A.

June 1917

WAR DIARY.

FOR MONTH OF JUNE, 1917.

VOLUME :- 4

UNIT :- R.A.M.C. 113th Field Ambulance

B.E.F.

SUMMARY OF MEDICAL WAR DIARIES OF 113th F.A. 16th Div.

8th Corps. 5th ARMY. from 22.6.17.

Western Front Operations - June - 1917.

Officer Commanding - Lt.Col. W. BENNETT.

SUMMARISED UNDER THE FOLLOWING HEADING :-

Phase "D" - Battle of Messines - June - 1917.

B.E.F.

113th F.A. 16th Div. 8th Corps.   5th ARMY.   WESTERN FRONT
Officer Commanding - Lt.Col. W. BENNETT.   June 1917.

Phase "D" - Battle of Messines - June - 1917.
Headquarters at Broxeele.

June 22nd.   Division entered 5th ARMY.

B.E.F.

SUMMARY OF MEDICAL WAR DIARIES OF 113th F.A. 14th Div.

8th Corps. 5th ARMY. (from 22.6.17)

Western Front Operations - June - 1917.

Officer Commanding - Lt.Col. W. BENNETT.

SUMMARISED UNDER THE FOLLOWING HEADING :-

Phase "D" - Battle of Messines - June - 1917.

B.E.F.

<u>113th F.A. 16th Div. 8th Corps.   5th ARMY.</u>
<u>Officer Commanding - Lt.Col. W. BENNETT.</u>

WESTERN FRONT
June 1917.

<u>Phase "D" - Battle of Messines - June - 1917.</u>
<u>Headquarters at Broxeele.</u>

June 22nd.   Division entered 5th ARMY.

WAR DIARY
or
INTELLIGENCE SUMMARY.

(Erase heading not required.)

Army Form C. 2118.

Instructions regarding War Diaries and Intelligence Summaries are contained in F.S. Regs., Part II. and the Staff Manual respectively. Title pages will be prepared in manuscript.

Place	Date	Hour	Summary of Events and Information	Remarks and references to Appendices
LOERE	1/10/1	21	Sent on many to A.D.S. Nothing of interest to report.	
"	2	22	Heavy bombardment material. Casualties increasing, all ready, cars went around the A.D.S's & R.A.P. today with the A.D.M.S. Things generally were going well.	
"	3	21		
"	4	22	Everything going well. Sent out forty to eventy our new A.D.S. at Roven Farm. cars.	
"	5	22	Things going well, can't get fast horse for Stones Splints so we have made them in ambulance. A cross piece of wood 6" high with 2½" cut out at each side where it comes on pole, a piece of wood 1½" by four inches let in have forward to pole which allows a wester of 1½" to project between the poles. Two pieces of about are connection when surface for stant with cap canvas. Racks supplied thus	[sketch]
"	6	23	Went around A.D.S, today found all ready & working smoothly have things ready here also. Have been reinforced by 15 & 56 Sanitary Sections of 112 F. Amb with 3 large distribu/ehicles & Ford. as well as 2 C.M.O's & 3 large Ambulances & 1 gave car.	

Army Form C. 2118.

WAR DIARY
or
INTELLIGENCE SUMMARY.
(Erase heading not required.)

Instructions regarding War Diaries and Intelligence Summaries are contained in F.S. Regs., Part II. and the Staff Manual respectively. Title pages will be prepared in manuscript.

Place	Date	Hour	Summary of Events and Information	Remarks and references to Appendices
LOCRE	7	22	The day we have been preparing for has come & gone. The arrangements proved adequate & tonight Devonshire Dressing Station is deserved. So are clear from Casualties due to enemy attack.	
"	8	22	It has been a quiet day. Our A.D.S. was hit by a fragment of a shell in the afternoon today yet the tent presently to in fairly comfortable circs.	
"	9	23	Our A.D.S. was evacuated today & I stood the journey well. I went up the line today to look into the evacuation. My ambulance car was running to the da front line. Everything was going well. Tonight is issued orders as to the handing over of our A.D.S. to the relieving Division.	
"	10	22	Handed over all my A.D.S.s today to relieving division.	
"	11	21	Started taking out again today. Serving the Staff we Cheered Officer Bristol 4, J. Onneuli 6, 65 Australians & R.A.H.S. Personnel (German) Officers 9, O.Rs 98. There was no hitch.	
"	12	23	Orders to march tomorrow.	

WAR DIARY
or
INTELLIGENCE SUMMARY.
(Erase heading not required.)

Army Form C. 2118.

Place	Date	Hour	Summary of Events and Information	Remarks and references to Appendices
Sht 24 W & 4 d.6.8	13	23	Got here after a 10 mile march. One of my wagons acted has been sent to Corps Salvage somewhere but could not carry my equipment without it. I have not got this today. We are not ordered for work here but are on rest after 4 months in the line, our	
"	14	22	A new A.D.d.S. has been appointed but has not got forward. Yesterday visited everything was alright was very much the worse for wear as	
"	15	23	Nothing to report cwB	
"	16	24	Received orders to march in the morning to Fourdrinoire, which means that after 4 months in the line the Ambulance has but 3 days in the back area on	
WOBURN CAMP	17	22	Marched this morning at 8.20 a.m. about 8 miles to WOBURN CAMP about 2 miles S of LOERE where we remained for today after trying to take over our old pitch. Tonight overran over-crowded & all available	
"	18	24	Returned to W 24 d.6.8. shot (28 Belgium & France)	

2353 Wt. W2514/1454 700,000 5/15 D. D. & L.   A.D.S.S./Forms/C. 2118.

4.

Army Form C. 2118.

WAR DIARY
or
INTELLIGENCE SUMMARY.
(Erase heading not required.)

Instructions regarding War Diaries and Intelligence
Summaries are contained in F.S. Regs., Part II.
and the Staff Manual respectively. Title pages
will be prepared in manuscript.

Place	Date	Hour	Summary of Events and Information	Remarks and references to Appendices
N 2 7 d 6.8	19	22	Tonight we cease to belong to 1st Corps. Capt Lowe rejoined. Lt chauvgnac U.S. She joined up 15/6/17. cws	
Q.19 e.26.	20	23	Marched to the farm today nothing to report.	
	21	20	Today we needed lessons of equipment etc cws	
BROXEELE	22	23	It has been out all day, & we got the benefit of it marching here.	
	23	22	We are in a farm house a hundred of so beds in a shed we are running here.	
"	24	21	Went around the Brigade today as we are now attached to own Brigade for duty with them, as we are Billeted in a very area area	
"	25	22	Nothing to report cws	
"	26	21	" cws	
"	27	21	Our new ADMS has not got some. Went to St Omer this afternoon	
"	28	21	Nothing to report cws	
"	29	23	" cws	
"	30	21	Brigade moved to new training area today, but ambulance still accompany, or billets several streets from here, expermentt	

2353 Wt W2514/1454 700,000 5/15 D. D. & L. A.D.S.S./Forms/C. 2118.

WAR DIARY.

FOR MONTH OF JULY, 1917.

VOLUME :- 18

UNIT :- 113th Field Ambulance
R.A.M.C.

COMMITTEE FOR THE
MEDICAL HISTORY OF THE WAR
Date 10 SEP. 1917

Confidential

War Diary

of

113th Field Ambulance

From July 1st 1917   To July 31st 1917

Volume 18

W Bennett
Lieut Col Kane
O.C. 113th Field Ambulance

B.E.F.

SUMMARY OF MEDICAL WAR DIARIES OF 113th F.A. 16th Div.

8th Corps.   5th ARMY.

19th Corps from 22nd July.

To 3rd Army on 22.8.17.

Western Front Operations - July - Aug. 1917.

Officer Commanding - Lt.Col. W. Bennett.

SUMMARISED UNDER THE FOLLOWING HEADINGS :-

Phase "D" 1. Passchendaele Operations,"July-Nov.1917.

    (a) - Operations commencing 1/7/17.

    (b) - Operations commencing 1/10/17.
         Canadians attacked Passchendaele, Oct. 30th.
         Canadians took Passchendaele, Nov. 6th.

B.E.F.

113th F.A. 16th Div. 8th Corps. 5th ARMY. WESTERN FRONT.
Officer Commanding - Lt.Col. W. BENNETT. July-Aug./17.

3rd Army 22.8.17.

19th Corps from 22nd July.

Phase "D" 1. - Passchendaele Operations, "July-Nov.1917"

    (a) - Operations commencing 1/7/17.

H.Q. at Broxeele.

July 1st-8th.	Operations R.A.M.C. Nothing of note.
9th.	Moves. To WINNIZEELE J.17.c.3.5.
18th.	Medical Arrangements. T.S.D. opened at WATOU.
22nd.	Transfer. To 19th Corps.
25th.	Moves. To LUNA PARK.

B.E.F.

113th F.A. 16th Div. 19th Corps. 5th ARMY.   WESTERN FRONT
                                              July-Aug./17.

Officer Commanding - Lt.Col. W. BENNETT.

3rd Army 22.8.17.

PHASE "D" 1. - Passchendaele Operations,"July-Nov.1917"

    (a) - Operations commencing 1/7/17.

H.Q. at Watou.

July 22nd.   Transfer. To 19th Corps.
    25th.   Moves. To LUNA PARK.
    26th-31st. Operations R.A.M.C.   "Work on new Hospital."

B.E.F.

113th F.A. 16th Div. 8th Corps. 5th ARMY. WESTERN FRONT.
Officer Commanding - Lt.Col. W. BENNETT. July-Aug./17.

3rd Army 22.8.17.

19th Corps from 22nd July.

Phase "D" 1. - Passchendaele Operations,"July-Nov.1917"

    (a) - Operations commencing 1/7/17.

H.Q. at Broxeele.

July 1st-8th.	Operations R.A.M.C. Nothing of note.
9th.	Moves. To WINNIZEELE J.17.c.3.5.
18th.	Medical Arrangements. T.S.D. opened at WATOU.
22nd.	Transfer. To 19th Corps.
25th.	Moves. To LUNA PARK.

B.E.F.

2.

113th F.A. 16th Div. 19th Corps. 5th ARMY.   WESTERN FRONT
                                             July-Aug./17
Officer Commanding - Lt.Col. W. BENNETT.

3rd Army from 22.8.17.

PHASE "D" 1. - Passchendaele Operations,"July-Nov.1917"

    (a) - Operations commencing 1/7/17.

H.Q. at Watou.

July 22nd.   Transfer. To 19th Corps.

             Moves. To LUNA PARK.

26th-31st.   Operations R.A.M.C.   "Work on new Hospital."

Army Form C. 2118.

WAR DIARY
or
INTELLIGENCE SUMMARY.
(Erase heading not required.)

Instructions regarding War Diaries and Intelligence Summaries are contained in F. S. Regs., Part II. and the Staff Manual respectively. Title pages will be prepared in manuscript.

Place	Date	Hour	Summary of Events and Information	Remarks and references to Appendices
Broxeple	1/7/22	22	Nothing to report. Last month's diary sent to A.D.M.S.	
"	2	23	Received instructions to clear from 45 Brig in addition to our own	
"	3	21	Nothing to report, except indeed that 5 have been granted leave for 10 days	
"	4	22	Capt. Parsons takes over the ambulance for the present arrangement. Lieut Col. Bennett D.S.O. left this p.m. having been granted leave to U.K. Nothing futher to report.	
"	5/7/17	21	Nothing to report.	
"	6/7/17	22	The H.Q. U.S. quartis W.T.A. two of transport -	
"	7	21	Nothing to report.	
"	8	22	Received orders from 49th Brigade to move to DE CROQUES FARM W.17.N.1.2.E.H.15. J.17.c.3.5. at 6.50 p.m. starting point Road junction B 27.5. O.C. 112th Field Ambulance. Under instruction from A.D.M.S. notifies O.C. 112th XIV Corp School and 45 Bde -	
Winnizeele	9	22	Arrived here. (DE CROQUES FARM J.17.c.3.5.) at	

WAR DIARY
or
INTELLIGENCE SUMMARY.
(Erase heading not required.)

Army Form C. 2118.

Place	Date	Hour	Summary of Events and Information	Remarks and references to Appendices
MIINIZEELE	9	22	(Cont.) 11.10 a.m. Received, on loan from Area Commdt. 16" Bath. which was erected for accumulation of convalescent R. aux. and A.S.C. one operating tent for patients; 3 L.D D. tents X I.K Corps. and H.Q. tents tents walked in this afternoon.	
"	10	23	Nothing to report — Leave from Dunmurry — Capt. B. Keevil Control Officer of cour Commando — Capt. R. Cavanagh still in attendance — WElateman	
"	11	23	The Ambulance was (by a 2 hrs worknunt from 10-12 noon under Lieut. Musgrave U.S.R. Bay Parade at 2.0 p.m. followed by a full kit inspection. J. Blaymush Capt.RAMC	
"	12	23	Lovely weather. Returning from temporary duty to its 14/K Royal Irish Fusiliers, I took over the tenporary command of the ambulance from Capt. J.B. Cavanagh. Nothing further to report B. T. van der Byrne Capt. RAMC. (S.R.)	

3

Army Form C. 2118.

Instructions regarding War Diaries and Intelligence
Summaries are contained in F. S. Regs., Part II.
and the Staff Manual respectively. Title pages
will be prepared in manuscript.

WAR DIARY
or
INTELLIGENCE SUMMARY.
(Erase heading not required.)

Place	Date July 5/7	Hour	Summary of Events and Information	Remarks and references to Appendices
WINNEZEELE	13	23	Fine warm weather. Sect 1 & 2 of Army Act men & both men on parade. Had a walk from S.A.D.M.S. in the afternoon. Issue from E.S. of ambulance of the note of new man Tuesday.	P.T.V.
"	14	21	Clear evening. The men and Emdering on the ground. Capt. R. J. Vernon + Pte. Roberts granted leave to 7th U.K. Two pack mules obtained in the ambulance	P.T.V.
"	15	21	Exceptionally good weather. Church parade at 11 a.m	P.T.V.
"	16	23	Returned from leave.	
"	17	22	Nothing to report	Aug 24
"	18	23	Opened a Band Subdivision at WATOU. Capt Van de Vijver in charge	184 d.19
"	19	21	Nothing to report	
"	20	22	Review French review on a moor on the 25".	
"	21	21	Nothing to report	
"	22	22	"	
"	23	21	Went & saw our new site. also the existing Corps Rest Station	Sheet 24
"	24	23	Sent on advance party	L.9 c.3.1
LUNA PARK	25	21	Marched from today & started getting here ready. Have got permission from my O.C. R.S. to draw some rations from R.C. Evans for the horse. WB	

2353 Wt. W2514/1454 700,000 5/15 D, D, & L. A.D.S.S./Forms/C. 2118.

Army Form C. 2118.

WAR DIARY
or
INTELLIGENCE SUMMARY.
(Erase heading not required.)

Instructions regarding War Diaries and Intelligence Summaries are contained in F. S. Regs., Part II. and the Staff Manual respectively. Title pages will be prepared in manuscript.

Place	Date	Hour	Summary of Events and Information	Remarks and references to Appendices
LUNA PARK	26	21	Went to Red Cross Depot today & drew some baths & other things for our new defences.	
"	27	22	Worked on new Hosp.	
"	28	21	Went up this morning to the line to see Aid Posts of A.D.S.	
"	29	22	The A.D.S. had an ambulance commander to a conference today.	
"	30	21	Sent W.E.O. & 2 men to establish a dump for us for water down the forward area. Nothing further to report.	
"	31	21	Today we added 200 Stretchers to our dump. Took in a few cases of concussion Shell from this mornings strafe, for an outing as a reception and for the very slightly wounded Consciously ged.	

OC 113 F.A.

WAR DIARY.

FOR MONTH OF AUGUST, 1917.

VOLUME 10

UNIT 113th Field Ambulance
R.A.M.C.

Confidential

War Diary
of
113th Field Ambulance

From 1st August 1917   To 31st August 1917

Volume 19

W Bennett
Lieut.ColonelL
O.C. 113th Field Ambulance

B.E.F.

SUMMARY OF MEDICAL WAR DIARIES OF 113th F.A. 16th Div.

8th Corps. 5th ARMY.

19th Corps from 22nd July.
To 3rd Army on 22.8.17.

Western Front Operations - July. - Aug. 1917.

Officer Commanding - Lt.Col. W. Bennett.

SUMMARISED UNDER THE FOLLOWING HEADINGS :-

Phase "D" 1. Passchendaele Operations, "July-Nov.1917.

    (a) - Operations commencing 1/7/17.

    (b) - Operations commencing 1/10/17.
        Canadians attacked Passchendaele, Oct. 30th.
        Canadians took Passchendaele, Nov. 6th.

Aug. 3rd.		Moves. To BRANDHOEK.
6th.		Casualties R.A.M.C. O & 5 killed.
12th.		Assistance. 50 Regimental Stretcher-Bearers sent to assist as ranks of unit bearers depleted by becoming casualties or exhausted by the arduous duties of carrying through mud over long distances.
16th.		Operations. Local attack in morning, was unsuccessful.
18th.		Moves. To WATOU Q 6a. (27).
22nd.		Moves and Transfer. To entraining point BAYENCHOVE on transfer to 3rd ARMY.

Aug. 3rd.   Moves. To BRANDHOEK.

6th.   Casualties R.A.M.C. O & 5 killed.

12th.   Assistance. 50 Regimental Stretcher Bearers sent to assist as ranks of unit bearers depleted by becoming casualties or exhausted by the arduous duties of carrying through mud over long distances.

16th.   Operations. Local attack in morning, was unsuccessful.

18th.   Moves. To WATOU Q 6a. (27).

22nd.   Moves and Transfer. To entraining point BAYENCHOVE on transfer to 3rd ARMY.

Army Form C. 2118.

WAR DIARY
or
INTELLIGENCE SUMMARY.
(Erase heading not required.)

Place	Date	Hour	Summary of Events and Information	Remarks and references to Appendices
BRAND-HOEK	10	22	A quiet day for this front. Nothing special to report. cw/3	
"	11	22	Nothing special to report. cw/3	
"	12	23	Sorry we are to be reinforced by 50 Regt Bearers, so as to give my men a little rest. They turned up to the strength of 33. S hope to get the Bearers in the morning. There is a fairly quiet day. Attent arrived the A.D.S. this morning. A nurse is attending sometime. cw/3	
"	13	21	Nothing special	
"	14	22	Weather still here, but we are ready when it improves. ADSs around the ADS. So today to see all were correct. One ADS was badly shaken, but is being cleared up tonight by some Elephants. Thus we line up. cw/3	
"	15	23	Everything ready. One of my officers died today (Bathgate) & SW (shelled) was asked this morning and had to pose back from shell of the carried territory. S hi made collection of wounded difficult but they are coming in steadily. cw/3	
"	16	22		
"	17	20	We have received orders to hand over this section tomorrow to another factory. Have announced camps	

Army Form C. 2118.

WAR DIARY
or
INTELLIGENCE SUMMARY.
(Erase heading not required.)

Place	Date	Hour	Summary of Events and Information	Remarks and references to Appendices
WARLOY	18	22	Came out of the line today & returned here. Location is in a Hospice, accommodation roughly 100 cooking our tents etc	
"	19	23	Nothing to report.	
"	20	22	Shifted camp today to a farm where we have past of Sheet 24 E 2 a.a. up	
"	21	23	Nothing to report	
"	22	22	Entrained today at BAVENCHONE & have just arrived at MIRAUMONT	
ACHIET le GRAND	23	19	Marched to ACHIET le GRAND where we have fixed up for 100 patients	
"	24	22	Nothing to report.	
"	25	22	Sent off an advance party today to LACOUCHIE where we are to open	
LACOUCHIE	26	21	Travelled off at 8 a.m. & arrived at this place at 12 noon. This is to be our main dressing station for the present. It really will be a sort of Rest camp for Divisional Convalescents	
"	27	19	Rained all day, so could do little with new fitted	
"	28	22	This was a fine day & we got started with our work etc	
"	29	22	Nothing to report. NB	
"	30	23	Visited R Ros Evan Sorby today to arrange for 40 Beds to complete thirteen	
"	31	23	Nothing to report. A/ Bennett	

WAR DIARY.

FOR MONTH OF SEPTEMBER, 1917.

VOLUME 20

UNIT:- R.A.M.C. 113th Field Ambulance

Confidential

War Diary
of
113th Field Ambulance

From Sept 1917   To Sept 30th 1917

(Volume 20)

W T Bennett
Arthur Rose
OC 113th Fd Amb

Army Form C. 2118.

WAR DIARY
or
INTELLIGENCE SUMMARY.
(Erase heading not required.)

Instructions regarding War Diaries and Intelligence Summaries are contained in F. S. Regs., Part II. and the Staff Manual respectively. Title pages will be prepared in manuscript.

Place	Date	Hour	Summary of Events and Information	Remarks and references to Appendices
LA ROUCHE	1/9/17		Last month's diary ready for A.D.M.S. CWB	
"	2	22	Nothing to report except last month's diary forwarded to A.D.M.S.	
"	3	23	Nothing special CWB	
"	4	22	Work has going well. Have been mainly completed, but also it is considered that we are too far from the line, & we are to be ready to move forward. CWB	
"	5	23	A.D.M.S. Divn gone on 10 days leave Senr to act.	
"	6	23	Nothing to report	
"	7	22	Sent off advance party to start work on our new field. The ground is covered with felled trees & wire & will take a lot of clearing. CWB	
"	8	22	Nothing to report	
"	9	22	Nothing special.	
"	10	23	Getting on with clearing field for my new main Dressing Station	
"	11	23	Nothing to report.	
"	12	22	Visited new site for Amb. today, everth there is going on well	
"	13	22	Nothing to report. CWB	
"	14	23	Nothing to report. CWB	

Army Form C. 2118.

WAR DIARY
or
INTELLIGENCE SUMMARY.

(Erase heading not required.)

Instructions regarding War Diaries and Intelligence Summaries are contained in F. S. Regs., Part II. and the Staff Manual respectively. Title pages will be prepared in manuscript.

Place	Date	Hour	Summary of Events and Information	Remarks and references to Appendices
LAROUE	15	23	Visited our new field again today. CURZONETT	
"	16	22	Nothing to report. WB	
"	17	23	I find it very hard to get transport to move up my Hospital Huts to our new site. Same allowed this service daily but as they only make one run and that between the two, I find it very slow and not between the fortnight it's hard. One	
"	18	22	Visited new site again today. A.D.M.S. has returned from leave.	
"	19	23	Nothing to report except in fact that two new officers their arrived today.	
"	20	22	Nothing to report.	
"	21	24	Visited my new site again today. We have now all the ground cleared & four of the huts up.	
"	22	23	Attended a conference of Ambulance Commanders today at A.D.M.S's office where the necessary precautions we are now given are as well as arriving the matter. Capt. Smyth who joined the Amb. on the 20th inst. was detailed off strength today having been detailed for duty in No 1 Br. Brigade was left us today having been posted to Base.	
"	23	23	Nothing to report	

Army Form C. 2118.

WAR DIARY
or
INTELLIGENCE SUMMARY.
(Erase heading not required.)

Instructions regarding War Diaries and Intelligence Summaries are contained in F. S. Regs., Part II. and the Staff Manual respectively. Title pages will be prepared in manuscript.

Place	Date	Hour	Summary of Events and Information	Remarks and references to Appendices
LECUWE HIE 24	24	23	Nothing to report. WB	
"	25	22	Nothing to report.	
"	26	23	Work at new site is going on wonders	
"	27	24	Our new site was inspected by O.S.M.S Corps today, work is going on well there. WB	
"	28	23	Nothing to report.	
"	29	23	Nothing to report. WB	
"	30	22	Was at new pitch again today. There is much sorting of rubbish & manure, so that our way back I got my men to clear what I take is an old gun wash cart for that purpose. The wheels are damaged as I have brought ten wheels, which I think will fit it. I am seeing the cart have about these wheels, as they are sent by a French peasant & seem to be civilians, but I can see no much outher thing except in this is to save wear on my G.S. carts, as I am with (1.10.19 M.S.d.) I am not away the several others but have next them back to where they were found. The cart I am told old right my authority is the WOF of the above. We have since others. MOR WB	

WAR DIARY

FOR MONTH OF OCTOBER, 1917.

UNIT 113th Fd Amb. R.A.M.C.

VOLUME NUMBER 21

Confidential.

War Diary
of
113th Field Ambulance

From 1-10-17   To. 31-10-17

(Volume 21)

G.T. van en Lyn
Capt. R.A.M.C.
for O/113th Fd Amb

Army Form C. 2118.

Instructions regarding War Diaries and Intelligence Summaries are contained in F. S. Regs., Part II. and the Staff Manual respectively. Title pages will be prepared in manuscript.

WAR DIARY
or
INTELLIGENCE SUMMARY.
(Erase heading not required.)

Place	Date	Hour	Summary of Events and Information	Remarks and references to Appendices
LA COUTURE	1/10	23	Visited our new site again today & arranged with the R.E. for trees which are rather in the way etc.	
,,	2	23	Spent the day around the place, & sent in report to D.D.M.S. 4th Corps on huts which are available in this neighbourhood etc.	
,,	3	22	Nothing to report.	
,,	4	23	Accompanied the A.D.M.S. today to the site of a proposed A.D.S. which he wishes us to establish, so as to shorten the present carry by the bearer divs.	
,,	5	23	Nothing to report.	
,,	6	22	,, ,, ,, except more cattle has caught us on our move & makes the putting up of huts difficult.	
,,	7	23	Still rain & wet, yet work goes on, but getting up of huts is difficult now.	
,,	8	23	Rain etc.	
,,	9	23	Nothing to report.	
,,	10	23	Received orders to send a party to prepare an A.D.S. in the forward area. Went up today & pointed them to their duties. One water detail from unit today for divisional work, in accordance with orders A.D.M.S.	
,,	11	23	Spent the day around home forming our Scheme tour, etc. to fly, & march in 2 & 5 Rd [?], 5, 6, 7, 8, 9, 10 ADS D Doct &c A.D.S.S. forms/C. 2118 they had not even a fortnight to get in as lorry.	

Army Form C. 2118.

WAR DIARY
or
INTELLIGENCE SUMMARY.
(Erase heading not required.)

Instructions regarding War Diaries and Intelligence
Summaries are contained in F. S. Regs., Part II.
and the Staff Manual respectively. Title pages
will be prepared in manuscript.

Place	Date	Hour	Summary of Events and Information	Remarks and references to Appendices
LA COUTURE	12	23	Again rain, work on our station is very difficult due to this break in the weather.	
"	13	23	Nothing to report.	
"	14	22	Nothing to report.	
"	15	24	Called at A.D.M.S. office this morning, where I was examined & found fit for Service (I'm graphic). Visited my company part at new site where things are going well.	
"	16	23	Nothing to report.	
"	17	23	We are to move up to our new site tomorrow.	
SAPIGNIES	18	22	Moved up here today.	
"	19	23	A threatening day with some rain.	
"	20	23	A fine day getting on with the work, military work party to our reserve posts.	
"	21	23	A conference of S.A. Commanders today.	
"	22	22	Went around part of line today with the A.D.M.S.	
"	23	24	Was inspected today by a Col.J of D.D.M Services. Wet day	
"	24	20	Going on leave, Capt. J. Van de Vyvere in charge	

2353 Wt. W2544/1454 700,000 5/15 D.D.& L. A.D.S.S./Forms/C. 2118.

Army Form C. 2118.

WAR DIARY
or
INTELLIGENCE SUMMARY.
(Erase heading not required.)

Instructions regarding War Diaries and Intelligence
Summaries are contained in F. S. Regs., Part II.
and the Staff Manual respectively. Title pages
will be prepared in manuscript.

Place	Date	Hour	Summary of Events and Information	Remarks and references to Appendices
SAPIGNIES	Oct 1917 25/5	20	Wet boisterous weather. Work progressing favourably.	Strength/......
"	26"	22	In the forenoon I visited the A.D.S at ECOUST, & took up 4 bearers.	G.T.V.
"	27"	22	- for the Aid Post at RAILWAY RESERVE. Showery wind, rain. Has a visit from our D.D.M.S. in the forenoon. Opened 1 surgical & 1 medical hut for patients.	G.T.V.
"	28"	22	Work progressing favourably. Operating hut [ ] completed to receiving patients.	G.T.V.
"	29"	22	Fine crisp weather. Hut for A.S.C. (horse transport) [ ] mentally finished. Construction of camp nrl.E. kept back on account of a temporary shortage of some of the material.	G.T.V.
"	30"	22	Weather wet, windy, rainy. Lt. Johnston of the M.T. S.R. M.C. arrived early this morning & is taken on our strength from that date. Re letter of Col. Cummins - left this Division yesterday on Duty elsewhere. War progressing well.	G.T.V. O C's
"	31"	23	Good weather. In the forenoon the A/A.D.M.S. had a Conference of ambulance. A week's supply of material received from Engineers. Hut nearly completed.	G.T.V.

Confidential

War Diary
of
113th Field Ambulance.

From 1st November 1914 to 30th November 1914

(Volume 22)

40/2578

COMMITTEE FOR THE
MEDICAL HISTORY OF THE WAR
Date 17 JAN. 1918

W J Bennett
Lieut Colonel RAMC
O.C. 113th Field Amb.

Army Form C. 2118.

Instructions regarding War Diaries and Intelligence
Summaries are contained in F. S. Regs., Part II.
and the Staff Manual respectively. Title pages
will be prepared in manuscript.

WAR DIARY
or
INTELLIGENCE SUMMARY.
(Erase heading not required.)

Place	Date	Hour	Summary of Events and Information	Remarks and references to Appendices
SAPIGNIES.	Nov. 1917 1st.	23	Pleasant weather most so cols. Received 6 patients from the M.I.R. Field Ambulance. 26 patients in our wards so far. Good progress being made with our work. Has a visit from the "C.R.E." in the afternoon. He seems very pleased with our work.	G.T.V.
"	2nd	22	Medy most so cols. In the afternoon I visited the A.D.S. at ECOUST, the two Aid posts in RAILWAY RESERVE, KNUCKLE Post, & the QUARRY Aid post. Line very quiet.	G.T.V
"	3rd	22.	Similar weather to yesterday's. Work here at M.D.S. progressing very favourably. 42 patients remaining; 7 to beds prepared for gomore.	G.T.V.
"	4th	23	Colder weather. Work going well. Nothing further to report.	G.T.V.
"	5th	23	Good progress being made c roads + drains New incinerator starts. 9 men being sent daily to help with work at ECOUST	G.T.V.
"	6th	22.	Cts mud. Improved Art water bottles even being made by Ambulance. Nearly all the actd timber, corrugated iron etc now dumped near pline hut. Other work going on well.	G.T.V
"	7th	23	Work going on satisfactorily. Had a visit from our new A.D.M.S. in the afternoon - Col Campbell.	G.T.V

Army Form C. 2118.

WAR DIARY
or
INTELLIGENCE SUMMARY.
(Erase heading not required.)

Instructions regarding War Diaries and Intelligence Summaries are contained in F. S. Regs, Part II. and the Staff Manual respectively. Title pages will be prepared in manuscript.

Place	Date	Hour	Summary of Events and Information	Remarks and references to Appendices
SAPIGNIES	Nov 1917 8th	19½	Showery weather. All our small box respirators are being fitted with the new containers. 56 patients now in Hospital. Has a visit from the D.D.M.S.	G.T.V.
"	9th	22	Much colder Johnny. In the forenoon I visited the A.D.S at PECOURT, + found everything going well. I had some blankets, hot-bottles, medical comfrts, etc. sent up to the N.C.O in charge.	G.T.V.
"	10th	20½	Cold Johnny. Work going on well, except that there is still a shortage of material, which is keeping us back. The C.O. returns from leave this evening.	G.T.V.
"	11	22	I passed in London on the 9th. I returned here last night. Today I visited our A.D.S. & Bearer Post with Dmvd our A.D.M.S. who was posted to the Division during my absence underneath,	
"	12	21	Nothing to report.	
"	13	22	Attended a conference of our Commanders at A.D.M.S. today.	
"	14	21	Nothing to report.	
"	15	23	Nothing to report.	
"	16	24	Visited my A.D.S.	

WAR DIARY
or
INTELLIGENCE SUMMARY.
(Erase heading not required.)

Army Form C. 2118.

Place	Date	Hour	Summary of Events and Information	Remarks and references to Appendices
SAPIGNIE	14	23	Nothing to report	
"	15	22	Sent reinforcements to two e.e.S today, which makes 36 men away from my Ambulance on this duty as well as two of O's. This is not very satisfactory, when one is in the line. One would think it better if each be arranged to reinforce the two out divisions of the Ambulances & let the enemy see the divisions of R.E.S. This were done one would know where one was instead of having to meet the emergencies of the line with depleted staff.	
"	19	23	Was up the line today, seeing things were going fair a little above which was expected in the near future.	
"	20	24	Active of wounded undertaken this morning. Cases were sent direct to e.e.S. which were reinforced from Ambulances. Ambs. A & D Brooks were also left there. This worked satisfactorily. cvs	
"	21	22	Things settled down, all cleaning finished early yesterday but I have not got my rearers back yet. cvs	

Army Form C. 2118.

Instructions regarding War Diaries and Intelligence
Summaries are contained in F. S. Regs., Part II.
and the Staff Manual respectively. Title pages
will be prepared in manuscript.

WAR DIARY
or
INTELLIGENCE SUMMARY.
(Erase heading not required.)

Place	Date	Hour	Summary of Events and Information	Remarks and references to Appendices
SAPIGNIE	22	23	Reserves returned yesterday, no casualties amongst them, a reserve platoon of	
"	23	23	Sent up 10 Reserves this afternoon in answer to a call from Hq in line, cuts	
"	24	23	Went round ADS & RAP's today. Last nights operations successful. Strong	
			withdrew extra Reserves.	
"	25	24	Nothing to report. W. Bennett	
"	26	23	This evening Strong 4 man reserving engaged. First night out this	
			this winter. Started Reserves marching to get them into good trim	
			again as things look unsettled again.	
"	27	23	Nothing to report	
"	28	22	" " "	
"	29	23	Received orders to take 2nd here again, instead of sending all cases	
			direct to CCS as we have been doing. We have received a preliminary	
			notice that we are to be ready to hand over	
"	30	21	Sent nights orders pleased in everyone for the present. Have got back	
			some of my men who were attached to C.C.S's W. Bennett Lt Col R.A.M.C

WAR DIARY

FOR MONTH OF DECEMBER, 1917.

VOLUME :- 25.

UNIT :- 113th Field Ambulance, R.A.M.C.

Confidential
War Diary
of
113th Field Ambulance.

From Dec 1st 1917 to Dec 31st 1917

(Volume 23)

W.J. Bennett
Lt Col R.A.M.C.
O.C. 113th Field Ambulance

Army Form C. 2118.

WAR DIARY
or
INTELLIGENCE SUMMARY.
(Erase heading not required.)

Instructions regarding War Diaries and Intelligence Summaries are contained in F. S. Regs., Part II. and the Staff Manual respectively. Title pages will be prepared in manuscript.

Place	Date	Hour	Summary of Events and Information	Remarks and references to Appendices
SAPIGNIES	1	23	Sent off last month's diary. Received notice that an advance party of 135 F.A. is to take over tomorrow. WB.	
"	2	23	Orders to move tomorrow but keep 4 places not yet given. Handed over this a.m. today with A.D.S. to advance party of 135 F.A.	
"	3	23	Very fine day. Marched to BARASTRE	
BARASTRE	4	22	Ready to march all day on advance with orders received, but still orders to start not received	
TINEOURT	5	23	Marched to Tineourt, distance about 12 miles.	
"	6	22	Sent an party today to take over the new line A.D.S. We take over the Main Dressing Station at VILLERS FAUCON at 10 A.M. Tomorrow	
V. FAUCON	7	24	Took over main dressing station here today. Visited A.D.S. WB	
"	8	22	Went around the 3 R.A.P.s on the Divisional front today. The evacuation from all is simple being by wheeled stretcher along main roads. There are however some very enforced as we also the R.A.P.s, which lie very near the front line, a good fault, but still in this area I am afraid still a fault as they are practically in the front line, with expected advance expected. WB	
"	9	22	Lt. Duncan USA C.A.R. reported the Amb today from 18 J. P. P. S. WB	

Army Form C. 2118.

WAR DIARY
or
INTELLIGENCE SUMMARY.
(Erase heading not required.)

Instructions regarding War Diaries and Intelligence Summaries are contained in F. S. Regs., Part II. and the Staff Manual respectively. Title pages will be prepared in manuscript.

Place	Date	Hour	Summary of Events and Information	Remarks and references to Appendices
V.F0ueoN	10	22	Nothing to report	
"	11	23	Went around line with a D.A.D.S today, arranging for new R.A.Ps	
"	12	22	Work at chain dressing station cuz3	
"	13	23	Last night we had about 40 crossed through largely owing to we enfayed the Oil tin warmer with firmer stove to great advantage.	
"	14	22	A.D.M.S went on leave today, having arranged around R.A.Ps. the Australian Div. relieved & went over our was a quiet day. lost.	
"	15	22	Nothing to report cuz3	
"	16	22	We here had a stormy evening, a number of shells burst around the loop at about 9-30 pm. We carried the hospital into a sunken road. After about half an hour we got the decents & staff back again as the shelling had ceased. We had no casualties but it was a near thing, as at least six shells burst in & around the track cuz around	
"	17	22	Heavy snow last night. Have been busy getting in some shell shelter for patients & personnel, as this is a very exposed site cuz3	

Army Form C. 2118.

WAR DIARY
or
INTELLIGENCE SUMMARY.
(Erase heading not required.)

Instructions regarding War Diaries and Intelligence Summaries are contained in F. S. Regs., Part II. and the Staff Manual respectively. Title pages will be prepared in manuscript.

Place	Date	Hour	Summary of Events and Information	Remarks and references to Appendices
V. FAUQN	18		Nothing to report.	
"	19	22	Went around the ADS as RAP. Today with the DADMS. cwr	
"	20	22	Quiet day nothing to report cwr	
"	21	23	Nothing to report	
"	22	24	One of our Rgt OR was killed today (shell). I have found a man through from 111 F.A. to take at his work. cwr	
"	23	23	Attended the funeral of Capt Singleton RAMC today. He was buried in the forward area. Salus intrepedemy at Secus	
"	24	22	Attended a meeting of ADsMS in at Couford H.Q. This afternoon the whole of this Recke area got a heavy bombardment from the enemy. We had no casualties in our Amb, but sent 40 wounded from coups around here came in. The bombardment was very heavy & lasted for about half an hour. I had the patients all ready to file into our shelter trench, which we have dug during the week. cwr	
"	25	22	Quietness day, over anxiously	
"	26	22	Nothing to report cwr	

WAR DIARY
or
INTELLIGENCE SUMMARY.
(Erase heading not required.)

Army Form C. 2118.

Place	Date	Hour	Summary of Events and Information	Remarks and references to Appendices
V. FAUCON	27 May	22	Quiet day, nothing to report. EWS	
"	28	24	Enemy used gas during answer drifts on roads, evacuations difficult EWS	
"	29	23	Still front & known. EWS	
"	30	22	2nd in Comd S. returned today, and also Capt Shields who was on leave. EWS	
"	31	21	This was a quiet day. I have orders some trouble about drinking water in the forward area, which has to be cleaned up. I saw the town chosen of the place in question & arranged with him about this matter. A Sennett.	

WAR DIARY

FOR MONTH OF JANUARY, 1918.

VOLUME :- 24.

UNIT :- 113th Fd. Ambce. R.A.M.C.

Confidential

War Diary
of
113th Field Ambulance

From Jan 1st 1918. to Jan 31st 1918.

(Volume 24.)

W.J. Bennett
Lieut Col RAMC
O.C. 113th Field Ambulance

Army Form C. 2118.

WAR DIARY
or
INTELLIGENCE SUMMARY.
(Erase heading not required.)

Instructions regarding War Diaries and Intelligence Summaries are contained in F.S. Regs., Part II. and the Staff Manual respectively. Title pages will be prepared in manuscript.

Place	Date	Hour	Summary of Events and Information	Remarks and references to Appendices
VILLIERS FAUCON	1/1/18	21	Sent off last monthly diary today. Snow & frost still persist. Cup attacked Raide attacks to this and this day reported 111 B.A.	
"	2	21	This was a warmer day, signs of thaw.	
"	3	22	Nothing to report cwB	
"	4	22	The A.D.M.S today kindly presented 5 shilling cheques to my men which they had been granted for good work in our two last shows	
"	5	21	Nothing to report cwB.	
"	6	21-36	Capt G. Hamden Bryon went on leave today wB	
"	7	22	Nothing to report cwB	
"	8	21	Went up the line today with A.D.M.S. Snowing heavily	
"	9	22	Nothing to report.	
"	10	24	Today was warm & the frost seems broken wB.	
"	11	22	Nothing to report. cwB	
"	12	21	Went up the line with R.E. Ryf today to look out a new A.D.S. camp	
"	13	21	Nothing to report cwB	
"	14	21	Nothing to report cwB	

Army Form C. 2118.

WAR DIARY
or
INTELLIGENCE SUMMARY.
(Erase heading not required.)

Instructions regarding War Diaries and Intelligence Summaries are contained in F.S. Regs., Part II. and the Staff Manual respectively. Title pages will be prepared in manuscript.

Place	Date	Hour	Summary of Events and Information	Remarks and references to Appendices
V. FACEON	15-	21	A very wet day. Capt Vervoe went to 2 R.D.F. for temp. duty. Lt Brown attached to us in his place. ayb	
"	16	21	Went up to advance area today with a D.I.S. to visit a R.A.P. which he proposes changing. ayb	
"	17	23	Great followed by rain last night, sea of mud today. Sent to Arras commandant for 12 Serves of Stretcher bearers for my wards which are burying of Revelly, attached officer (Lt Brown) evacuates today with Rose Ireneles. ayb	
"	18	21	Nothing to report ayb	
"	19	22	Went up to A.D.S. today, work is going on well there ayb	
"	20	21	Nothing to report ayb	
"	21	22	" " " ayb	
"	22	22	Shelling was heavy around here today but none hit in the Hospital ayb	
"	23	21	Lt Col & E Skinner attached to Amb. from today ayb	
"	24	22	Nothing to report ayb	
"	25	21	Nothing to report ayb	

WAR DIARY
or
INTELLIGENCE SUMMARY.
(Erase heading not required.)

Army Form C. 2118.

Place	Date	Hour	Summary of Events and Information	Remarks and references to Appendices
V. FAUON	26	22	Nothing to report.	
"	27	21	O.i/c D.a.D.S visited the Hosp today & saw Pte Clifford who had asked to see him and neglected to leave cits	
"	28	21	Nothing to report.	
"	29	21	Same front again. It On Davies returned from leave today at 13	
"	30	22	A section of 6" Hows appears to have been placed within 200 yards of our dressing station, which makes things a bit uncomfortable for patients & staff. aub	
"	31	21	Went around our line today to see some new R.A.Ps.	

CWJBennett
Lt. RMC Racke.

WAR DIARY.

FOR MONTH OF FEBRUARY, 1918.

VOLUME:- 25

UNIT:- 113th Field Ambulance R.A.M.C.

Confidential
War Diary
of
113th Field Ambulance.

From Feby 1st 1918.   To Feby 28th 1918.

Volume 25

W Bennett
Lieut Col A.M.C.
O.C. 113th Field Ambulance

Army Form C. 2118.

Instructions regarding War Diaries and Intelligence Summaries are contained in F.S. Regs., Part II. and the Staff Manual respectively. Title pages will be prepared in manuscript.

WAR DIARY
or
INTELLIGENCE SUMMARY.
(Erase heading not required.)

Place	Date	Hour	Summary of Events and Information	Remarks and references to Appendices
VILLIERS FAUCON	1/2/18	23	Went to this Army H.Q. today, as the Surgeon General (D.ch.S.) wanted to see two of us Amb. Commanders. Capt Van der Byner returned from leave today	
"	2	22	Nothing to report cwB	
"	3	21	Nothing to report cwB	
"	4	22	Went at the Line today with A.D.M.S with views to relieving a near R.A.P. _____ cwB	
"	5	22	Nothing to report cwB	
1	6	21	Am attending at H.Q. 39 Divn for instructions in duties of A.D.M.S. cwB	
"	7	22	Nothing to report cwB	
"	8	21	Nothing to report cwB	
"	9	21	Went to A.D.S today to pay detachment, work is going on well there cwB	
"	10	22	Went around the next Division I went today with a view to our taking over their Aid Posts & A.D.S. cwB	
"	11	21	Nothing to report	
"	12	22	Nothing to report	
"	13	24	Received orders to take over, fresh sector of Line mentioned above	

Army Form C. 2118.

WAR DIARY
or
INTELLIGENCE SUMMARY.
(Erase heading not required.)

Instructions regarding War Diaries and Intelligence Summaries are contained in F. S. Regs., Part II. and the Staff Manual respectively. Title pages will be prepared in manuscript.

Place	Date	Hour	Summary of Events and Information	Remarks and references to Appendices
V. FAUCON	14	21	Took over another ADS today from Bray onward. MB	
"	15	21	One Car arrived from 111 F.d Amb. last night to help us with the new ADS	
"	16	22	A ch. A. Car from 112 F.A today attached for duty. MB	
"	17	22	Nothing to report.	
"	18	21	A.D.M.S. visited Amb. today & gave me notice of a raid which is to take place tonight. Reinforcements arranged for at R.A.P's MB	
"	19	22	Arrangements for raid worked out well. All wounded evacuated direct from A.D.S. to C.C.S.	
"	20	24	Nothing to report MB	
"	21	24	" " MB	
"	22	23	Went around our O.Ps today with the A.D.M.S. The Corps Commander inspected Ambulance today. The A.D.M.S. also had a parade & presented Personal Honour Certificate to some of the men.	
"	23	22	Went around line today with A.D.M.S. of Division in attempt to retire items	
"	24	21	Nothing to report MB	
"	25	22	Nothing to report MB	

WAR DIARY
or
INTELLIGENCE SUMMARY.
(Erase heading not required.)

Army Form C. 2118.

Place	Date	Hour	Summary of Events and Information	Remarks and references to Appendices
V. FAUCON	26	22	Nothing to report. WB	
"	27	21	Went with A.D.M.S. to see a site (proposed for us in Back Area)	
"	28	22	Sent off advance party to new area, but had to recall them as move off. Have handed over part of my line to an incoming division this evening, my remaining party being withdrawn to H.Q. W.J. Bennett Lt Col. RAMC O.C. 113 Fd Ambce	

140/25an?

113th Field Ambulance

March
9/10/19

Confidential

War Diary

113th Field Ambulance

From 1st March 1918 To 31st March 1918

(Volume 26)

E.T. van der Byun
Capt. RAMC
OC 113th Field Ambulance

Army Form C. 2118.

WAR DIARY
or
INTELLIGENCE SUMMARY.
(Erase heading not required.)

Instructions regarding War Diaries and Intelligence
Summaries are contained in F. S. Regs., Part II.
and the Staff Manual respectively. Title pages
will be prepared in manuscript.

Place	Date	Hour	Summary of Events and Information	Remarks and references to Appendices
VILLERS FAUCON	1-3-18	22	Handed over ADS on extreme R to another Division in accordance with orders from ADMS. We are now concentrated on our old front & our relief seems off for the present. Use the Avesnes area with ADMS.	
"	2	22	Snow storm all day. Our front quiet cwB.	
"	3	22	Went around line today with A.D.M.S	
"	4	24	Nothing to report cwB.	
"	5	22	Have been granted 1 months rest leave home from tomorrow. Capt G. van der Bijver will be in command whilst I am away cwB.	
"	6	21	Took over temporary command of the ambulance today. In the afternoon I went up made arrangements with Major Whittle for the construction of the walking wounded post & new artillery dressing station. Dr W. G. Unwin Inspects the horse lines. G. T. van der Bijver.	
"	7	21	In the afternoon we had a visit from the Consulting Surgeon of this army, + our D.D.M.S + A.D.M.S. Work progressing well. G.T.V.	
"	8	21	Weather fine. the nurses Baths, dressing room etc for Scarics nearing completion. 9 nurses the N.C.O's men in the G. Unwin G.T.V.	

WAR DIARY
or
INTELLIGENCE SUMMARY.

(Erase heading not required.)

Army Form C. 2118.

Place	Date	Hour	Summary of Events and Information	Remarks and references to Appendices
VILLERS FAUCON	March 1918 9	2.3	Capt. G.E.E. Nichols attended a short course of instruction at the D.M.S. Corps Gas School. Enjoyed amusing new numbers of G.	G.T.V.
"	10	23	Very hard sunny weather. On the forenoon I went up the line with the A.D.M.S. We visited the A.D.S. + Wrote to chigour A.D. Posts. H.Z.K	
"	11	22	Capt Ropwell detailed to report to the D.D.M.S. ROUEN. 1st Lieut Gregg M.O.R.C. U.S.A. arrived 1st Army to take his place, went up to N.Z. + relieve Capt Pearson in the afternoon. Everything being quiet on the — construction of the dug-outs, not built out hours for front lines G.T.V.	
"	12	22	Gloomy november weather. Capt Pearson being sent up to Trench stores instead. Capt A Massey has report. to me for temporary duty in his place. We had a visit from the G.O.C. the A.D.M.S. on the forenoon. & the	
"	13	21	Daily Stats shown number of admissions as 45. nor nothing further to report, except clothes was a good deal of artillery activity during the night. G.T.V.	
"	14	23	In the forenoon I took up some of the Season N.C.O.s/men to reconnoitre the 4 overland tracks leading up to L'EMPIRE + RONSSOY. Received orders to complete with Army new Shooting order by 5 a.m. to-morrow. G.T.V.	A.D.M.S. 9/14-15-43. 9/15 9/14-15-43/A 12/71

2353 Wt. W 2544/1454 700,000 5/15 D.D.&L. A.D.S.S./Forms/C. 2118.

Army Form C. 2118.

WAR DIARY
or
INTELLIGENCE SUMMARY.
(Erase heading not required.)

Instructions regarding War Diaries and Intelligence Summaries are contained in F. S. Regs., Part II. and the Staff Manual respectively. Title pages will be prepared in manuscript.

Place	Date	Hour	Summary of Events and Information	Remarks and references to Appendices
VILLERS FAUCON	March 1918 15	23	All sick personnel from other hrs. evacuated — including 2 Bearers from Ambulance. Orders were issued now except the Bearers glts M.F. Field Ambulance. Under instructions from A.D.M.S., Capt J.S. Cavanagh M.C. R.A.M.C. Engg. M.O.R.C. U.S.A. were withdrawn from the A.D.S. in the afternoon, the becoming the combined M.D.S. & A.D.S. — the A.D.S. at LEMPIRE the combined Aid Posts for their battalions. In the afternoon Corps G.S.O. Meulder to recommend utmost & "A" Track. As to last night we are still on readiness in the event of the enemy attacking.	G.T.V.
"	16	21½	Hospital admissions returned to between 30 + 40. 9 wounds open to men in the event of the Division becoming inhabitable owing to shellfire. Patients' personnel allotted to the various dug-outs. Very little artillery activity to-day. Gas alert went out from the A.D.M.S. in the forenoon. Nothing to report.	G.T.V. G.T.V.
"	17	23		
"	18	22	Capt W.H. Panin M.C. to went on leave to the United Kingdom. Eni arrangements + accommodation very near completion.	G.T.V.
"	19	20	Spell of good weather broken — dull wet. Visited the A.D.M.S. in afternoon.	G.T.V.

WAR DIARY or INTELLIGENCE SUMMARY

Army Form C. 2118.

(Erase heading not required.)

Instructions regarding War Diaries and Intelligence Summaries are contained in F. S. Regs., Part II. and the Staff Manual respectively. Title pages will be prepared in manuscript.

Place	Date	Hour	Summary of Events and Information	Remarks and references to Appendices
VILLERS FAUCON	March 1918. 20	22	Good work being done on the dug-outs. We are being kept employed a new one we discovered across the road.	
TINCOURT	21	2.4	The bombardment started at about 5 a.m. unmercifully. I got the sick, wounded & personal transport to the dug-outs. The enemy starts shelling the town (VILLERS FAUCON) at about 8 a.m. but in spite of this we managed our work wonderfully well. 20 M.O.s can never seem to help us. We were unable to evacuate wounded from the front line - we lost 9 bearers we did not were all wounded. We were able to run the 6 a.m. Section very successfully until 3 p.m. when the shelling became much worse. The A.D.M.S. writes us an experience & Lt. Colonel. Captain Marshalls, Watson D.S.O, M.D. of the W.R. Orders Ambulance. ran M.O. of 45 C.C.S. Field Ambulance came to reinforce us. at 8 p.m. I moved my D.S. back to TINCOURT. having Capt. J.B. Cavanagh M.C. with a Section at VILLERS FAUCON.(A.D.S)	Rout 32.º W 23 & 25.
DOINGT	22	19	Capt Cavanagh & his personnel returned to TINCOURT at 7.30 a.m. Very luckily we suffered no casualties during the move from VILLERS FAUCON.	

WAR DIARY or INTELLIGENCE SUMMARY

Army Form C. 2118.

Place	Date	Hour	Summary of Events and Information	Remarks and references to Appendices
DOINGT	1918 March 22	19	Finished dbh. after breakfast & went back to establish my mess Siney at DOINGT. Taking 2 sections t the hainkers along with me. The site at TINCOURT being the A.D.S. I left one section there with Capt. G.E.E. Nichols in charge Lt Grigg M.O.R.C. U.S.A. G.H.R. in Under instructions from A.D.M.S. 9 also lent a Gd. N.S. servant to Capt. Turner R.A.M.C. - our Sapper M.D. An people were lddy the green line. The wounded went well back until Capt Nichols sent the party has to move back here at 2 p.m. Too few men being killed .... several them wounded, and I to the A.D.S. being shelled. To look up my communication with the line, I made instructions from the A.D.M.S. I sent out a motor cyclist to reconnoitre for wounds along the DOINGT - BUSSU - TEMPLEUX-LA-FOSSE - R.T.V. TINCOURT roads	Map 52a J. 36, 25, 2.
near BIACHES	23	20	Capt G.E.E. Nicholls the party reported into the Advanced H.Q. of the Army ? the A.D.S. OTTINGCOURT back on account of heavy hostile shells	Map 62d H 29.a.t.d.

2353 Wt. W2544/1454 700,000 5/15 D. D. & L. A.D.S.S./Forms/C. 2118.

WAR DIARY
or
INTELLIGENCE SUMMARY.
(Erase heading not required.)

Army Form C. 2118.

Place	Date	Hour	Summary of Events and Information	Remarks and references to Appendices
nr BIACHES	1918 March 23	20	The majority of them removing our cars were working hard all the time evacuating wounded. After breakfast the A.D.M.S. instructed me to move on to meet 8 BIACHES, on the main BIACHES—HERBECOURT road. I left Capt. Cavanagh with orders and all the available A.T.DOING and what shelter Bussings my 2nd 3rd span. etc. He kept our wounded though at the front and 8 BIACHES, & Capt Cavanagh the party joined me there at 1½ p.m. my 4 ambers being ordered to return. At 5 p.m. 8 of my men party or 10 a junr 200 yd west of HERBECOURT to assist the Main Dressing Station while I established an advanced dressing station at 2 pm/2500 east 8 BIACHES on the main road to HERBECOURT. The latter party remained there until 12 midnight 23rd—24th. During all this time we evacuated any few cases through the A.D.S. Was in constant com. with A.D.M.S. I instructed the A.D.S. personnel to join up the main party, + at 1 a.m. (X 205) marched the whole Field Ambulance back 6 a.m. 1 1800 yds west of CAPPY.	Sheet 62.S. & 50 cent. ALBERT [coordinates] 27⁰53N 03⁰04E [coordinates] 27⁰06 62⁰ 411 L 30 u 0.9. map AMIENS.
nr CAPPY	24	24	We arrived at this point at about 4 a.m. Bivouaced off the road north of the 111th Field Ambulance. Had freedom + afternoon on had a first night + at 5 p.m. on got orders to move further west to QUERRIEU.	17.

2353 Wt. W2544/1454 700,000 5/15 D. D. & L.   A.D.S.S./Forms/C. 2118.

WAR DIARY
or
INTELLIGENCE SUMMARY

Army Form C. 2118.

Place	Date	Hour	Summary of Events and Information	Remarks and references to Appendices
QUERRIEU	25	15	We marched to this front along the main CAPPY — BRAY sur SOMME — CORBIE — QUERRIEU road. The traffic was very congested, & it took us two hours to get to BRAY. The enemy planes dropped some bombs on the town, but none landed near the road. It was a clear moonlight night. The men marched splendidly. We arrived here at 5 a.m.	AMIENS 1/7
N.W. of BOIS DE VAIRE	26	20/½	A.M. Some tea & a feed, we all turned-in & slept until about sharp 4 p.m. At 4 p.m. we started off for the front, marched via DAOURS — AUBIGNY — FOUILLOY. The men all turned in as soon as they had a feed & slept apart night rest. There was very little doing during the day; rite men were able to have a thorough rest.	X Sheet 57.D P.20 & 21.B. (Ref 2 S.29)
+ rond junction S. of BLANGY TRONVILLE	27	22	At 4 p.m. we received orders to be on the move again, & marched via FOUILLOY — AUBIGNY — & BLANGY TRONVILLE to the ridge. Camping just got the men under ½ G.T.V. was junction on ST NICOLAS — BLANGY TRONVILLE — AMIENS road.	Sheet 62 N. 28 & 28. S. G.T.V.
S. of BLANGY TRONVILLE	28	24	Activity on front very much quieter. Re-packed wagons.	G.T.V.
S. of BLANGY TRONVILLE	29	19	All the men resting, with exception of 1 N.C.O. & 7 men sent up to AUBIGNY to run a coffee stall for stragglers. At 6 p.m. an ambulance convoy duly took our wounded & wounded rec'd S.T.V. (Returns 111 sick and 11 wounded)	

Army Form C. 2118.

WAR DIARY
or
INTELLIGENCE SUMMARY.
(Erase heading not required.)

Instructions regarding War Diaries and Intelligence Summaries are contained in F. S. Regs., Part II. and the Staff Manual respectively. Title pages will be prepared in manuscript.

VIII

Place	Date	Hour	Summary of Events and Information	Remarks and references to Appendices
S. of BLANGY TRONVILLE	1915 March 30	22	Very wet muddy. Our ambulances were on duty here to the allotment reservations of all wounded for the last 24 hours, ending at 6 p.m.. We had a great rush of cases during the afternoon. Under instructions from the A.D.M.S. two horse ambulances from each of the three ambulances were sent up to the A.D.S. at FOUILLOY to help work the evacuation. G.T.V.	*Phots[?] N.28.c.8.5
S. of BLANGY TRONVILLE	31	22	Cold, windy, showery. Very little doing. In the afternoon the 1st sent two horse ambulances up to the A.D.S., FOUILLOY; shortly remain required. Church parade at 11 a.m.. G.T.V.	

Gifford Tremayne[?] Lynn
Capt R.A.M.C.

2353 Wt. W²2544/1454 700,000 5/15 D. D. & L. A.D.S.S./Forms/C. 2118.

Confidential

War Diary
113th Field Ambulance

From April 1st 1918
To April 30th 1918

(Volume 21)

No 27
140/2983

COMMITTEE FOR THE
MEDICAL HISTORY OF THE WAR
9 JUL 1918

G.T. Watkyn
Lieut Col RAMC
O.C. 113th Fd Ambce

ORDERLY ROOM
30/4/18
113th Field Ambulance
R.A.M.C.

Army Form C. 2118.

WAR DIARY
or
INTELLIGENCE SUMMARY.
(Erase heading not required.)

Instructions regarding War Diaries and Intelligence Summaries are contained in F. S. Regs., Part II. and the Staff Manual respectively. Title pages will be prepared in manuscript.

Place	Date	Hour	Summary of Events and Information	Remarks and references to Appendices
S.W. g BLANGY TRONVILLE	April 1/7/18	24	Weather greatly improved. Aylin Lunch was moved about a mile further east along the main VILLERS-BRETONNEUX - AMIENS road. at 8 a.m. an ambulance went on duty to the attention reservation of cases passing through him from the A.D.S's AT FOUILLOY & HAMEL. G.T.V.	Sheet 62 x N26&5.b
S.W. g BLANGY TRONVILLE	2	24	Very few cases evacuated during the night. during the 24 hours, we only had 180 cases approximately. neturing sit lightly sick. From German aeroplanes flew over in the afternoon, their agostive apparently being AMIENS. we drew 2 water carts & 2 limber wagons to complete Mot. T. Aysonvoir, counts by loss in action. G.T.V.	
SALEUX	3	21	At Lunch time we received orders from the A.D.M.S. to come on here, marching through LONGUEAU, along the outskirts g AMIENS, & on through SALOUEL. Aylin posting a guard & horse piquet, we all retired early for a good night's rest. G.T.V.	AMIENS 17.
SALEUX	4	23	Miserably wet muddy. at 7 a.m. Capt J.G. Cavanagh lyt with all the transport, except the motor ambulances, in route to ERCOURT. Lieut R.M. Davis left at 11 p.m. to do its billeting. Capt G.E.E. Nichols	"

2353 Wt. W2544/1454 700,000 5/15 D. D. & L. A.D.S.S./Forms/C. 2118.

Army Form C. 2118.

WAR DIARY
or
INTELLIGENCE SUMMARY.
(Erase heading not required.)

Instructions regarding War Diaries and Intelligence Summaries are contained in F. S. Regs., Part II. and the Staff Manual respectively. Title pages will be prepared in manuscript.

Place	Date	Hour	Summary of Events and Information	Remarks and references to Appendices
	April 1918			
SALEUX	4	23.	Took charge of 10 motor ambulances, this not going into ines at SALEUX station at 9.30 p.m. G.T.V.	AMIENS. 7.
ERCOURT	5	20	By 6.5 detraining at BLANGY at 8 a.m, we had breakfast, then marched on Kine via TRANSLAY along the main ABBEVILLE to far as ST. MAXENT, where we branched off to ONICOURT & ERAULT MESNIL. We arrived here just before me p.m, & the transport soon after. Saw A.D.M.S. called on R.C. of Limousin. G.T.V.	map. ABBEVILLE
"	6	23	All the N.C.O's. were meeting, with the exception of orderly sergt. & gunner, present, phone on hospital duties. G.T.V.	"
ERCOURT	7	20	Lovely spring weather. On the afternoon motored along to see the A.D.M.S. & later on drew some money from the Field Cashier. The men were paid at 5 p.m. G.T.V.	"
"	8	12	Returned from leave last night. I found orders waiting for me to join 62 Division as A.D.M.S. I am accordingly today instructions from A.D.M.S. & am command of Amb. to change & over to be RACHE as a temporary measure. 62 Div went to be at Dyffryn	"

WAR DIARY
or
INTELLIGENCE SUMMARY.
(Erase heading not required.)

Army Form C. 2118.

Instructions regarding War Diaries and Intelligence Summaries are contained in F.S. Regs., Part II. and the Staff Manual respectively. Title pages will be prepared in manuscript.

Place	Date	Hour	Summary of Events and Information	Remarks and references to Appendices
ERCOURT	April 1918 8	21½	Drill met. On the 2nd instant Capt W. Lancaster (T.C.) reported to O.C. ambulance for duty; yesterday Capt L.C. Ferguson (T.C.) + Capt R. Asher (T.F.) all three of whom having been taken on the strength from the absentee of their respective arrivals. At mid-night 7/K/8/K Col W. Bennett D.S.O. + Capt W.H. Ransom M.C. returned off leave. In the afternoon the C.O. left for his new appointment as A.D.M.S. 32nd Division, y/h having handed over the command of the ambulance as a temporary measure. Capt W.A. Ransom received orders to report for duty at the War Office, London. Left along with the Colonel. S.T.V	Map ABBÉVILLE
MENESLIES	9	22	Cloudy but fair. We were on the march at 12 midday; + came on here via TOURS-en-VIMEU, FRESSENNEVILLE, FEUQUIÈRES, MOYENCOURT arriving here at 8.45 p.m. We were all-out good billets, most of them immediately the outgoing troops had vacated them — at 8 p.m. S.T.V.	
MENESLIES	10	17	A small reception room has opened in hospital admission. Misty weather; roads soft. S.T.V.	

Army Form C. 2118.

WAR DIARY
or
INTELLIGENCE SUMMARY.
(Erase heading not required.)

Instructions regarding War Diaries and Intelligence Summaries are contained in F.S. Regs., Part II. and the Staff Manual respectively. Title pages will be prepared in manuscript.

Place	Date	Hour	Summary of Events and Information	Remarks and references to Appendices
ASSINGHEM.	1918 April 11	21	At 7.19 A.M. on the previous day we entrained at EU for ARQUES arriving at 8.19 P.M. & arrived at H.Q. de Tanny Station at 7.15 this morning after having some breakfast on markets on the site of station. My journey through BLENDECQUES, NOIR CORNET, WIZERNES, CREPEN, & REMILLY, WIRQUIN. In the afternoon I received a copy of medical distribution (D.M.S. 1st Army); also a list of Return to be rendered to me now as in the XIII R Corps of the 1st Army. Weather good, roads dry. At 9 P.M. I received orders from the Staff Captain H.Q. 49th Infantry Brigade to be ready to move at an hour's notice. Ambulances all here very running. G.T.V. welle is good. F. Castant. S.J.V.	A.S. & N. L. 4.12 = Brave No. 5 a.
ASSINGHEM.	12	19.	Delightful sunny weather. We were busy all day getting the new attains cleaned up. Sgt Cochrane Q.S.C. (M.T.) left for the United Kingdom to him for a commission in the R.A.C. Cpl.	49 R Bay Note order No. 4
ASSINGHEM.	12	21.	Captain R.G. Vernon, Lieut R.A. Johnson M.O.R.C. U.S.A returned to us after doing temporary duty with no 32 C.C.S. Daily state of sick showing of afternoon, 7 of which are remaining. Cloudy sky today. We now have our full establishment of medical Officers, namely 8. G.T.V.	D.M.S 1st Army

Army Form C. 2118.

WAR DIARY
or
INTELLIGENCE SUMMARY.
(Erase heading not required.)

Instructions regarding War Diaries and Intelligence Summaries are contained in F.S. Regs., Part II. and the Staff Manual respectively. Title pages will be prepared in manuscript.

Place	Date	Hour	Summary of Events and Information	Remarks and references to Appendices
ASSINGHEM	April 1916 14	20	Cloudy sky, cold. Lieut T.M.G. Town M.C. proceeds this day to ROUEN. Late in the winter B.D.M. B.12. General Hospital. In the forenoon I received orders from D/y Capt. Wing J 29/R. Sg. Bde. for its ambulance to move to another area, but later on this order was countermanded. We received 10 reinforcements - a Cpl. + 9 privates, now only require 13 more men to complete our R.A.M.C. establishment; + 6.S.C. (3 H.T. + 1 M.T.) establishment.	HAZEBROUCK 5A. G.T.V.
ASSINGHEM	15	21	Cloudy, cold. In the afternoon I visited the A.D.M.S.; but didn't see him. An Armoured Rearguard has moved to AIRE.	G.T.V.
"	16	21½	nothing to report.	G.T.V.
"	17	23	Cloudy, cold. Much instruction from A.D.M.S. I proceeded to BLENDECQURT in the forenoon for an interview with HQ D.I.M.S. Present Ambulance site greatly improved. All rubbish removed, new latrines + incinerator built. Men were paid in the afternoon.	*GLENS. " B.T.V.
"	18	21	Cold showery. During the forenoon the Area Commandant informed me that the 'Paper Factory' our present ambulance site, was to be handed over to G Central Ammo. Park, electrical men observed workshop. Major J.B. Cavanagh	

Army Form C. 2118.

WAR DIARY
or
INTELLIGENCE SUMMARY.
(Erase heading not required.)

VI.

Instructions regarding War Diaries and Intelligence Summaries are contained in F. S. Regs., Part II. and the Staff Manual respectively. Title pages will be prepared in manuscript.

Place	Date	Hour	Summary of Events and Information	Remarks and references to Appendices
ASSINGHEM	April 1916 18	21	I went rather what accommodation the village of CAMPAGNETTE offers, but decided to remain on here. Found a suitable place for the hospital. Our division was sanctioned by the A.D.M.S. who pays on a visit the afternoon.	May HAZEBROUCK 5 A. G.T.V.
"	19	24	Weather quite wintry. According to D.R.Os, I'm entitled to wear the badge of Lieut. Col. while temporarily commanding the ambulance, my pay remaining as before.	G.T.V.
"	20	21	Weather improved, although still rather cold. By the time we have emptied the stores out of J. Paper factory, moved our Transport lines Kelly is made tenable north from here. Our men wants for the work on my satisfactory.	G.T.V.
"	21	21	Lovely spring weather. Our new Quartermaster, Lieut St Georges, arrives in the afternoon. I In the forenoon we fail to complete our establishment O.S.c (H.T.) now only requiring one Private to complete our establishment. T.S.V.	G.T.V.
"	22	21	14 cases remaining in hospital. Our officers + I.O.R. amounts to C.C.I.	G.T.V.
"	23	24	In the forenoon I inspected all the billets, the cook house, latrines + Transport lines. Everything very clean + satisfactory.	G.T.V.
"	24	23	According to Kings Regs, Section 1648 the Army Ret was sent out to all the ambulance by Major G.B. Granagh M.C. One officer admitted to hospital	G.T.V.

Army Form C. 2118.

WAR DIARY
or
INTELLIGENCE SUMMARY.
(Erase heading not required.)

Instructions regarding War Diaries and Intelligence Summaries are contained in F. S. Regs., Part II. and the Staff Manual respectively. Title pages will be prepared in manuscript.

Place	Date	Hour	Summary of Events and Information	Remarks and references to Appendices
BLÉQUIN	25	24	Received orders from A.D.M.S. to Capt N[...] altho(T.C.) to report to A.D.M.S. 50th Division (T.C.) He left us that day more direct off the ambulance altogether accordingly. I also received a warning order from 4th Infantry Bde. to move to the BLÉQUIN area. Re Brigade Billeting Party, including Capt R. J. Kenny, our ambulance, left at 1.30 a.m. Orders came in at 1.15 a.m; we marched to BLÉQUIN we left ASSINGHEM at 2 p.m. marched via WAVRAN, ELNES, FOURDEBECQUE, WISMES, DRIONVILLE, T LEDINGHEM, arriving here at 8 p.m. E.T.V.	Map CALAIS, 13.
"	26	23	One of our motor ambulance drivers was wounded — whether 15 m. & stationary Hospital. Also one of the Rams Thunder. The billets here are jerry of bad; Hospital accommodation for our transport lines worth talking about. There was a lot of clearing & tidying up to do. No ambulance was left at 5 p.m. The A.D.M.S. gave us a visit before he that a look at our new site. E.T.V.	
"	27	23	Nothing to report.	
"	28	23	Weather — dull, cold, showery. Good progress has been made in the laying up improvement of the hospital, Q.M. stores, Mess, Sanitary arrangements have been very much improved. E.T.V.	

Army Form C. 2118.

WAR DIARY
or
INTELLIGENCE SUMMARY.
(Erase heading not required.)

Instructions regarding War Diaries and Intelligence Summaries are contained in F. S. Regs., Part II. and the Staff Manual respectively. Title pages will be prepared in manuscript.

Place	Date	Hour	Summary of Events and Information	Remarks and references to Appendices
	April 1918			maps CALAIS 13
BLÉQUIN	29	20/2	Weather still dull & showery. In the afternoon the O.C. Subaltern & 2 others went to No. 32 C.C.S. for temporary duty in the 2nd of 3 attempts. Others to rise. The remainder 18 N.C.O.s & men one batman Rams returned presently with Capt R.J. Vernon, & Lieut. R. of Germane M.O.R.C. to the afternoon 'C' Section even received its medical equipment & general service equipment all made up & established. The notice of green expected the packing unpacking & wagons.	
"	30	20/2	No improvement in the weather. In the afternoon B' Section practices packing unpacking their wagons. The orderlies attached to wagons are doing excellent work in getting them thoroughly clean, well oiled & their work polished up.	

G.T. van der Byrn
Lt Col R.A.M.C.

May 1918.

Vol 28

140/2983.

Confidential
War Diary
of
113th Field Ambulance

From 1/5/18. To 31/5/18.

(Volume 28)

COMMITTEE
MEDICAL HIS[TORY]
Date. 9 JUL 1918

E. T. van Nijven
Lieut Col b RAMC
O.C. 113th Field Ambulance

Army Form C. 2118.

WAR DIARY
or
INTELLIGENCE SUMMARY.
(Erase heading not required.)

Instructions regarding War Diaries and Intelligence Summaries are contained in F. S. Regs., Part II. and the Staff Manual respectively. Title pages will be prepared in manuscript.

Place	Date	Hour	Summary of Events and Information	Remarks and references to Appendices

BLÉQUIN	May 1916 1	23	Weather - dull, cold. Under instruction from A.D.M.S. the u/m Officers had to report for duty to the A.D.M.S. of Division on above typed their names. Lieut. R.F. Johnson M.O.R.C. U.S.A. 3rd Division
			   Capt. G.E.E. Nichols Reeve (T.C.) 46th Division
			   Capt. C.K. Benjamin Reeve (T.C.) 55th "
			   Capt. M. Lumsden Reeve (T.C.) 50th "
				map C.A.2118 13

"	2	24	These officers are being put to the strength of the ambulance from to-day. From to-day we started a course of physical drill for all ranks, a series of lectures + demonstrations to nurses, + small two inspections. Squads + stretcher drill for all ranks. G.T.V. Weather improved - sunny much warmer. In the afternoon I inspected all ambulance all self to billet. G.T.V.	
"	3	21.	Under instruction from A.D.M.S. we had to send two of our motor ambulances to report for duty to D.M.S. L of C. including the two M.T.C. A.S.C. (M.T.). These men + cars are struck off our strength from to-day. Very sunny weather. G.T.V.	

2353 Wt. W2544/1454 700,000 5/15 D. D. & L. A.D.S.S./Forms/C. 2118.

Army Form C. 2118.

WAR DIARY
or
INTELLIGENCE SUMMARY.
(Erase heading not required.)

Instructions regarding War Diaries and Intelligence Summaries are contained in F. S. Regs., Part II. and the Staff Manual respectively. Title pages will be prepared in manuscript.

Place	Date	Hour	Summary of Events and Information	Remarks and references to Appendices
BLÉQUIN	May 1915 4	24	"A" + "B" Sections were re-inoculated with mixed Typhoid + para Typhoid vaccine. Weather very oppressive sultry.	Map S.A.D.118 /3. A.T.V. B.T.V.
"	5	23	Nothing to report.	
"	6	23	In the prison A + B Section des Eynois extricate drill while C section men in the armoury Tidying up & etc wagons. Four men remaining in hospital. Weather - pleasant but showery.	G.T.V.
"	7	22	Nothing to report.	G.T.V.
"	8	22	Three patients remaining in hospital, three detained. Two hospital is still being [struck] emptied, + drawn away normally. Three of our men were granted a more [?] convalescent leave to & Kingdom	G.T.V.
"	9	23	In this of Senior the 46th Infantry Brigade has to have shown weight 1st message for best turnout of limber wagon + 2nd. for best washed out water cart	G.T.V.
"	10	23	C Section + Hdq of A.S.C. personnel were inoculated in the forenoon. 5 Officers + 23 other ranks are now required to complete the establishment of the ambulance. Two more men were granted special leave to U.K. Weather - cold & cloudy.	G.T.V.

WAR DIARY
or
INTELLIGENCE SUMMARY.

(Erase heading not required.)

Army Form C. 2118.

Place	Date	Hour	Summary of Events and Information	Remarks and references to Appendices
BLEQUIN	11	22	Another man granted special leave to U.K. In U.K. at Linton a case of doubtful Diphtheria was removed by an to the C.C.S.	G.T.V.
"	12	21	Two cases remaining in hospital both in general progressing well. G.T.V.	
"	13	22	Weather - dull wet. In the afternoon the Divisional Hygien Gave us a lecture, dealing specially on the various Gas shells employed by the enemy. G.T.V.	
"	14	23	Nothing to report G.T.V	
MENNEVILLE	15	21	Fine summers day. We got orders - only two hours before the appointed time - 10.30 a.m. We came along the main BLEQUIN - DESVRES road through through to LA CALIQUE, arriving here 2.12.45 p.m. We had a long halt for lunch, - wanted the billeting N.C.O has fixed up the billets, because our first order to proceed to DESVRES was cancelled. G.T.V.	
MENNEVILLE	16	23	Divisional Headquarters moved to SAMERS to-day. No casualties of any sort. The case we evacuated to the C.C.S on the 11th fortunately, proved not to be a case of Diphtheria. G.T.V.	

2353 Wt. W2544/1454 700,000 5/15 D. D. & L. A.D.S.S./Forms/C. 2118.

Army Form C. 2118.

WAR DIARY
or
INTELLIGENCE SUMMARY.
(Erase heading not required.)

Instructions regarding War Diaries and Intelligence
Summaries are contained in F. S. Regs., Part II.
and the Staff Manual respectively. Title pages
will be prepared in manuscript.

Place	Date	Hour	Summary of Events and Information	Remarks and references to Appendices
MENNEVILLE	17	21	In the afternoon we had a visit from the D.O.C. – Major General Riddell, CALAIS – Brig. Gen. Benta, commanding the 149th Infantry Brigade. The men were kept in the afternoon. Received instructions from A.D.M.S. sent north the remainder to Mt BOULOGNE area, including ambulance troops. B.T.V.	map CALAIS 13
NIEMBURG	18	22	In the afternoon we had a great inspection of the whole ambulance. Just before lunch I received orders from the A.D.M.S. to try the ambulance in here. The billeting party came on in advance. We marched via DESVRES, SAMER, then along the SAMER-VERLINTHUM road as far as the cross roads, and I the halt place when we proceeded almost due South to here. Billets not very satisfactory but quite passable. B.T.V.	"
NIEMBURG	19	21.	We got a horse for the # Hospital T.M. store. Just before lunch side had a visit from the A.D.M.S. & lt. J. clearing up was down in the afternoon. The place pretty improved. Church parade at 12 midday.	"
NIEMBURG	20	23	Very warm weather. Men ask home now strongly cleaned up in the orchard. Drains were made into general sanitation & its site improved	B.T.V.

WAR DIARY
or
INTELLIGENCE SUMMARY.

(Erase heading not required.)

Army Form C. 2118.

Instructions regarding War Diaries and Intelligence Summaries are contained in F. S. Regs., Part II. and the Staff Manual respectively. Title pages will be prepared in manuscript.

Place	Date	Hour	Summary of Events and Information	Remarks and references to Appendices
NIEMBURG	21	22	Exceptionally warm weather. Men with horse previously ready to be moved on. The 4th American Division arrived in the area 2 days ago. Our Division providing its Transport staff for them, & the train 3 rode their medical sgn Battalion - number 12 - at 14:45 turns to arrange about their departure & evacuation. We had a short visit from the A.D.M.S. after tea. G.T.V.	
"	22	21	Men then remaining in Hospital, whilst evacuated to the Base hospital in the afternoon. Two cases of mumps were admitted - 4th American Divisional Engineers. 'A' section went on a continued route march plant to the Gun returned in the cool of the afternoon. G.T.V.	
"	23	24	Some cases - sick - evacuated to the Base hospital in the afternoon. Many extra ments into their new toilettes to-day, Many improvements are still being carried out - Attention has been completing. G.T.V. I will record all day. Recently return from the A.D.M.S. that the unit under my command will most probably be transferred to the 4th American Division from the 26th of the month. Two more cases of mumps were admitted "from the American" - remounts to no. 14 General Hospital. G.T.V.	

2353 WT W2514/1454 700,000 5/15 D. D. & L. A.D.S.S./Forms/C. 2118.

WAR DIARY
or
INTELLIGENCE SUMMARY.
(Erase heading not required.)

Army Form C. 2118.

Instructions regarding War Diaries and Intelligence Summaries are contained in F. S. Regs., Part II and the Staff Manual respectively. Title pages will be prepared in manuscript.

Place	Date	Hour	Summary of Events and Information	Remarks and references to Appendices
NIEMBURG	25	23	"B" Section went for a continued Route March are quite to place at GABRIEL. 5 cases remaining in Hospital. Another case of mumps admitted. Transferred to No. 14 General hospital. Good progress being made in the improvement of the ambulance site. G.T.V.	MAP, CALAIS 13
"	26	23	"C" Section went for a continued Route March was taken. Determine nothing to report. G.T.V.	
"	27	23	Pleasant weather. In the forenoon I visited the A.D.M.S. & got its training cadre from him. In each ambulance it is to consist of the C.O., 2 M. Sgt. Major, 2 Staff Sgts., 3 Sergeants (Bearers), 4 Sgt. C.T.R., 9 & 15 other ranks. 5 cases remaining in the ambulance. G.T.V.	
"	28	23	In the forenoon the Sgt. Major selected 15 men to receive Divisional Orders explains my name amongst those who had been honoured with its Military Cross. G.T.V.	
"	29	22	Pleasant weather. This morning I will now finishes on the furnace are had a visit from our new Brigade Commander – Brigadier General MACK. 2 Case remaining on the ambulance. G.T.V.	

Army Form C. 2118.

WAR DIARY
or
INTELLIGENCE SUMMARY.
(Erase heading not required.)

VII

Instructions regarding War Diaries and Intelligence Summaries are contained in F. S. Regs., Part II. and the Staff Manual respectively. Title pages will be prepared in manuscript.

Place	Date	Hour	Summary of Events and Information	Remarks and references to Appendices
NIEMBURG	30	23	Outposts work progressing well. Major is unable to find the cut tree rings incinerator, so we are awaiting a supply of these cemented from the Engineer of the Garrison. Has arrived from the M.O. the new American Machine Gun Company - no. 10. Lousy weather.	
"	31	23	Sick cases remaining in the H.Q. Ambulance 5 Officers, 24 other ranks, + 2 heavy draft horses required to complete establishment of ambulance.	

B.T. van Nijven
Capt RAMC

CONFIDENTIAL.

WAR DIARY

of

113 FIELD AMBULANCE.

FROM 1ST JUNE 1918 TO 30TH JUNE 1918.

VOLUME 29.

W.O. 29
140/3076

4
June 1918

COMMITTEE FOR THE
MEDICAL HISTORY OF THE WAR
Date 7 AUG 1919

Army Form C. 2118.

WAR DIARY
or
INTELLIGENCE SUMMARY.

(Erase heading not required.)

Instructions regarding War Diaries and Intelligence Summaries are contained in F. S. Regs., Part II. and the Staff Manual respectively. Title pages will be prepared in manuscript.

Place	Date	Hour	Summary of Events and Information	Remarks and references to Appendices
NIEMBURG	June 1	23	Exceptionally fine weather. The 11th American machine gun Battalion arrives in this area, on our platforms at FRENOD. G.T.V.	Map CALAIS 1.3
"	2	22	Lt. R.J.M.S. George was granted two weeks leave to the North Riding. In the afternoon we had a visit from the A.D.M.S. G.T.V.	
"	3	23	Sick aid remaining in the ambulance. All the horse-drawn wagons we are re-painting & overhauling. G.T.V.	
"	4	23	Several work of the ambulance is good. Engraving will be in the forenoon we has small Box Regiments drill for the A.S.C.(M.T.), who practice in adjusting the horse respirators. G.T.V.	
"	5	23	Lovely weather. Yesterday we are re-horse-drawn not Remount depot in exchange for some of our own. We have now eleven sick cases remaining in the ambulance. Two officers, one Corp of Nimph admitted 6th day from the 12th American machine Gun Battalion. We receives some of its orderlies as its orderlies for from the Engineers. B.T.V.	
"	6	23	Good weather continues. Two more cases of Nimph admitted - American	G.T.V.

Army Form C. 2118.

WAR DIARY
or
INTELLIGENCE SUMMARY.
(Erase heading not required.)

Instructions regarding War Diaries and Intelligence Summaries are contained in F. S. Regs., Part II. and the Staff Manual respectively. Title pages will be prepared in manuscript.

Place	Date	Hour	Summary of Events and Information	Remarks and references to Appendices
NIEMBURG	7	22.	Fine weather. Seventeen sick cases now in the ambulance. Work progressing well. Range on men patients. Work horse jumpers, all latrines improved, made fly proof, new manorial slates. We are still hoping to draw our men to complete our strength. G.T.V.	Map CALAIS 13
"	8	23.	Good weather. Sixteen sick cases in the ambulance, & two examined to the B are hospital in the afternoon. The 4th American Division leaves this area to-morrow, & will march to their entraining area; MONTREUIL - BEAURAINVILLE - MARESQUEL - HESDIN. Sent one horse ambulance to 15.4 A. Engineer Regiment at WIDEHEM, one to H.Qs. 4th Divisional Train at DALLE at 7 p.m. this evening. On completion of entraining they will return here. G.T.V.	A.D.M.S. No. 42/281(A) 8/5/9 um
"	9	23.	Showery weather. At 7 a.m. ten motor ambulances proceeded to the 4th American Division in two days duty - one to the 4th Engineer Regiment at WIDEHEM, the other 5-15- to the Infantry regiment at DOUDEAUVILLE. Nineteen sick cases remaining in the ambulance to-day. Another case of Mumps was admitted. G.T.V.	

WAR DIARY or INTELLIGENCE SUMMARY.

Army Form C. 2118.

(Erase heading not required.)

Place	Date	Hour	Summary of Events and Information	Remarks and references to Appendices
NIEMBURG	10	23	Part of the 60th American Division arrived in our area to-day. I went round with the car collecting the sick in the premises, & brought five sick from HUBERSENT with me.	G.T.V.
"	11	21	Weather good. In the afternoon I managed some of the tents. Turned up another meeting, went to Medical case. We have 19 sick cases remaining in the ambulance, & evacuated 2 to No.13 General Hospital	G.T.V.
"	12	21	Lovely weather. In the afternoon I visited the R.E. dump, & A.D.M.S. Saw Col. Bowen has gone on leave to UK the day before. I got attention to him. No sick afternoon, & 18 cases remaining in the ambulance.	G.T.V.
"	13	23	Cloudy day, but fair. We managed to draw some material from the Engineers — one G.S wagon load.	G.T.V.
"	14	23	We drew another G.S. wagon load of material from the Engineers. Seven cases remaining in the ambulance & nine evacuated to the Base. Four officers & 24 other ranks are required to make up the strength of the ambulance.	G.T.V.

Army Form C. 2118.

WAR DIARY
or
INTELLIGENCE SUMMARY.
(Erase heading not required.)

IV

Instructions regarding War Diaries and Intelligence Summaries are contained in F.S. Regs., Part II. and the Staff Manual respectively. Title pages will be prepared in manuscript.

Place	Date	Hour	Summary of Events and Information	Remarks and references to Appendices
NIENBURG	15	23	Lovely weather. We had a wire from the D.A.D.M.S. in the prison. Fourteen sick cases remaining in the ambulance. Three removals to the base. G.T.V.	
"	16	23	Nothing to report, except one evacuation – P.U.O. G.T.V.	
"	17	23	Capt. E.H. Sevills R.A.M.C. having been posted to this unit, is taken on the strength from to-day. Lieut. G.M. St George returned of leave this afternoon. Our officers were admitted yesterday to the Base – Case of Venereal Eczema. We erected a bath house to-day – three things both. G.T.V.	
"	18	23	Good weather. Our Divisional Brigade Staff, including A.D.M.S. Staff, along with Battalion Training Staff, left for SAMER area yesterday evening en route for BOULOGNE, prior to proceeding to the United Kingdom. We are now under the A.D.M.S. of the 34th Division. G.T.V.	
"	19	23	Nothing to report. G.T.V.	
"	20	23	Weather showery. There are now only 12 sick cases remaining in the ambulance. In the prison front the A.D.M.S. of the 34th Division. One of our motor ambulance cars has been at the work shop in town. G.T.V.	

Army Form C. 2118.

WAR DIARY
or
INTELLIGENCE SUMMARY.
(Erase heading not required.)

Instructions regarding War Diaries and Intelligence Summaries are contained in F. S. Regs., Part II. and the Staff Manual respectively. Title pages will be prepared in manuscript.

Place	Date	Hour	Summary of Events and Information	Remarks and references to Appendices
NIENBURG	21	23	Weather - cloudy mild. Three of our men have developed P.U.O. Two of them were on our supply wagon - 144 A.S.C. Coy., where there seems to be quite an epidemic of it at present. G.T.V.	
"	22	23	Weather - windy cold. Twenty sick cases remaining in the Ambulance. Four men of our men have been admitted with P.U.O. - eight altogether now. This type of fever seems like Influenza, so I took Major R. of Vernon R.A.M.C. (T.C.) + Capt. Smillie R.A.M.C. (T.C.) went on leave to the United Kingdom to-day. Very cold weather in general. Two more cases of Influenza - the Sgt Major + one of the Sergeants. G.T.V.	
"	23	23		
"	24	22	Weather - cold showery. According to D.M.S., First Army no. 677/68, this epidemic of fever is not Influenza; but caused by a diplococcus. It is spoken of by some as the "three day fever". There are 20 sick cases remaining in the Ambulance to-day; one case of O.W.M. nosis (? meningitis) was evacuated to the Base. G.T.V.	

Army Form C. 2118.

WAR DIARY
or
INTELLIGENCE SUMMARY.

(Erase heading not required.)

Instructions regarding War Diaries and Intelligence Summaries are contained in F. S. Regs., Part II. and the Staff Manual respectively. Title pages will be prepared in manuscript.

Place	Date	Hour	Summary of Events and Information	Remarks and references to Appendices
NIEMBURG	25	23	Weather - cloudy but not so cold. Twenty two cases remaining in the Ambulance. There were no movements to the Base — one a case of Appendicitis. The kitchen has all been plastered & improved, & a cement floor & drain made for the back house. E.T.V.	
"	26	22	Pleasant weather. Two more cases were admitted, more were evacuated to 2nd Base. One of our riding horses died this morning, following upon a severe attack of Colic. As a prophylaxis against the Horse Day Flays, all the men are having their throats sprayed night morning. E.T.V.	
"	27	23	Weather - 70th. In the afternoon I visited the A.D.M.S. - 34th Division. Four of our men were discharged from hospital to-day, & four more admitted. Two of the latter were evacuants to the Base. E.T.V.	
"	28	23	Major J.B. Cavanagh M.C. visits all yesterday & remains with us three days from. From to-day we come under the administration of the A.D.M.S. of the 39th Division. I went all with the Horse to-night, & went early to bed. Body state about 2.9, and cases remaining in the Ambulance. E.T.V.	

Army Form C. 2118.

WAR DIARY
or
INTELLIGENCE SUMMARY.
(Erase heading not required.)

VII.

Instructions regarding War Diaries and Intelligence Summaries are contained in F.S. Regs., Part II. and the Staff Manual respectively. Title pages will be prepared in manuscript.

Place	Date	Hour	Summary of Events and Information	Remarks and references to Appendices
NIEMBURG	29	23	Very anxious day but all day felt pretty miserable. My temp. jumped from 103° to 102°. Major Cavanagh in charge to hospital all right. G.T.K.	
"	30	23	Kindly excuse. We had a rumour to see the station division would be returning to Hanover tomorrow but nothing final yet. G.T. van der Byl Lt. Col. Reine O.C. 11th SA Battalion	

CONFIDENTIAL

WAR DIARY

of

113 FIELD AMBULANCE.

FROM 1ST JULY 1918 TO 31ST JULY 1918.

VOLUME 30.

Army Form C. 2118.

WAR DIARY
or
INTELLIGENCE SUMMARY.
(Erase heading not required.)

Instructions regarding War Diaries and Intelligence Summaries are contained in F. S. Regs., Part II. and the Staff Manual respectively. Title pages will be prepared in manuscript.

Place	Date	Hour	Summary of Events and Information	Remarks and references to Appendices
NIEMBURG	July 14/18 1	23	Lovely warm weather. There are 29 sick cases remaining in the Ambulance. Two more of our own men were admitted with Pure Stay Fever, & two were discharged to duty. G.T.V.	
"	2	21	Weather – good. Twenty two sick cases remaining. 1 & 14 were experienced at the base. In view of our own being on the move again, Sie. sick C Sections wagons all packed. G.T.V.	
"	3	22	Weather – good. Our 4 G.S. Wagons on command were returned to us from 143 A.S.C. Coy. to-day. Eight of our men were discharged to duty. Twenty one sick cases remaining in the ambulance. G.T.V.	
"	4	22	Weather – clean, sunny roads. In the afternoon we received orders from the 117 Inf. Bde, 39th Division, stating that we would be attached to the 30th American Division, & move along with them to the 3rd Army Area. – The move of the Division start to-day. We got our own wagons packed, also all the sick cases onwards to & there but not our own. All the sick cases onwards were to duty. G.T.V.	

MS. 1st Class Army
D. D. & L., London, E.C.
(A6091) Wt. W1771/M2031 750,000 5/17 Sch 52 Forms C2118/14

Army Form C. 2118.

WAR DIARY
or
INTELLIGENCE SUMMARY.
(Erase heading not required.)

Instructions regarding War Diaries and Intelligence Summaries are contained in F. S. Regs., Part II. and the Staff Manual respectively. Title pages will be prepared in manuscript.

Place	Date	Hour	Summary of Events and Information	Remarks and references to Appendices
NIEMBURG	5	23	Weather - cloudy & dry. At 10.30 a.m. our Transport minus motor Ambulances, left this new area by road. There are still twelve of our men down with "three day" fever.	
BREVILLERS	6	24	Warm weather. Major J.B. Cavanagh's mounted 1st Team to its entraining station at GAM - DÉSVRES. Our train left at about 2 p.m. We arrived at BOUQUEMAISON at about midnight. The men who were sent with "three day" fever came on by the motor ambulances. G.T.V	Map L5N811
"	7	22	It was about 4 a.m. before we got settled down for a rest, as there was no one to meet us when we got to our billets. The Transport didn't arrive until 7 p.m. so beyond slightly arranging about billets we weren't able to get very much done. This is Lucelli, this is a great deal of trouble in it. There are 26 sick cases remaining in the Ambulance including 20 of our own men. G.T.V	
"	8	23	Lovely warm weather. Our men are still very sick with the Three Day fever. We now have 25 in hospital. A large number are convalescing too. So that altogether we are having rather a serious epidemic.	

WAR DIARY
or
INTELLIGENCE SUMMARY.
(Erase heading not required.)

Army Form C. 2118.

Instructions regarding War Diaries and Intelligence Summaries are contained in F. S. Regs., Part II. and the Staff Manual respectively. Title pages will be prepared in manuscript.

Place	Date	Hour	Summary of Events and Information	Remarks and references to Appendices
GREVILLERS	8	23	Wi. had a bit of cleaning up to do. A man showing himself was once hit. The hospital filled, mainly managements employed work generally. A Ford Van was made in this direction anyway. G.T.V.	
"	9	22	Showery weather. Rather more of our men were wounded & with three Bay Gunners. Major R.G. Vernon Capt C.H. Seville returned by leave to the U.K. this afternoon. G.T.V.	
"	10	23	Weather - showery. Forty two cases remaining in the ambulance, forty of which are our own men. In the afternoon I visited the D.D.M.S. 4th Corps, the Surgical Surgeon of the P.O.R. American Division. G.T.V.	
"	11	23	Weather - mild; showery in the afternoon. Fifty sick cases remaining in the ambulance, forty three of which are our own men. A truck horse is in course of construction. In the afternoon we had a ride from the D.D.M.S. 6th Corps. G.T.V.	
"	12	21	Excellent weather except for one or two small showers. Fifty six sick cases remaining in the ambulance, no more of our own men being admitted with the three Bay fever. One or two cases have relapsed. To complete the strength of the ambulance we require 4 Officers, D. D. & L. 3 this month, 3 A.S.C. (M.T.), 1 riding horse & 2 heavy draught	

WAR DIARY
or
INTELLIGENCE SUMMARY.

Army Form C. 2118.

(Erase heading not required.)

Place	Date	Hour	Summary of Events and Information	Remarks and references to Appendices
BREVILLERS	12	21	Vehicles to complete mechanical transport: 2 large motor ambulances, 1 horse ambulance, 1 water cart. G.T.V.	
"	13	20	Weather - good. Nine more of our men were admitted with Three Day Fever - altogether 65 such cases remaining in hospital. G.T.V.	
"	14	22	Two more of our men were admitted with pyrexia. G.T.V.	
"	15	22½	Weather - close & showery. Twelve more of our own men were admitted with Three Day Fever to-day. Out of 267 told off 69 sick remaining in the ambulance, 62 are our own men. Ten were discharged to duty. G.T.V.	
"	16	22	Very close & warm. Three more of our men were sick & sent to fever to-day. So far we have had three groups 1,2,+ others march days up with the fever. According to the postponed of the 3rd Army in all there were the 1st Army became a hundred something. Yesterday we received our new horse ambulance from Kalhoot. This day before the water cart. G.T.V.	
"	17	23	Still close thundery weather. Four more of our men were admitted with Suppressed to-day... Murphy Smith all of 261 rifle men ah Llkay + Pu E. Larron Clarke, a Sapling Ken Ward left morning. G.T.V.	

Army Form C. 2118.

WAR DIARY
or
INTELLIGENCE SUMMARY.
(Erase heading not required.)

Instructions regarding War Diaries and Intelligence Summaries are contained in F. S. Regs., Part II. and the Staff Manual respectively. Title pages will be prepared in manuscript.

Place	Date	Hour	Summary of Events and Information	Remarks and references to Appendices
BREVILLERS	18	23	A few minor sickness today, it not nearly so close. We have on till horses now completed, but nearly as many at men, as discharges to duty. G.T.V.	
"	19	23	11 sick & our men were discharged to duty. Weather - warm, cloudy. Three of our men were admitted with influenza & 12 discharged to duty. Request to complete strength of Ambulance; 4 officers & 24 others, 1 A.S.C. (M.T.) and 12 motor ambulances; 1 cooking & Heavy Chiff Lorries. G.T.V.	
"	20	10	Having been granted 15 days leave to the U.K., I am handing over the temporary command of the Ambulance to my second in command, Major J.B. Cavanagh M.C. Lt. Van der Vyver.	
"	"	"	Lt. Col. Van der Vyver proceeded on leave to United Kingdom this evening. There have been no fresh admissions to Hospital - five men have been discharged to duty, and T/2/016757 Pte Nevin J.A.S.C. Att² has been evacuated with relapse of P.U.O. J.B.C.	
"	21	22	Strong S.W. wind, rain, and no rain. Four men discharged to duty. No fresh case of influenza. J.B.C.	

Army Form C. 2118.

WAR DIARY
or
INTELLIGENCE SUMMARY.
(Erase heading not required.)

Instructions regarding War Diaries and Intelligence Summaries are contained in F. S. Regs., Part II. and the Staff Manual respectively. Title pages will be prepared in manuscript.

Place	Date	Hour	Summary of Events and Information	Remarks and references to Appendices
BREVILLERS	July 22nd	21	A fine day Today. No 38208 Pte Brooks and No 594833 Pte Bond H (15th Sqdn Regt. Attached) proceed on leave to United Kingdom (23/7/18 - 6/8/18). No 7/12267 S/L McKinley T. (A.S.C. AH) returned from leave having been granted 5 days extension of leave. Men were discharged to duty today. No fresh admission to hospital from P.V.O. since routine administration of 4 grains Quin. Sulph. evening parade, and gargle int. Calfate mixture on morning parade - commenced on 18/7/18. Capt Kerbrowis (C.F.) now reports over to 57th Div. M.F.S. at MARIEUX. J.S.G.	
"	23rd	22	A very hot day, hindering all outdoor work. One admission to hospital and one discharge. No fresh cases of influenza. J.S.G.	
SAULTY	24th	23	Field Ambulance left BREVILLERS at 2.0pm and proceed to SAULTY, attached to 319 + 320 Regts of the 80th A. Div. Our Bick and Convalescent were conveyed on motor Ambulances. Billeting accommodation for Officers + Hospital acceptable, poor at present. 2 Heavy Draught train from reinforcements arrived Today. J.S.G. No admission to Hospital Today.	
"	25th	21	A showery day, work consisted of clearing up and rearranging Ambulance Sick Hospital accommodation for about 50. Epidemic of influenza appears to be finished. Col Hinge D.D.M.S. VI Corps came to look round; we are to admit cases only from American units at present. Col. Hinge D.D.M.S. VI Corps came to look round; we are to admit cases only from American units at present. J.S.G.	
"	26th	20	Heavy showers throughout the day. Visit by 80th Am. Div. Surgeon. 4 men discharged from Hospital. No A.S.C. arrived as reinforcement from Div. Train. J.S.G.	

Army Form C. 2118.

WAR DIARY
or
INTELLIGENCE SUMMARY.
(Erase heading not required.)

Instructions regarding War Diaries and Intelligence Summaries are contained in F. S. Regs., Part II. and the Staff Manual respectively. Title pages will be prepared in manuscript.

Place	Date	Hour	Summary of Events and Information	Remarks and references to Appendices
SAULTY.	27th	21.	Heavy showers on and off all day. Making our Amb. Site in a large scale. Work on Canteen and Dining Hall also new roads by for Motor Ambulances. Pte. Meat proceeded on 14 days special leave to United Kingdom. 2 NCOs & 8 men proceeded to WARLUZEL to take over Ambulance site from 6th F.A. 9.36.	
"	28th	21.	No rain. Prep. for a change. D.D.M.S. III Corps came to look round this morning. 15 men arrived as reinforcement from Godwit Base Depot — these men come from Nieuport, E.F. and Salonica E.F. and consequently have not had leave for 2 years or more. Instructions received tonight that F.A. Site at WARLUZEL is to be handed over to 67th Div. F.Amb.	
"	29th	22.	Hot and rather close. Ambulance went to the Baths today 9.36. Order re- WARLUZEL cancelled. Dining Hall finished.	9.36.
"	30th	23	A fine hot day. Two discharges and one admission. Ambulance personnel. No.72/015011 St. For. Taylor F. P.S.C. 112 F.A. att. returned to A.S.C. Base Depot to-day.	
"	31st	21.	Quite hot today. Ambulance moves to Amb. site at WARLUZEL 11 am. 9.6. Major Boland and Amb. Train 80th American Div. A arrive for billets for Train. Which is to arrive tomorrow and be attached to this unit for instruction. Ambulance site is still held at SAULTY — nursing staff, general A/S staff and 2 Ambulance cars to collect regimental sick.	
WARLUZEL				

John Bernard Cavanagh
Major R.A.M.C.
O/C. 112 E F.C.) Ambulance

CONFIDENTIAL

WAR DIARY

OF

113 FIELD AMBULANCE.

From 1st August 1918 To 31st August 1918

VOLUME 31.

Army Form C. 2118.

WAR DIARY
or
INTELLIGENCE SUMMARY.
(Erase heading not required.)

Instructions regarding War Diaries and Intelligence Summaries are contained in F.S. Regs., Part II. and the Staff Manual respectively. Title pages will be prepared in manuscript.

Place	Date	Hour	Summary of Events and Information	Remarks and references to Appendices
WATRULZEEL	Aug. 1.	20	Hot and fine. Provisions have not arrived today. Expected Thomas took consisted of tidying up camp - one new of Mongrel leaving 3 men of Trench admitted) and 2 men discharged from hospital. N°708843 Pte Patterson S. and N°699349 Pte Robson C. handed over to A.P.M. II Corps for 14-28 days F.P.N°.1 respectively.	J.B.C.
"	2nd 21.		Very wet today. Field Hospital Section and Ambulance Company section of the 306th American Sanitary Train arrived at 2.0 p.m. Today, D.D.M.S. II Corps came over to arrange about disposal. This American Unit is to be reorganised and trained on British Field Ambulance lines.	J.B.C.
"	3rd 22		Wet. Rearrangement of billets of both American and our own unit as result of new instruction by 7mm Major after complaint to VI Corps. 319 Am. Field Hosp. left and 319th Am. Ambulance Coy amalgamated and divided into 'A' 'B' + 'C' sections on lines of British F. Ambulance. Explained new organisation to Officers & N.C.O's. Div. Surg. 80th Am. Div. paid a visit. The reorganisation & training promises to work smoothly.	J.B.C.
"	4th 24		Fine. 319th Am. F.A. began their course of instruction this morning. Gas Drill, stretcher work and First Aid by the Sections in rotation - in the afternoon training of motor & Horse Ambulance wagons and a lecture on the work of a F.A. on Active Service.	J.B.C.
"	5th 23		Heavy Showers interfering with outdoor training. Training Scheme carried out on the same lines as yesterday - in the afternoon lectures	

Army Form C. 2118.

WAR DIARY
or
INTELLIGENCE SUMMARY.
(Erase heading not required.)

Instructions regarding War Diaries and Intelligence Summaries are contained in F.S. Regs., Part II. and the Staff Manual respectively. Title pages will be prepared in manuscript.

Place	Date	Hour	Summary of Events and Information	Remarks and references to Appendices
WARLUZEL	5th	23.	Lnt Shaw. Barricks Att and Thos Surgical PS and the Water Cart. The instruction was well carried out, and the men are keen and quick to grasp what is told them. 120112 S/Sgt Sargester G. appears in R.A.M. Corps Orders as promoted to Quartermaster Sgt with effect from 13/9/18. J.C.B.	
"	6th	24	Showery day. Visited detachment at SAULTY and Mor attached D.D.M.S. III Corps Conference at BAC du SUD. Gas alarm for both 113 & 319 F.A.s 11.10 - 11.15 Today. Schedule of training carried out. No 57100 Pte Crompton proceeds on 14 days leave to U.K. No 79306 Pte Barnes, F.A. transferred to England. Has been struck off the strength for 6 months home duty, has been struck off the strength. J.C.B.	
"	7th	21.	A fine day. Able to get on well with work in camp J.C.B. and training schedule. Lt-Col. Paulson Nyier has obtained a trans syllabus of lecture J.C.B.	
"	8th	22..	No rain today. 319 F.A. can now be said to have been through all the chief points connected with Ambulance Equipment and work, once. No 42083 Pte Stanford.E. RAMC. 112th F.A. attd reports here last night having over-stayed his leave by 3 days - unmade for trial by C.M. 'Anti aircraft' MG Crew began Today in Ambulance Me- GOft Pionette Rifle. J.C.B.	
"	9th	21.	Fine. No 23416 Dr Richardson A.S.C. MM2 proceeds on leave to U.K. Work proceeded well, also training. Fine sunbeams two Fords for M. Cycles and personnel arrived this afternoon for 319th Am. Py. Ambulance paid Today. Col. Linton A.D.M.S. 59th Div came to look round and see American unit. J.C.B.	

Army Form C. 2118.

WAR DIARY
or
INTELLIGENCE SUMMARY.
(Erase heading not required.)

Instructions regarding War Diaries and Intelligence Summaries are contained in F.S. Regs., Part II. and the Staff Manual respectively. Title pages will be prepared in manuscript.

III

Place	Date	Hour	Summary of Events and Information	Remarks and references to Appendices
WARLUZEL	Aug. 10	21	A fine hot day. Organised a field day for the 319 Am FA. Fifty "wounded" distributed over "front" S.W. of COULLEMENT. These cases were well treated in the field evacuated by Stretcher Squads to A.D.S. stations, afterwards between WARLUZEL & COULLEMENT and evacuated by Motor Ambulances to M.D.S. at WARLUZEL. The work in all Departments was good and altogether a very creditable finish to 2 weeks Training. This took from 12:00 noon to 5:30 pm before all was clear. Ambulance Transport and equipment for 319 Am FA. arrived here this evening. Book the M.T. & H.T. Personnel for this unit are temporarily attd. to us for rations & messing. (Col. Pollard D.D.M.S. IIIrd Corps) paid a visit to the Ambulance.	J.G.
"	11	23	A fine hot day. Church Parade for Amb. 9.30 am. Afternoon off. Visited detachment at SAULTY.	J.G.
"	12	22	Another fine day. Pitched two of the I.P.E.P. Hosp Tents in place of the other marquees. Brivous Rmb. sent up 1 Off and 20 O.R. to each of the 3 A.D.S.' at IVANLLY, BLOMONT MILL, RANSART, for 3 days instruction. Detachment at SAULTY (change) and relieved from 20 to 10.	J.G.
"	13	23	Fine warm weather. Returned off learn to-day. I found the ambulance in better than many excellent order. Great credit is due to Major Cavanagh for the very fine work he has done during my absence. The training schedule for the 319th American F.A. is running a close 2nd, & to-day they were busy packing and their equipment Mackay. Capt. A.M.S. formerly attached. R.T. Vanden Byron Lieut Reeve

Army Form C. 2118.

WAR DIARY
or
INTELLIGENCE SUMMARY.
(Erase heading not required.)

Instructions regarding War Diaries and Intelligence Summaries are contained in F.S. Regs., Part II. and the Staff Manual respectively. Title pages will be prepared in manuscript.

Place	Date	Hour	Summary of Events and Information	Remarks and references to Appendices
WARLUZEL	Aug 14	22	Fine warm weather. In the afternoon I attended a conference at BAC-DU-SUD. held by the D.D.M.S. VI th Corps. Work in general progressing well. No. 62390 Pte Platt E. has been granted leave to the U.K. from the 13-8-18 to 27-8-18. No. 1511 Sgt Hobson R., No 64181 Pte Garvey A.J.R., No. 64601 A/Cpl Sgt Harrison H. from the 15-8-18 to 29-8-18 - Medal leave in the case of the latter. Capt. D.S. Bodmoch R.A.M.C. (S.R.) having been posted to this unit is taken on the strength from to-day. G.T.V.	
"	15	23	Good weather continues. Two more parties of the American unit proceeded to the A.D.S.s at WAILLY & RANSART for instruction. Under instruction from G.D.M.S. 3rd Division, the R.I.R. Field Ambulance took over the site at SAULTY. The officers, returning a detachment of our own men who returned to Head quarters. G.T.V.	
"	16	22½	Warm sunny day. Three Officers & 10 other ranks are now required to bring the ambulances up to full strength. With the exception of two motor ambulances & one inlay horse, there are no transport shortages. One of our M.T.O.S. as notified to-day. G.T.V	
"	17	23	Sky - cloudy. A new hut and the cook house has been cemented & greatly improved upon. Sickly as number of sick & wounded very few; only about 20 cases per diem on the ambulance. Received orders from D.D.M.S. VI Corps	G.T.V

Army Form C. 2118.

WAR DIARY
or
INTELLIGENCE SUMMARY.
(Erase heading not required.)

Instructions regarding War Diaries and Intelligence Summaries are contained in F. S. Regs., Part II. and the Staff Manual respectively. Title pages will be prepared in manuscript.

Place	Date	Hour	Summary of Events and Information	Remarks and references to Appendices
WARLUZEL	Aug 17	23	To return to our own Division to-morrow. The march is to be done in two stages. To-morrow our destination is TINQUES, on the following day we are to go on to BARLIN. G.T.V.	
LIGNY-ST.FLOCHEL	18	23	Cloudy, not so warm. During the forenoon we packed up, handed over to the 7th. Field Ambulance. The transport left at 12 midday, rail 2 p.m. I brought on the main party. We marched via GRAND RULLECOURT - LIGNEREUIL - AMBRINES - MAIZIERES + AVERDOINGT, and came on here, on the town major at TINQUES gave an "Ellets" there - no accommodation being available. G.T.V.	
RUITZ	19	23	Warm pleasant weather. We came on here at 9 a.m. the transport going on in advance; marched through BAILLEUL-aux-CORNAILLES, MAGNICOURT, LICOMTE, RANCHICOURT, where we got orders to proceed to RUITZ instead of BARLIN — authority A.D.M.S. He also instructed me to be prepared to relieve the 141st Field Ambulance — relief to be completed in the 21st. The ambulance arrived here at 6 p.m. A/c to the C.D. of No. 141 F.A. to send up the load trades the three A.D.S's "4 aid posts." G.T.V.	

WAR DIARY or INTELLIGENCE SUMMARY

Army Form C. 2118.

Place	Date	Hour	Summary of Events and Information	Remarks and references to Appendices
RUITZ	Aug. 20	23	Fine warm weather. In the forenoon the A.D.M.S. exhibitions his way up the line with the A.D.M.S. of the 1st Division. After breakfast went up small ?trench to each of the A.D.Ss, & R.A.Ps., in the afternoon a motor car to the walking wounded post at LABOURSE. G.T.V.	
"	21	22½	Exceptionally hot day. At 9 a.m. went up Major Kennon, Capt Babington & Sindle - with personnel - to the A.D.Ss. to the men from the Officers of the 141/1st Field Ambulance. Reynard taking over & completed here by 12 noon. The medical organisation hitherto opened to what we normally experienced. The entire forward work is done by our ambulance. The heavy guns are only heavy here at the W.D.S., which is to be seen by the 112 F.A. Through the their A.D.Ss. in stopped with a heavier ant-shower each. G.T.V.	
"	22	23	Swelteringly hot weather. After breakfast the 2 m.o. visits the A.D.Ss. Major Kennon is in charge of us at CAMBRIN, Capt Babington at = ANNEQUIN FOSSE, & Capt Sindle = at MADELEINE. The line was quiet; about 10 casualties were sledded to the two more during the / / R. both over from the 2 m.o. in the of Kennon. G.T.V.	

Army Form C. 2118.

WAR DIARY
or
INTELLIGENCE SUMMARY.
(Erase heading not required.)

Place	Date	Hour	Summary of Events and Information	Remarks and references to Appendices
RUITZ	Aug 23	20	Cloudy sky, not nearly so warm. I walked round our feels on portion of the camp. Had a trip from the A.D.M.S. in the afternoon. G.T.V.	
"	24	23	Lovely weather. Weekly returns rendered. G.T.V.	
"	25	23	Weather good. In the afternoon I visited the A.D.Ss. + R.A.P. G.T.V.	
"	26	23	Still showery. In the afternoon I visited all the A.D.Ss. + R.A.P. again with the A.D.M.S. Lima very quiet. G.T.V.	
"	27	22	Nothing to report. G.T.V.	
"	28	23	Still showery. Got the carpenters started on the new meat stores. G.T.V.	
"	29	23	Pleasant weather. In the afternoon I visited the A.D.Ss. Note Major West with me — he took over in command of abt 112.15 Field Amb. G.T.V.	
"	30	23	Lovely weather. We now have our full complement of motor ambulances, having received two additional ones 3 days ago. "Red Cross" at Madeleine A.D.S. is now complete. The rest of the work at the A.D.Ss. is progressing well. G.T.V.	

Army Form C. 2118.

WAR DIARY
or
INTELLIGENCE SUMMARY.
(Erase heading not required.)

Instructions regarding War Diaries and Intelligence Summaries are contained in F. S. Regs., Part II. and the Staff Manual respectively. Title pages will be prepared in manuscript.

VIII

Place	Date	Hour	Summary of Events and Information	Remarks and references to Appendices
RUITZ	Aug. 31	20	Cloudy sky; cool. Monthly weekly returns rendered up to time. To complete establishment of Ambulance, we now require 3 Officers & eleven other ranks. Also we require horses or a rider.	

G.T. van der Nyen
Lt.Col. R.A.M.C.

WR 32

14/3259

Confidential.

War Diary

of

113 Field Ambulance

From 1st September 1918   To 30th September 1918.

Volume 32.

COMMITTEE FOR THE
MEDICAL HISTORY OF THE WAR
Date 9 NOV 1916

Army Form C. 2118.

WAR DIARY
or
INTELLIGENCE SUMMARY.
(Erase heading not required.)

Instructions regarding War Diaries and Intelligence Summaries are contained in F. S. Regs., Part II. and the Staff Manual respectively. Title pages will be prepared in manuscript.

Place	Date	Hour	Summary of Events and Information	Remarks and references to Appendices
RUITZ	Sept 1	23	Weather - colder. In the forenoon I went round the "A.D.M.S., visited all the A.D.Ss & R.A.P.s. for details that we do away with the aid post in "railway cutting". G.T.V.	
"	2	23	Pleasant weather, but quite cold towards evening. We got all the preparing the emergency aid posts ready along our position of the camp. I got round from Major Vernon at noon that owing to the Bosch having moved back opposite our left sector, the R.A.P. at Winople Street has been moved forward to the tunnel. G.T.V.	
"	3	23	Lovely weather. I visited the A.D.Ss. in the forenoon. Heard from Major Vernon that the M.O. of the right battalion of the left sector has moved his R.A.P. back to Winople Street. Major J.B. Cavanagh proceeded on special leave to the U.K. to-day – in this weather. We received eleven re-inforcements to-day – all private R.A.M.C. G.T.V.	
"	4	22	Warm sunny day. Built a hundred gassed cases (shell) were evacuated through the A.D.S. at CAMBRIN. Nearly all the 2nd H. Lomers regiment". G.T.V.	
"	5	23	Close stinking weather. All work progressing steadily. Meanwhile Clove completion. Another 100 gassed cases (shell) were evacuated through MADELEINE – 9/2 BLACK WATCH. G.T.V.	

Army Form C. 2118.

WAR DIARY
or
INTELLIGENCE SUMMARY.
(Erase heading not required.)

Place	Date	Hour	Summary of Events and Information	Remarks and references to Appendices
RUITZ	Sept 6	23	Very warm. In the afternoon I visited the A.D.S. with the D.A.D.M.S. There are still a number of gassed cases (mild) being evacuated through A.D.S., CAMBRIN. Also a number of wounded. G.T.V.	
"	7	22	Close, thundery weather. Lieuts. R.M. Devereux & C.A. Barker, R.A.M.C. having been posted to this unit, are taken on the strength from the 6/9/1918 inclusive. Forage & fuel sheds have been erected, & all other work progressing well. At 11 a.m. there a horse harness inspection. During last 24 hours 21 sick + 48 wounded came through MADELEINE A.D.S., + 7 sick + 48 wounded were evacuated through CAMBRIN. G.T.V.	
"	8	22	Cloudy showery. At 10 a.m. the A.D.M.S. & I went up the line & visited the A.D.S. & R.A.Ps.. Lieut. Barker we took up to CAMBRIN with me. I re attached him to Major Vernon for a course of instruction in A.D.S. work. G.T.V.	
"	9	19	Windy wet. Lieut. Devereux I sent up for a course of instruction at both ANNEQUIN & MADELEINE A.D.Ss. Forage presses arrived from the afternoon. Received a warning order from the A.D.M.S. to have everything packed, & be ready to move to a new site tomorrow morning. G.T.V.	

Army Form C. 2118.

WAR DIARY
or
INTELLIGENCE SUMMARY.
(Erase heading not required.)

Instructions regarding War Diaries and Intelligence Summaries are contained in F. S. Regs., Part II. and the Staff Manual respectively. Title pages will be prepared in manuscript.

Place	Date	Hour	Summary of Events and Information	Remarks and references to Appendices
BARLIN	10	23	Showery weather. According to A.D.M.S's instructions, attached, we moved to this site. Lieut. R.M. George, as billeting officer, made suitable arrangements with the Town Major for our accommodation. Our move was completed by 1.30 p.m. B.T.V.	A.D.M.S. 1645 Su No 8 147/285 9th Sept 1916
"	11	23	Heavy rain during the forenoon. In the afternoon 9 visits to A.D.Ss.: arrangts. for Capt. Babcock to return to head quarters for a rest, Lieut. Severance in his place. Arranged a detailed return of wounded and being evacuated through the A.D.S. at CAMBRIN. Other A.D.S.s very quiet. B.T.V.	
"	12	23	Still very showery. During the early hours of the morning Major Vernon sent down for 2 cars to evacuate some wounded. By noon midday the Signal people had the never fired up to our phone. On the afternoon there's a court of Enquiry held, on the cause of death of our heavy drays horse. The court came to the conclusion that the animal was accidentally strangled, that no one was in any way to blame. B.T.V.	

Army Form C. 2118.

WAR DIARY
or
INTELLIGENCE SUMMARY.
(Erase heading not required.)

Instructions regarding War Diaries and Intelligence Summaries are contained in F. S. Regs., Part II. and the Staff Manual respectively. Title pages will be prepared in manuscript.

Place	Date	Hour	Summary of Events and Information	Remarks and references to Appendices
BARLIN	13	22	Dull showery. In the afternoon Greenwood moved from Capt. Gentle's with his R.M.O. at Factory dug-out. Has moved his R.A.P. forward to "Munster Tunnel". Capt. Gentle sent up four additional R.A.M.C. bearers with Factory dug-out to act as a relay to those trying the cases down from the new R.A.P. One Green only reported now to complete 16 slightly & the ambulance. In all other respects we are up to strength. R.T.V. — one heavy day! none	
"	14	22	Still a tendency to be showery. In the forenoon I visited the horse lines. Past the men there. I arranged for him & the bearers at the "walking wounded" post to go up to MADELEINE A.D.S. as a reinforcement. Two of our bearers were slightly wounded while bringing some patients down from "BARTS" R.A.P. S.T.V.	
"	15	23	Warm sunny weather. After my orderly Room Travaux Inead-up the line with the A.D.M.S. & the Divisional Surgeon of the 60th American Division. We visited their A.D.S.s & all the R.A.P.s. Two of these have been moved forward — Henley St. to "Mountain Keep" & Factory to "Munster Tunnel". And we visited "Barts" Tunnel, where Bart is being moved up to to-night. Right Sector { Munster Tunnel - Right Battalion — R.R.Z.H. / Mountain Keep - Left " } S.T.V.	

Army Form C. 2118.

WAR DIARY
or
INTELLIGENCE SUMMARY.
(Erase heading not required.)

Instructions regarding War Diaries and Intelligence Summaries are contained in F. S. Regs., Part II. and the Staff Manual respectively. Title pages will be prepared in manuscript.

Place	Date	Hour	Summary of Events and Information	Remarks and references to Appendices
BARLIN.	Sept. 16.	2.3	Lovely warm weather. The M.O. of the Rifle Bde. on the Right Section notifies me of his move up to "Kemp's Cron" (Barts Tunnel). We are trying the horse lines in movement, & intend to go to look at Prale, which we are drawing to-morrow. One of our motor ambulances has been repainted, their Plates on another one to-day. One of the water carts. The horse ambulance is almost ready to be removed. G.T.V.	
"	17	2.11½	Exceptionally hot + close. Nothing special to report. G.T.V	
"	18	22⅓	Warm weather. A second motor ambulance has been re-painted. To-day a float was made on a third. In the afternoon I went over our new D.A.D.M.S. - Major Trayer round the whole A.D.S. + told the Relay + R.A.Ps. Twenty two wounded gassed cases were evacuated through CAMBRIN A.D.S. to-day. The Boche still seems to be throwing over a lot of yellow cross gas shells. G.T.V.	
"	19	23	Cloudy, rather strong east wind blowing. Nothing to report. G.T.V.	

Army Form C. 2118.

WAR DIARY
or
INTELLIGENCE SUMMARY.
(Erase heading not required.)

Instructions regarding War Diaries and Intelligence Summaries are contained in F. S. Regs., Part II. and the Staff Manual respectively. Title pages will be prepared in manuscript.

VI

Place	Date	Hour	Summary of Events and Information	Remarks and references to Appendices
BARLIN	Sept. 20	23	Showery weather. I visited the A.D.M.S. after breakfast, received a warning order that we'd have to move to our Headquarters in a couple of days time. With that object in view I visited VAUDRICOURT to find out what billeting accommodation there was there. Re granting of weekly cash grants to-day; we got starts on a second one. Six privates having been posted to this unit are taken in the strength from to-day. We given an surplus of 5 other ranks; we are now two officers short, the establishment having been brought up to 10 again. G.T.V.	
"	21	22	Good weather. Very few wounded rank cases evacuated through the A.D.S. to-day. G.T.V.	
"	22	22	Dull & wet. In the forenoon I went along to VAUDRICOURT with one of my sergeants & had a look at the billets & ambulance site we are to take over to-morrow. I arranged with the C.O. of the 2/1st Wessex Field Ambulance to send up some of my wagon in the afternoon, & received an advance party of 1 N.C.O. & 6 men. 16th Division R.A.M.C. operation order No. 28 received at 8.45 p.m. The same is attached. G.T.V.	

Army Form C. 2118.

WAR DIARY
or
INTELLIGENCE SUMMARY.
(Erase heading not required.)

Instructions regarding War Diaries and Intelligence Summaries are contained in F. S. Regs., Part II. and the Staff Manual respectively. Title pages will be prepared in manuscript.

VII

Place	Date	Hour	Summary of Events and Information	Remarks and references to Appendices
VAUDRICOURT	Sept. 22		Strong, & a good deal colder. Our move was complete by 11.30 a.m. The site is quite a good one for an ambulance running the line, only the horse lines are far too close to its sick hut workhorses. All the tents are quite good. Ammunition organisation - 1st Corps, 5th Army. G.T.V.	
"	23		Fresh Autumn weather. All day we were busy clearing tidying up the camp. In the forenoon we had a visit from the A.D.M.S. By 7 p.m. we had our telephone forces up, communication established with the Divisional Exchange. G.T.V.	
"	25	22	Strong in the morning. In the forenoon the A.D.M.S. & Lieut-Col. A.D.S. & R.A.P.s. Owing to the narrowing of the Divisional front, Bath Alley post & Kings Cross R.A.P. are now out of our area; most of the casualties & sick are evacuated through CAMBRIN A.D.S. & only have 2 bearer now at Mendi's Tunnel, & withdrawn all his bearers at Railway Keep Relay post. Col. Bowen to investigate the area in the vicinity of Loos Alley for a new R.A.P. which would function for the whole frontage, the communication near its light railway leading E. CAMBRIN Mountain. Keep R.A.P. has been evacuated by us. G.T.V.	

Army Form C. 2118.

WAR DIARY
or
INTELLIGENCE SUMMARY.
(Erase heading not required.)

Instructions regarding War Diaries and Intelligence Summaries are contained in F. S. Regs., Part II. and the Staff Manual respectively. Title pages will be prepared in manuscript.

Place	Date	Hour	Summary of Events and Information	Remarks and references to Appendices
VAUDRICOURT	Sept 26	22	Weather-good. We sent for several loads of straw to improve its rough parade ground. On the 23rd we received an allotment of horses - one place to stay- until the 7th. Of next month, I was right, we received our allotment fine. In the afternoon Major J.B. Cavanagh returned off leave. Incurred orders from the A.D.M.S. to send three down their heavy Army horses to the Area Commandant towards area VIRGUINEUL for temporary duty. Have arranged for the men to be billeted. the horses to be stabled at our W.W.C.R. LABOURSE. G.T.V.	
"	27	23	Lovely weather. In the forenoon went up to meet an R.E. officer at CAMBRIN, under instructions from the A.D.M.S. arranged with him to the construction of a new R.A.P. At Major — Cavanagh & selected a site at approximately A 22 d 2·3 just behind AUCHY (Gone trench map) Major J.B. Cavanagh M.C. relieves Major R.G. Vernon at CAMBRIN A.D.S.. Good progress is being made with construction of new shelters at Cambrin. One of the two huts down here we actually up as a m.R. Room. salvage store. G.T.V.	

Army Form C. 2118.

WAR DIARY
or
INTELLIGENCE SUMMARY.
(Erase heading not required.)

Place	Date	Hour	Summary of Events and Information	Remarks and references to Appendices
VAUDRICOURT	Sept. 28	20	Showery in the forenoon, somewhat colder. W.E. & B. Smith in everyplace this week; + deficient of 2 officers, 72 heavy draft horses. Our attn: under cont: is being met. Parrots at present. All their work is progressing well. For the last 4 or 5 days very few wounded have been evacuated from the line. G.T.V.	
"	29	23	Cold raw. In the forenoon lined up + visited the A.D.S. work at A.D.M.S. I have detailed a work party of 12 R.A.M.C. bearers for the new R.A.P. + arranged for them. 15 beds at Mauritz Tunnel during the period of duty. G.T.V.	
"	30	20	Showery cold. All lying wounded are being evacuated to no 15 C.C.S. RUITZ. Sick + other wounded to no 13 C.C.S. PERNES, + no 15 C.C.S. RUITZ on alternate days. Made mixed arrangements. D.M.S. 5ᵗʰ. Army, no 89 dated 25-9-18. Very few cases being evacuated from the line just now — yesterday 9 sick + 1 wounded during 12 hours ending 6 a.m.	1st Corps med instruction no 62 dated 27-9-18.

G.T. van der Vijver
Lt. Col. R.A.M.C.

SECRET   A.D.M.S.16th Divn.No.S.192/280.

Copy No. **6**

16th DIVISION MEDICAL ARRANGEMENTS.
-o-o-o-o-o-o-o-o-o-o-o-o-o-o-o-o-o-o-o-o-o-o-

Ref.Sheets:- 44B 1/40,000 & Trench Map "GORRE"   9th September, 1918.

The Main Dressing Station, RUITZ, 112 Field Ambulance, will close tomorrow the 10th instant and be handed over with certain remaining patients to No.6 Casualty Clearing Station.

The personnel of No.112 Field Ambulance with the Headquarters personnel of 113 Field Ambulance will be billeted in BARLIN and 112 Field Ambulance will remain closed for the present. Arrangements for billets to be made direct between Officers Commanding, Field Ambulances and Town Major, BARLIN.

111 Field Ambulance will, from tomorrow, act as Main Dressing Station for 16th Division sick except those from the line.

Under arrangements with A.D.M.S., 55th Division, all wounded and sick from the line will be admitted direct to 1/3 West Lancs Field Ambulance, RUITZ K.20.a. as a temporary measure.

Reference page 2, para 4, of my S.192/284 dated 1st September, for Main Dressing Station, RUITZ, 112 Field Ambulance, read 111 Field Ambulance, BARLIN.

The dispositions of Horse Lines will be as follows:-
    111 Field Ambulance at BARLIN) arrangements with
    112 Field Ambulance at BARLIN) Town Major.
    113 Field Ambulance at J.24.d.4.7.

Revised Medical Arrangements will be issued later.

ACKNOWLEDGE.

                                             A. Bonn
Headquarters,   Colonel, AMS.,
16th Division.   A.D.M.S., 16th Division.

Copies to:-
Nos. 1 - 2	O.C.111 F.A. (2 Copies)	32	D.A.P.M., 16th Divn.
3 - 4	O.C.112 F.A. (2 Copies)	33	O.C., 16 Div.Train.
5 - 6	O.C.113 F.A. (2 Copies)	34	S.C.F., D.C.G.Dept.
7 -11	47th.Inf.Bde.(5 Copies)	35	S.C.F., P.C's Dept.
12-16	48th.Inf.Bde.(5 Copies)	36	A.D.M.S., 15th Divn.
17-21	49th.Inf.Bde.(5 Copies)	37	A.D.M.S., 55th Divn.
22	O.C.11th Hants Rgt.	38	D.M.S., First Army.
23	O.C.16th M.G.Battn.	39	D.D.M.S., 1st Corps.
24	C.R.E., 16th Divn.	40-41	Diary (2 copies)
25-28	C.R.A., 16th Divn.(4 copies)	42	File.
29	16th Div."G"		
30	16th Div."A" & "Q"		
31	D.A.D.V.S.16th Divn.		

SECRET.   COPY No:- 6

16th. DIVISION R.A.M.C. OPERATION ORDER No. 28.
-o-o-o-o-o-o-o-o-o-o-o-o-o-o-o-o-o-o-o-o-o-o-o-o-o-o-

Ref.Sheets:- 44B.1/40,000 & Trench Map "GORRE"   22nd.SEPTEMBER, 1918.

1. Until further orders No.111 Field Ambulance will remain open at BARLIN, as a temporary measure, for the treatment of the Sick from the Forward Area.

2. No.112 Field Ambulance will move on the morning of 24th. Sept. to BRUAY (old site of No.22 Casualty Clearing Stn.) and open there by 12 noon 25th.instant for the reception of the sick of the Brigade in Reserve.

3. The Headquarters of No.113 Field Ambulance will move to VAUDRICOURT on the morning of 23rd. Sept. and take over all billets, horse lines etc. at present occupied by 2/1st.Wessex Field Ambulance 55th.Division, who will be clear of the site by 12 noon.
   No.113 Field Ambulance will continue to be responsible for the evacuation of the Sick and Wounded of the Forward Area.

4. The sick of the 47th.Infantry Brigade will be collected on the mornings of the 23rd. and 24th.Sept. by No.111 Field Ambulance.
   Commencing on the morning of the 25th.instant No.112 Field Ambulance will be responsible for the collection of all sick from the 47th.Infantry Brigade in Reserve.
   Location of Units of the Brigade in Reserve is as follows:-

   Bde.H.Q................HESDIGNEUL.
   "A" Battn..............HESDIGNEUL.
   "B" Battn..............   LOZINGHEM.
   "C" Battn..............MARLES-LES-MINES.
   T. M. Batty............HESDIGNEUL.
   Train Coy..............MARLES-LES-MINES.

   From the morning of the 24th.inst. No.112 Field Ambulance will cease to supply Horse Ambulance Wagons for conveying sick from Casualty Clearing Stn.RUITZ to No.111 Field Ambulance BARLIN. This duty will be carried out from the 24th.inst. by No.111 Field Ambulance.

5. Details of the moves will be arranged between the O's.C. Units concerned.

6. Receipts for any stores taken and handed over will be sent to this office in duplicate.

7. The completion of all moves will be reported to this office by wire.

8. The office of A.D.M.S. will close at RUITZ at 5 p.m. 23rd. inst. and re-open at DROUVIN (K.4.c.5.2.) at the same hour.

9. ACKNOWLEDGE.

Headquarters,   G Bowen.
16th.Division.   Colonel, AMS.,
AK.   A.D.M.S., 16th.Division.

Issued at 7 p.m.

For distribution see over.

DISTRIBUTION.

Copies to:-

```
      Nos.1 - 2  O.C.111 F.A.(2 copies).
          3 - 4  O.C.112 F.A.(   -do- ).
          5 - 6  O.C.113 F.A.(   -do- ).
          7 - 11 47th.Inf.Bde(5  -do- ).
         12 - 16 48th.Inf.Bde(   -do- ).
         17 - 21 49th.Inf.Bde(   -do- ).
            22.  O.C.11th.Hants Regt (P).
            23.  O.C.16th.M.G.Battn.
            24.  C.R.E.,16th.Divn.
         25 - 28 C.R.A.16th.Divn(4 copies).
            29.  16th.Div."G"
            30.  16th.Div."A" & "Q"
            31.  D.A.D.V.S.16th.Divn.
            32.  D.A.P.M.16th.Divn.
            33.  O.C.16th.Div.Train.
            34.  S.C.F.,D.C.G.Dept.
            35.  S.C.F.,R.C's.Dept.
            36.  A.D.M.S.,15th.Divn.
            37.  A.D.M.S.,55th.Divn.
            38.  O.C.6 C.C.S.
            39.  D.G.O.16th.Divn.
            40.  D.M.S.,Fifth Army.
            41.  D.D.M.S.,I Corps.
         42 - 43 Diary (2 copies).
            44  File.
```

COMMITTEE FOR THE
MEDICAL HISTORY OF THE WAR
4 DEC 1916
Date

Army Form C. 2118.

21 113th Fld Amb

WAR DIARY
or
INTELLIGENCE SUMMARY

NM 33

Place	Date	Hour	Summary of Events and Information	Remarks and references to Appendices
VAUDRICOURT	Oct 1918 1	23	Lovely fresh weather. In the forenoon I went along to see the A.D.M.S. at his Office. CAMBRIN was being shelled in the afternoon. Some of our men at the A.D.S. were slightly gassed, Major Cavanagh among the O.C. received slight wounds. B.T.V.	
"	2	23	Cloudy & damp. Received instructions from the A.D.M.S. to open up a dressing centre at our W.W.C.P., LABOURSE. Made arrangements after dark in the afternoon. Our new sergeant Corp. (1st Corps type) is now clerk in the afternoon. All this work is progressing well. B.T.V.	
"	3	24	Cloudy & dull. The enemy having with drawn to the HAUTE DEULE CANAL, I over line having accordingly been moved forward, I went up the line to investigate the disposition of the new R.A.P's. I took Major Cavanagh with me, & we reconnoitred as far forward as DOUVRIN, the enemy holding DOUVRIN, has been detailed as the R.A.P. to the Bn. in its line - map ref. Sheet 44 A. 13.2.6 & 3.3. There were arranged to have a Relay Post in HAINES next to the R.A.P. for LG 13,, in support. Map ref. m B. 25.2.3.2. In AUCHY are selected a site for an advanced A.D.S. - map ref. A.23 29.7.	

Army Form C. 2118.

WAR DIARY
or
INTELLIGENCE SUMMARY.
(Erase heading not required.)

Place	Date	Hour	Summary of Events and Information	Remarks and references to Appendices
VAUDRICOURT	Oct 1918 3	24	From - the R.A.P. at Hersin today the cases will be evacuated by wheeled stretcher carrier to the Advanced A.D.S. to by twenty stretcher bearers along the line DOUVRIN — HAISNES — AUCHY road. A ford car will be dispatched at the Advanced A.D.S. it's convey them to the A.D.S. at CAMBRIN. The dressing centre is now to be established at A.D.3. ANNEQUIN. B.T.V.	
"	4	19	Good weather. In the forenoon I took the A.D.M.S. up to see the new front & advanced A.D.S. Under his instruction I gave orders for the W.W.C.P. at LABOURSE to be closed, & all the equipment to be conveyed to ANNEQUIN. He also instructed me to move my headquarters to CAMBRIN tomorrow. We're receiving a new allotment of cases for the move to start to-morrow. We will be at the rate of two a day until the 24th. Ambulances – 5 Car. m. the P.R. at the rate of two a day until the 24th. Number of cases evacuated thro' A.D.S. yesterday. – 6 sick + 7 wounded. B.T.V.	
"	5	22	Cloudy mild. In the forenoon the 2.m. & I went up to CAMBRIN to arrange about billets. I got most of the equipment sent up to-day, & itching the train (by lt motoring) too late, & not medical stores. We now have a large amt. car at AUCHY, & a ford at HAISNES, where the Relay post was. The R.A.P. has moved from Sugar factory DOUVRIN to BILLY. met by B 23 C 2.8.-. My Relay host at Kl symph factory about ½ mile To. of Lacolin. Evacuates thro' A.D.3. wounded 9, including two German prisoners, & 9 sick. B.T.V.	

Army Form C. 2118.

WAR DIARY
or
INTELLIGENCE SUMMARY.
(Erase heading not required.)

Instructions regarding War Diaries and Intelligence Summaries are contained in F.S. Regs., Part II. and the Staff Manual respectively. Title pages will be prepared in manuscript.

Place	Date	Hour	Summary of Events and Information	Remarks and references to Appendices
CAMBRIN	Oct 1918 6	23	Good weather. Our move from VAUDRICOURT was completed by 11.30 hours. In the afternoon major Cavenagh & myself went over to look out a suitable property. the A.D.S. in BILLY. We found that R.A.P. of No.73 holding the land but moving forwards to the Chateau in BILLY – that 44 A B 23 c 6.5 arranged for a pool car to be on duty at the Riley post – Sugar factory, DOUVRIN. G.T.V	
"	7	22	Cold showery. A.D.S. I work was done cleaning up the site, arranging suitable the villetly accommodation. All personnel equipment for new A.D.S. ready to move at a moment's notice. Hear a raid from the D.D.M.S. in the forenoon. G.T.V	
"	8	23	Cloudy cold. All the G.S. waggons were re-packed, with the contents withness according to the scale laid down in G.R.O. 5175. The reduction has allowed us to pack all the G.S. wagons equipment in each section – in 5 to 6 wagons. By this arrangement we have 9 spare G.S. wagons which shews utilized for the following purposes: 4 for dispensary 2 " M. store 1 " Carpenters tools 1 " Tailor 1 " Bootmaker	

(A8o4) D. D. & L., London, E.C.
Wt. W1777LM2 31t 750,000 5/17 **Sch. 52** Forms/C2118/14

Army Form C. 2118.

WAR DIARY
or
INTELLIGENCE SUMMARY.
(Erase heading not required.)

Instructions regarding War Diaries and Intelligence Summaries are contained in F. S. Regs., Part II. and the Staff Manual respectively. Title pages will be prepared in manuscript.

Place	Date	Hour	Summary of Events and Information	Remarks and references to Appendices
CAMBRIN	Oct 12/15	20	Misty mild. I sent down timber corrugated iron to the dressing centre at ANNEQUIN - Lieut Durrence Party - for a shed to be erected, in which the die-gassed clothing can be hung. Also went round the 4 advanced chambers. Very few casualties, week are being evacuated in now. G.T.V.	
"	13	22	Cold extremely windier pouring rain. Broken + two running, reports to O.C. 34 C.C.S. for temporary duty & instructions. G.T.V.	
"	14	22	Clear sky sunny in the forenoon 9 weeks this great progress has been made in the improvement - all the cellars have been thoroughly cleared + cleaned out, good entrance has been made, also a wooden + iron wooden sleds for taking stretcher cases into the dressing room. The cellars are being stay-kased, one specially prepared for the treatment of clothing of gassed cases. G.T.V.	
"	15	23	Cloudy; made muddy as result of rain during the night. In the afternoon I received word from Major Cornnegy [?] stating that our 3 party were across the canal DEHLIA-HAUTE-DEULE Canal + turning on towards PROVIN. He reported against A.D.S. due at BERCLAU - B18 20 75	

WAR DIARY
or
INTELLIGENCE SUMMARY.

(Erase heading not required.)

Army Form C. 2118.

Place	Date	Hour	Summary of Events and Information	Remarks and references to Appendices
CAMBRIN	April 15	23	Also visited the 2nd R.A.P. has moved forward to the Brewery today - B.24 d.3.2. I went to the A.D.S. DOUVAIN & arranged for Major Browney & his party - 6 men - to move to BERCLAU & his earlier conversation the following morning. B.T.V.	
"	16	21	Clearing & damp. The A.D.S. men & stretchers at BERCLAU & from h + at 10.00 the 2nd R.A.P. moves forward to the PROVIN - Q.27.d.29.7.30. Sulphur men in Bn. M.O. positioning the R.A.P. in BAUVIN & the former WOODS meets 40 O.D.S. Bn at BERCLAU from army in to PROVIN & carrying the sufficient from troops arrived to move to A.D.S. till further orders we shall be mixed up PROVIN - Q.27.a.5.6 - At 22.00 3 men arrived Major Downey (H.Q.) had complete service to PROVIN, also the L.C.R.A.P (M.O. Royal Army Medical) Red been stopped in ANNEBULIN we are all ready to move on the Main Downy station forward to BERCLAU & taken an advance party of 1 Junior N.C.O. + 12 men & sent up at 2.00 m. the instruction from A.D.M.S. have written to Lieut-Col ... A.D.Ss... B.T.V.	

Army Form C. 2118.

WAR DIARY
or
INTELLIGENCE SUMMARY.
(Erase heading not required.)

Place	Date	Hour	Summary of Events and Information	Remarks and references to Appendices
PROVIN	Oct 1914 17	23	Fairly good weather. Under instruction leaving CAMBRIN at 09.15. Lived on wheat rations & horse meat. Supplies & horse lines arranged. Our move over the spurs, streets, ditching soon arranged. We were just settling in when I got word from Major Cavanagh that he was moving the A.D.M.S. forward to CAMPHIN - D 21 C 2.1. - so without unpacking 9 classes to 20 sought on to go forward to PROVIN this rather more was completed by 15.15. Very few casualties.	B 1862.75.
CAMPHIN-EN-CAREMBAULT	18	22	Good weather. We had a tremendous lot of work cleaning up the kit, washing the personnel &c. I got all equipment & kits cut down to a minimum. The meant unpacking & repacking the wagons. Major Cavanagh his one G.S. wagon attached to him temporarily. I received word from him saying he had moved forward to PONT A MARCQ. As a temporary measure I sent on an officer & 9 other ranks to establish a relay car collecting post at PHALEMPIN - D 23 d 3.6 - came in here at 18.00 o'clock, taking on the men an ambulance and went a German hospital I may think. We have had to send two of our large horse into the workshop - broken chains. S.T.V.	

WAR DIARY
or
INTELLIGENCE SUMMARY.

(Erase heading not required.)

Army Form C. 2118.

Place	Date	Hour	Summary of Events and Information	Remarks and references to Appendices
RUMES	Oct 1918 22	20	Misty, raining. Roads very muddy. Undress instructions from the A.D.M.S. in camp on here at 09.30 by is being relieved by the 112 R. Field Ambulance. The Ambulance site is at the school - Huts 27 T 28 b.s.s. Joint instruments. Tenty with Lieut Bowman in charge. Move was completed at 12.50. 16th Division R.C.M.C. Opens in Order No. 31 is attached. I received news from Major Cavanagh that he had taken over available units. A heavy spirits to church, TAINTIGNIES – U25 d 6.3. – as a dressing room + place for cases. Saidson he reports that they had been shells, and 5 lying by sitting cases were expecting more. G.T.V.	
"	23		Clear sky again. Major Cavanagh came down for a short time, reports all going well at the A.D.S. I had a visit from the A.D.M.S. in the afternoon; the instructions are to detain all slight cases, so that three rooms prepared as wards. Our cars only evacuate as far as TEMPLEUVE where the M.T. cars, & they evacuate from there by M.A.C. cars to the C.C.S. All cases of the general show are there on the A.D. books. G.T.V.	

Army Form C. 2118.

WAR DIARY
or
INTELLIGENCE SUMMARY.
(Erase heading not required.)

Instructions regarding War Diaries and Intelligence Summaries are contained in F. S. Regs., Part II. and the Staff Manual respectively. Title pages will be prepared in manuscript.

Place	Date	Hour	Summary of Events and Information	Remarks and references to Appendices
RUMES	Oct 1918 24	23	Good weather. In the forenoon I visited the A.D.S., TAINTIGNIES. Lieut. Devine went with me to where Capt Saville, who has been slightly wounded, received rather a shaking up. G.T.V.	
"	25	20	Good weather. Hardly any rounds, but a good number of sick being admitted - mostly Enteritis. Capt Mitchell, Lieut Baker, + 3 m.r.s returned from No. 54 C.C.S. today, after being temporarily attached there for instruction. G.T.V.	
"	26	23	Weather - frost morning. Opened up new aeroplane hut for patients in the field Amm - own ambulance site. G.T.V.	
"	27	20	Fresh sunny day. I visited the O.D.S. in the forenoon + with Capt Mitchell up with me to where Major Cavanagh, D.A.C. & Forman, the A.D.M.S. called in on his way up to the A.D.S. G.T.V.	
"	28	22	Lovely weather. For the last 24 hrs ending at 0800 today we had 53 admissions to Hospital. Of these 17 were sick - chiefly Influenza - 11 wounded, + 25 gassed. Many of the latter has the typical signs + symptoms of mustard gas, while the other half were more or less suggestive of Phosgene or Chlorogene. All the gassed cases belong to the 34th London Regiment. G.T.V.	

XI

Army Form C. 2118

WAR DIARY
or
INTELLIGENCE SUMMARY.
(Erase heading not required.)

Instructions regarding War Diaries and Intelligence Summaries are contained in F. S. Regs., Part II. and the Staff Manual respectively. Title pages will be prepared in manuscript.

Place	Date	Hour	Summary of Events and Information	Remarks and references to Appendices
RUMES	Oct 1918 29	23	Fine weather. During last 24 hours ending 0800 K-day, in x no 5 6 wounded & 8 sick cases. 34 cases have been admitted. Sent to the 112 Tk Field Ambulance. - 3 detainees. Prevailing diseases Influenza & P.U.O. G.T.V.	
"	30	23	Fine sunny weather. In the forenoon I went up M/ofs to No 1 A.D.S. T investigate its water supply & the place. Also visited No 2 A.D.S. / G.T. Capt Metcalfe to investigate the water supply of TAINTIGNIES. Cases during last 24 hours — 3 wounded, 9 pront (3 malaria & typhoid) + 1 N.Y.D.; Gas. Sick sent to 112 T.F.A. — 23. Sick detained — 9. Prevailing diseases — Influenza & P.U.O. G.T.V.	
"	31		Cloudy damp. Cases during last 24 hrs — admitted: 3 wounded, 80 cases, 1 2 N.Y.D.? Gas. Two passed to case detained. Sick — 24 similars to detained. Prevailing diseases - P.U.O. & N.Y.D.N. & T. van der Nyre Capt RAMC O.C. 113 F. field Ambulance	

CONFIDENTIAL

War Diary

of

113 Field Ambulance.

1 Nov. 1918 — 30 Nov. 1918

Volume 34.

Army Form C. 2118.

WAR DIARY
or
INTELLIGENCE SUMMARY.
(Erase heading not required.)

Place	Date	Hour	Summary of Events and Information	Remarks and references to Appendices
RUMES	Nov 1918 1	19	Cloudy day but fine weather. We extended our hospital accommodation, opening up an Influenza P.U.O. ward, an extra reception & waiting room, & a room for gas cases. Personnel :- 1 officer deficient, + 1 Pte. surplus. 1. A.S.C. driver deficient. 1 heavy draft horse deficient. Cases during last 24 hours ending at 0600: Wounded 3, Gassed 26, Sick 3.5, five of which were detained. Prevailing diseases: Influenza & P.U.O. G.T.V.	
"	2	23	Cloudy & damp. On the afternoon I visited the A.D.S. Cases during 24 hours ending 0600:- 3 wounded, 17 gassed, + 7 N.Y.D: Sic. Admissions 27, + 1 case detained. Prevailing diseases: Influenza & Pyrexia. G.T.V.	
"	3	19	Showing milder. Cases during last 24 hours :- 2 wounded + 4 gassed. Sick admissions 22, + detained 6. — 7 Cases of Influenza + 4 of P.U.O. G.T.V.	
"	4	22	Lovely dry weather. Under instructions from the A.D.M.S. I detailed Lieut. Barker to report to the 111th Hampshire Regiment for temporary duty, in relief of Capt. Whyte who returned to his ambulance. Cases during last 24 hours - wounded 10. Sick 31. 12 g whom were detained. Prevailing diseases Influenza, Diarrhoea, + P.U.O. G.T.V.	

WAR DIARY
or
INTELLIGENCE SUMMARY.
(Erase heading not required.)

Army Form C. 2118.

Place	Date	Hour	Summary of Events and Information	Remarks and references to Appendices
RUMES	Nov 1918 5	20	Showing much return. We are still having a good number of urgent civilian cases & attacks to chief by influenza Pneumonia. I sent Major Keenan up to the R.D.S. to relieve Capt. Mitchell, who has been so rocked. Admissions during last 24 hours – 5, wounded – 30 sick. Two additional such cases sent to Tournai. G.T.V.	
"	6	22	Rained continuously all day. In the forenoon I visited the A.D.S. & Pioneers R.A.P. The village was shelled from 1000 – 1200 Hr. & 7.9 am during the night. Counter battery wonderfully light – 2 soldiers killed, & half a dozen slightly wounded. Civilian cases as rather during last 24 hrs. enemy aircraft 0800 in – 15 wounded, 20 gassed, & 35 sick. Six of these were detained, & the being evacuated through the 41.42 15.FA.6 The 6 C.C.S. Presiding Ordnance – Influenza. G.T.V.	
"	7	22	Cloudy & dull. 0.5 inch man rain. 24 hrs ending 0800 hr. – Wounded 9, Gassed 14, Sick 28. Three of the latter were detained. Prevailing diseases – Influenza. In this afternoon I had a visit from the A.D.M.S. G.T.V.	

Army Form C. 2118.

WAR DIARY
or
INTELLIGENCE SUMMARY.
(Erase heading not required.)

Instructions regarding War Diaries and Intelligence Summaries are contained in F. S. Regs., Part II. and the Staff Manual respectively. Title pages will be prepared in manuscript.

Place	Date	Hour	Summary of Events and Information	Remarks and references to Appendices
RUMES.	Nov.1918 8	19	Atmosphere very damp. Very cloudy. In the forenoon 9 clients up by by B.D. A.Ds start our patrols and 1 passed forward to the ESCAUT Canal. Went forward with my 2 partners to investigate A.D.S. site at MERLIN r/c Convent. Railway on the WEZ-VELVAIN - JOLLAIN-MERLIN road. Hospital accommodation - 9 wounded + 2 sick. Room of other casualties returned, there were only 5 stretcher cases. An enquiries will 20 yesterday. J.T.V.	
"	9	19	Fine frosty. Owing to the enemy having been pushed back on the front, we have extracted a new collecting point in BRUXELLES - Wez-37. U.26.a.8.2. Admissions during 24 hours many wounded. 9 wounded 3 gassed +47 sick. So my only great battle, has been journey. Returns. J.T.V.	
ANTOING	10	21	Fine, clear morning. Incurred access from the A.D.M.S. during the early hours g. 115 moving to come in here with the ambulance - left BRUXELLES R.A.M.C. evacuation order no. 32 attached. Main party left RUMES at 09.30, marched via TAINTIGNIES. GUIGNIES. WEZ-MERLIN. MERLIN + BRUYELLE. Main convoy left at 14.15. Very bad roads caused by the road being very congested. Scheme or other required arrangement.	

Army Form C. 2118.

WAR DIARY
or
INTELLIGENCE SUMMARY.
(Erase heading not required.)

IV

Instructions regarding War Diaries and Intelligence Summaries are contained in F.S. Regs., Part II. and the Staff Manual respectively. Title pages will be prepared in manuscript.

Place	Date	Hour	Summary of Events and Information	Remarks and references to Appendices
ANTOING	Nov 1918 10	21	The sick we have taken over are one of them German hospitals. Their men are. Accommodation is excellent, but the place has been left in a filthy condition. Beds in the utmost confusion. G.T.V.	
"	11	23	Very cold. Armistice signed by the enemy & our terms accepted. Hostilities ceased at 11.00 hrs. Ambulance set in an excellent one, only that is a tremendous amount of cleaning to do. We had 15 evacuate practically all our patients to the 113 F.A. Field Ambulance, as we were unable to turn up the wounds. G.T.V.	
"	12	22	Rainy fresh weather. The whole hospital building has been cleaned up & renewed. It is certain action, now we turns up a large surgical day a medical ward. Under instructions from the A.D.M.S. we started our own Ajmangin to achieve Both from 12.00 to day. G.T.V.	
"	13	23	Some frosty weather. In all persons 3 wards the A.D.M.S. Two more wards have been prepared to furnish. Special progress made on the cleaning up of the whole building. G.T.V.	

Army Form C. 2118.

WAR DIARY
or
INTELLIGENCE SUMMARY.
(Erase heading not required.)

Instructions regarding War Diaries and Intelligence Summaries are contained in F. S. Regs., Part II. and the Staff Manual respectively. Title pages will be prepared in manuscript.

Place	Date	Hour	Summary of Events and Information	Remarks and references to Appendices
ANTOING	Nov 14 1918	23	Lovely weather – cold – dry. Festivities general all over France & neighbouring countries. All whole hospital building fairly well completed on programme. Stores & other supplies handed in. Intend in the Hospital at 15.00 o'clock. 68. 41. at moderate + 27 cases obtained. After Tea I got a summary order from the A.D.M.S. telling me that I am on events probably be moving to-morrow morning. Received all the cases kits & present an order from the A.D.M.S. that we would remain near the 98th Infantry Brigade. Rain rather to 74 i.e. attacks. G.T.V.	
ELBAIR	15	19	Smoky weather. The Brigade out on Divil Tes. The company to be in support somewhere. The C.O. Gs. Murrels came out on our Brigade advance on 44. Moved to LS LARAD. G.T.V.	
LA POSTERIE	16	22	Very cold, frosty. A.P.R. Infantry Bde. order no. 45 attacks. The attacking point from did not refer to us. Our Regt. ELBAIR at 14.00 was sent to somewhere from there during the Taken embarcation to go through RUMES. Move was completed at 15.5.5 o'clock. We collected both A.P.Rs & 14 J.R. By Rumes Both made with the exception of sent wagon caves all taken were casualty. The 1/2 R-shell ambulance we ordered from Rumes another to all our here. G.T.V.	

D. D. & L., London, E.C. (A5001) Wt. W1771/M2031 750,000 3/17 Sch. 52 Forms/C2.—8/14

Army Form C. 2118.

WAR DIARY
or
INTELLIGENCE SUMMARY.
(Erase heading not required.)

Place	Date	Hour	Summary of Events and Information	Remarks and references to Appendices
ARDOMPRETZ	Nov 1918 17	22	Very cold & frosty. 3 details & cars to collect 40 R.Dy. Guns went to 0610 o'clock. War horse ambulance wagon to follow in rear of the line of march. Detail of march given in attached Order No. 46. March completed at 12.20 o'clock. From the G. day, not come with the 23 minutes Light T. informed G. to 151st Army Field Amb. and asked for an E.T.V.	
"	18	23	6 mls clear & dry, but not for long. Kindle invitation from the A.D.M.S. Rest Stations were detailed to report to the A.D.M.S. 65th Division for duty. I visited the A.D.M.S. in the forenoon, got permission from him to get billets in PARADIS. E.T.V.	
PARADIS	19	19	Very cold & frosty. The ambulance moved from here at 11.15 o'clock, completing the move in three & one half hours. Billeting facilities are better here, we are able to accommodate every officer in the Ech. & 45 men. 9 days up a scheme for training in military reconnaissance, & cross road. E.T.V.	
"	20	23	Frosty & misty. In the forenoon all the heads were sharing up, in memento perfume this made, in the afternoon we had a sports meeting. E.T.V.	

Army Form C. 2118.

WAR DIARY
or
INTELLIGENCE SUMMARY.
(Erase heading not required.)

Instructions regarding War Diaries and Intelligence Summaries are contained in F. S. Regs., Part II. and the Staff Manual respectively. Title pages will be prepared in manuscript.

Place	Date	Hour	Summary of Events and Information	Remarks and references to Appendices
PARADIS	Nov. 1918 21	23	Very cold snow. Ambulance equipment was collected, sorted out in sections. A good deal of work to necessary that its condition of its smalls into accomplishment generally a return of men (space workers only) is called for. G.T.V.	
"	22	23	Lovely clear day. Started scheme of Ambulance Training - Personnel is being demobilised. Any drill in forenoon, exercise in the afternoon. Arrangements are being made to start its educational training soon. G.T.V.	
"	23	19½	Fine weather. Nothing to report except extra leave & 9. M. Boys. Parades with M.R. to 14 days special leave. G.T.V.	
"	24	22	Cloudy, cold snow. Instructions from the A.D.M.S. Scottches Capt Lewis to report to the 180 R.F.A Bde. for temporary duty - as M.O. Similarly I detail Capt Badenock to sit at in this bivouac to the O.C. 5th Royal Scots Fusiliers for temporary duty. G.T.V.	
"	25	23	Much milder morning toward evening. In the forenoon travelled to A.D.M.S. place to see Lt. Col. D.A.D.M.S about surplus medical equipment. Through our Evacuation Groups in report G.T.V.	

WAR DIARY
or
INTELLIGENCE SUMMARY.

(Erase heading not required.)

Army Form C. 2118.

Place	Date	Hour	Summary of Events and Information	Remarks and references to Appendices
PARADIS	Nov. 1918 26	21	Mostly rain, in the afternoon 3 Sergt. a 100 O.R. marched to Champs et de TEMPLEUVE by the O marched Disinfector. We also drew Timber material from R.E. dump for improving the billets sanitary arrangements. G.T.V.	
	27	22	Mild weather. This my parade a 09.00 hrs. T.O. to my Q. were work. At the Q. Amb. to O.Q. duel. At 20.00 hrs. we had a sports meeting to make arrangements about races, hockey, games and running competitions. G.T.V.	
	28	23	Dull showery. Had to go to hdqs of the branch to arrange to Influenza so got Major Conway to carry on for me. The Companies are working on the new billets getting them made more comfortable. G.T.V.	
	29	22	Still showery. Each platoon is busy made itself its canteen more work, with only interesting difficulty is the shortage of boards. G.T.V.	

Army Form C. 2118.

WAR DIARY
or
INTELLIGENCE SUMMARY.
(Erase heading not required.)

Instructions regarding War Diaries and Intelligence Summaries are contained in F. S. Regs., Part II. and the Staff Manual respectively. Title pages will be prepared in manuscript.

Place	Date	Hour	Summary of Events and Information	Remarks and references to Appendices
PARADIS	Nov 19/18	2.2	Colder, showers weather. Work – general routine. Sanitation of places being improved upon every day in lieu of unknown stay. A wire from the A.D.M.S. 2nd Div Capt. Whyle gave the condolence on decline on the history of Parliament. G.T. Van Nyppen Lt. Col. R.amc. O.C. 113th Field Ambulance	

SECRET.   COPY NO:- 6

16th. DIVISION R.A.M.C. OPERATION ORDER No.32.

Ref.Sheets:- 37 & 44A.1/40,000.   9th.NOVEMBER,1918.

1. No.111 Field Ambulance will move on the morning of the 10th. inst. to RUMES, taking over the present site of No.113 Field Ambulance, and open for the reception of sick.
    All remaining cases at PONT-A-MARCQ will be evacuated.
    O.C., No.111 Field Ambulance will leave a guard for the Hospital Equipment at PONT-A-MARCQ which will be taken over by O.C., No.32 Casualty Clearing Station, and on handing over the guard will proceed to RUMES.

2. No.113 Field Ambulance will proceed on morning of the 10th. inst. to ANTOING (old German Hospital) and establish a Main Dressing Station.
    Billets vacated at RUMES will be handed over to advance party of No.111 Field Ambulance.

3. No.112 Field Ambulance will remain in TEMPLEUVE until further orders, and will arrange for the collection of the Sick of Brigade in Reserve.

4. O's.C., Field Ambulances will arrange their own march table.

5. Completion of moves to be reported to this office.

6. A.D.M.S.Office will close at TEMPLEUVE at 1000 hours on 10th. inst. and open at TAINTIGNIES at same hour.

7. FIELD AMBULANCES ACKNOWLEDGE.

Headquarters,   A. Bowen
16th.Division.   Colonel, AMS.,
9-11-18.
AK.   A.D.M.S.16th.Division.

Issued at:- 1230 hours.

Copies to:-
    Nos.1 - 2. O.C.111 F.A.(2)   33. D.A.D.V.S.16th.Divn.
       3 - 4. O.C.112 F.A.(2)   34. D.A.P.M.16th.Divn.
       5 - 6   O.C.113 F.A. (2)   35. D.M.S.,Fifth Army.
       7 - 11. 47th.Inf.Bde.(5)   36. D.D.M.S., I Corps.
      12 - 16. 48th.Inf.Bde.(5)   37. S.C.F.,D.C.G.Dept.
      17 - 21. 49th.Inf.Bde.(5)   38. S.C.F.,P.C's.Dept.
         22.   O.C.11th.Hants Regt.(P) 39. A.D.M.S.15th.Divn.
         23.   O.C.16th.M.G.Bn.   40. A.D.M.S.55th.Divn.
         24.   C.R.E.16th.Divn.   41. O.C.12 M.A.C.
      25 - 28. C.R.A.16th.Divn.   42. O.C.32 C.C.Stn.
         29.   16th.Divn."G"   43.)
         30.   16th.Divn."A" & "Q"   44.) Diary.
         31.   O.C.16th.Div.Train.   45. File.
         32.   16th.Div.Gas.Offr.

SECRET   Copy No. 13.

48th INFANTRY BRIGADE ORDER No. 44.

Reference Maps 37 and 44, 1/40,000.   14.11.18.

1. (a) 16th DIVISION is moving Westwards, and is to be W. of a N. and S. line through RUMES by 1200 16th NOV.1918.

   (b) Moves for tomorrow (15th inst) will be as in attached table.

   (c) Further orders for move on 16th and subsequent dates will be issued later.

2. Division H.Q. remains at TAINTIGNIES 16th inst.

3. Attention is drawn to the orders contained in paras. 19, 20, and 21 of S.S.724 "March Discipline and Traffic Control", which must be strictly adhered to.

4. Brigade H.Q. will close at ANTOING at 1230 and open at WEZ VELVAIN or GUIGNIES at the same hour. Exact location will be notified later.

5. A C K N O W L E D G E.

H.P. Bowen.
Captain.
Brigade Major, 48th Infantry Brigade.

Issued at 2300, 14.11.18.

Copies to:-

1. G.O.C.
2. Staff Captain
3. Bde.Sig.Offr.
4. Bde.Int.Offr.
5. 22nd North'd Fus.
6. 18th Sco.Rif.
7. 5th R.Irish Fus.
8. 48th T.M.Battery
9. 155 Field Coy.,R.E.
10. 145 Coy.,A.S.C.
11. "D" Coy.,16.M.G.Bn.
12. 11th Hants (P)
13. 113rd Field Ambulance
14. 157 Field Coy.,R.E.
15. 16th Division "G"
16. C.R.E.,16th Div.
17. A.D.M.S.
18. 16th M.G.Bn.
19. 16th Div.Train
20.)War
21.)Diary.
22. File.

UNITS in order of march.	Starting Point	Time	ROUTE	Destination
Bde.H.Q. and 48th T.M.Battery.	TRESTLE BRIDGE at V.15.d.0.3.	1015	BRUYELLE - WEZ VELVAIN - GUIGNIES - TAINTIGNIES.	WEZ VELVAIN CHAU. or GUIGNIES CHAU. (See note (a) below).
22nd North'd Fus.		1025	do.	L'ECUELLE
18th Sco.Rif.		1040	do	VELVAIN
5th R.Irish Fus.		1105	do.	GUIGNIES
155 Field Coy.,R.E.		1120	do.	FLORENT
157 do. do.		1130	do.	PETIT RUMES
11th Hants (P)		1140	do.	WEZ VELVAIN
"D" Coy.M.G.Bn.		1205	do.	PETIT RUMES
113rd Fld.Amb.		1210	do.	ELBAIL.

NOTES:- (a) Battalions billeting in WEZ VELVAIN or GUIGNIES will exclude the chateaux and adjoining billets from their billeting area until location of Brigade H.Q. is definitely notified.

(b) Units make their own billeting arrangements in the areas allotted.

UNITS	STARTING POINT	TIME TO PASS STARTING POINT	ROUTE	DESTINATION
Brigade H.Q., and 48th T.M.Battery	C.3.b.3.2	1005	C.7.c.9.5 - C.7.a.8.5 - CROISETTE - BERGU - FOURNES	GENECH
22nd North'd Fus.	C.7.d.1.9	1050	As for Bde.H.Q.	GENECH
18th Sco.Rif.	VELVAIN CHURCH	1025	As for Bde.H.Q.	GENECH
5th R.Irish Fus.	C.8.c.6.5	1125	C.7.c.9.5 - C.7.a.8.5 - CROISETTE - B.9.d.6.5.	COBRIEUX
11th Hants (P)	VELVAIN CHURCH	1100	As for 5th R.Irish Fus.	BACHY
"D" Coy., M.G. Bn.	C.12.a.9.3	1225	As for Bde.H.Q.	LA CROIX (A.17.a.)
157 Field Coy.,R.E.	C.12.a.9.8	1230	CROISETTE - B.9.d.C.5	PLACE COMTE (B.1.b.)
155 Field Coy.,R.E.	BRUXELLE	1100	GUIGNIES - C.7.c.9.5 - CROISETTE - C.7.a.8.5 - B.9.d.5.5.	PLACE COMTE (B.1.b.)
113 Fld.Ambulance	C.12.a.9.8	1245	CROISETTE - B.9.d.5.5	LA POSTERIE (A.G.c.)

NOTES:-

(a) Billeting representatives of 22nd North'd Fus., and 18th Sco.Rifles will meet Staff Captain at GENECH CHURCH at 1130. All other units will make own billeting arrangements in areas allotted to them.

SECRET   Copy No. 14.

48th INFANTRY BRIGADE ORDER No. 45.

Reference Maps TOURNAI and VALENCIENNES
Sheets 1/100,000 & Sheet 44 1/40,000.   15.11.1918.

1. (a) The 16th Division is to concentrate and halt in the area roughly ATTICHES - AVELIN - ENNEVELIN - TEMPLEUVE - BERSEE - MONCHEAUX - OSTRACOURT - LIBERCOURT.

   (b) Moves of 48th INFANTRY BRIGADE Group to the Area GENECH - FOURNES - PLACE COMME - BACHY - COBRIEUX tomorrow (16th) will be as laid down in attached table.

   (c) Orders for final move of 48th Brigade Group on 17th will be issued later.

2. Lorry arrangements for 16th will be notified later to all concerned.

3. Distances to be observed on the march are:-
   100 yards between Companies
   100 yards between rear company of a battalion and its transport
   500 yards between battalions.

4. Brigade H.Q. will close at GUIGNIES at 1000 and open at GENECH on arrival. Reports to head of column while on the march.

5. A C K N O W L E D G E.

H F Bowen
Captain.
Brigade Major, 48th Infantry Brigade.

Issued at 2300 15.11.1918.

Copies to:-

No. 1 G.O.C.   12 "D" Coy., M.G.Bn.
    2 Staff Captain   13 11th Hants (P)
    3 Bde.Sig.Offr.   14 113 Field Ambulance
    4 22nd North'd Fus.   15 16th Division "G"
    5 18th Sco.Rif.   16 C.R.E., 16th Div.
    6 5th R.Irish Fus.   17 A.D.M.S.   "
    7 48th T.M.Battery   18 16th Div.Train
    8 155 Field Coy.,R.E.   19 16th M.G.Bn.
    9 157   do.   20)War
   10 145 Coy.,A.S.C.   21)Diary
   11 Bde.Int.Offr.   22 File.

P.T.O.

Reference Brigade Order No. 45.

A halt will be made at 12.50 for dinners and will not exceed 1 hour's duration.

In recommencing the march care is to be taken not to alter the order of march.

Addressed all recipients of B.O.45.

SECRET   Copy No. 13

48th INFANTRY BRIGADE ORDER No.46.

Reference Map Sheets 44.A and 44. 1/40,000.   16.11.1918.

1. 48th Brigade Group marches tomorrow (17th) in accordance with attached table.

2. Distances to be observed are as laid down in Brigade Order No.45 of 15.11.18.

3. Brigade H.Q. will close at GENECH at 1100 and open at F.11.d.5.1 at same hour.

4. Location of H.Q's of all Battalions, 48th T.M.Battery, and 113th Field Ambulance will be sent to Brigade H.Q. immediately on arrival.

5. A C K N O W L E D G E.

H F Bowen
Captain.
Brigade Major, 48th Infantry Brigade.

Issued at 2230 16.11.1918.

Copies to:-

No. 1 G.O.C.
 2 Staff Captain
 3 Bde.Sig.Offr.
 4 22nd North'd Fus.
 5 18th Sco.Rif.
 6 5th R.Irish Fus.
 7 48th T.M.Battery
 8 145 Coy.,A.S.C.
 9 155 Coy.,R.E.
 10 157 Coy.,R.E.

No.11 11th Hants (P)
 12 "D" Coy.,M.G.Bn.
 13 113 Fld.Amb.
 14 16th Div."G"
 15 C.R.E.
 16 A.D.M.S.
 17 16th Div.Train
 18 16th M.G.Bn.
 19)War
 20)Diary

No.21 FILE.

UNITS in order of March.	STARTING POINT	TIME TO PASS S.P.	ROUTE	DESTINATION
11th Hants (P)	BACHY	0800	GENECH - CAPPELLE - BERSEE - MONS.	LA NEUVILLE EN PHALEMPIN (K.7.b & d)
155 Field Coy.,R.E.	PLACE COMTE B.1.a.3.0.	0810	GENECH - CAPPELLE - BERSEE.	LESTREZ - MONCHEAUX RUE DE MONCHEAUX.
157 Field Coy.,R.E.	B.1.a.3.0	0820	do.	do. (Billets from C.R.E.)
"D" Coy.,M.G.Bn.	A.16.a.9.6	0930	GENECH - CAPPELLE - BERSEE - MONS-EN-PEVELE.	THUMERIES, and comes under orders of O.C., 16th M.G.Bn.
48 Bde.H.Q. and 48 T.M.Battery.	A.15.b.3.4	1000	Direct	TEMPLEUVE
5th R.Irish Fus.	A.16.a.9.6	1000	GENECH - CAPPELLE - MOLFAS	Squares K.6 and K.12 L.1 and L.7. (Sheet 44.A.)
22nd North'd Fus.	A.15.a.5.0	1030	Direct	TEMPLEUVE
10th Sco.Rif.	do.	1045	Direct	Squares F.27,28,29, L.3,4,& 5.a (Sheet 44.A)
113 Field Ambulance	LA POSTERIE	1040	Direct	TEMPLEUVE

NOTES:- (a) Billeting representatives of 22nd North'd Fus. and 113th Field Ambulance will meet Staff Captain at TEMPLEUVE CHURCH at 0930. Other units make own billeting arrangements in areas allotted.
(b) Brigade H.Q. and 48th T.M.Battery will occupy their former billets.

No 113 Field Ambulance

WAR DIARY or INTELLIGENCE SUMMARY

Army Form C. 2118.

113 Fd Amb   Vol 35

Place	Date	Hour	Summary of Events and Information	Remarks and references to Appendices
PARADIS	Dec 1918			
"	1	22	Frosty weather. In the forenoon Capt. B.E.E. Nicholls, NCO, & 19 ORs proceeded to No. 13 C.C.S. for temporary duty. Others work of the programme progressing well. G.T.V.	
"	2	23	Dull showery. Nothing to report. G.T.V.	
"	3	22	Mild cloudy. A few of the men are reporting sick with minor ailments — one or two cases of Influenza, but not of a serious nature. G.T.V	
"	4	23	Mild weather. In the forenoon I visited the acting A.D.M.S. Lt. Col. Bell. With Capt. Whyte along with me to see MT Trials and schemes for temporary duty — A.D.M.S.'s instructions. G.T.V.	
"	5	22	Cloudy, but fair. In the forenoon I inspected all the huts & in the educational class rooms we have 7 classes going now — two I watched were I.B. regimental students. G.T.V.	

WAR DIARY or INTELLIGENCE SUMMARY

Army Form C. 2118.

(Erase heading not required.)

Instructions regarding War Diaries and Intelligence Summaries are contained in F.S. Regs., Part II. and the Staff Manual respectively. Title pages will be prepared in manuscript.

Place	Date	Hour	Summary of Events and Information	Remarks and references to Appendices
PARADIS	Dec 1918 6	22	Cloudy mild. We took over a new billet for our all from 17th + enjoying the gd turn games and good hygiene now - Dream party during Divrs, r came country racing. Maps Ry Vernon has been given to Divn.	
"	7	23	65 the N.K. from 65 7-12-18 to 21-12-18 inclusive. G.T.V. Good weather in the forenoon I inspire its its weapons + Foeler - Horse Reserves. Our stable, turn out in full, will supply 2 now rly 2 officers + 10 other ranks requires to hang up wire to pull strings. G.T.V.	
"	8	21	Lovely sunny weather. Church parade at 09.30 o'clock G.T.V.	
"	9	22	Lovely weather. Educational work progressing well G.T.V.	
"	10	23	Still no news. I put in a party of 3 N.C.O.'s + 20 dogs none to see LILLE. Horse Ambulance left at 8:00 o'clock. G.T.V.	
"	11	23	Rained steadily all day. Under instructions from A.D.M.S. I shall to detail an M.O. to visit the sick of the Divnround them each morning. minimum eight-left for La Daparoul while to-day G.T.V.	

WAR DIARY
or
INTELLIGENCE SUMMARY.
(Erase heading not required.)

Army Form C. 2118.

Instructions regarding War Diaries and Intelligence
Summaries are contained in F. S. Regs., Part II.
and the Staff Manual respectively. Title pages
will be prepared in manuscript.

Place	Date	Hour	Summary of Events and Information	Remarks and references to Appendices
LE PARADIS	Dec 1918 12	22	Dull showery. In the morning SAS, 15.6 to the Cinema at LILLE. Taken winter, the 13 R.C.S. at TOURCOING. Lieut. Gray returned from leave. G.T.V.	
"	13	28	Cloudy mild. A second batch of 7 men left for the depot in the forenoon. One Sergeant, now Hands on Fatima - approved Centre. E 2nd Lieut. 22 Rances the Ladr, T.S — Q.S.C. (T.T) Arrives G.T.V	
"	14	22	Good weather. In the forenoon there a rendezvous at Retiny/2.D.M.S	
"	15	23	Cloudy mild morning. No Dewi plank batch of men - eight left for the Retired Ce(?) in the morning, one shower of the strongth from G.T.V.	
"	16	22	16 day. mild rebady day. Turn to day. See details on Appen to med the sick of the 108th Army (R.F.A.) - may or Cameron Ritchie is also attending that sick unit of the Divisional Train. G.T.V.	
"	17	23	Cloudy morning. Capt. C.H. Todd having been ordered to to No. 17 C.C.S. via 11 F.A. of the Ambulance is thinking off. He stayed from 14-12-1918. G.T.V.	

WAR DIARY
or
INTELLIGENCE SUMMARY.

Army Form C. 2118.

(Erase heading not required.)

Place	Date	Hour	Summary of Events and Information	Remarks and references to Appendices
Le PARADIS	Dec 14/18 18	23	Dull showery. In the forenoon a party of N.C.O's men went to LILLE for the day by the Divisional lorry. Further arrangements were made for Tommy Xmas puppies. G.T.V.	
"	19	22	Very cold, cloudy. In the forenoon I inspected some of the billets, & visited the O.C. 112th Field Ambulance. G.T.V.	
"	20	23	Cold raw. In the forenoon I visited the Divisional Canteen & spoke to the Return/O.D.M.S. Educational & recreational training preparing well. G.T.V.	
"	21	19.	Very cold. Under instruction from O.D.M.S. I detailed 2 B.S. Wagons & harness to report for duty temporary duty to the O.C. 145 Coy R.A.S.C. Two R.A.S.C. drivers were sent to us from the Divnal train to-day. G.T.V	
"	22	23	Cold showery. In the forenoon I spoke today to the 155 Coy R.E. to see about some work to their spring. Major R.G. Vernon returned off leave to-day. G.T.V.	
"	23	23	Dull showery. Preparation being made for Xmas. G.T.V.	

Army Form C. 2118.

WAR DIARY
or
INTELLIGENCE SUMMARY.
(Erase heading not required.)

Instructions regarding War Diaries and Intelligence
Summaries are contained in F. S. Regs., Part II.
and the Staff Manual respectively. Title pages
will be prepared in manuscript.

Place	Date	Hour	Summary of Events and Information	Remarks and references to Appendices
LE PARADIS	Dec 1918 24	22	Clear frosty weather. Xmas preparations in full swing. G.T.V	
"	25	23	Lovely frosty day. The men had their dinner at 12.30 o'clock, & were waited on by the sergeants. In the afternoon they had a football match, in the evening a concert & dance. Everything went splendidly, there was ample in this way & good grub. G.T.V.	
"	26	24	Clear frosty under instructions from A.D.M.S. 9 Divisional Major R.G Vernon to report to the O.C. 1/2/17 Field Ambulance for temporary duty in the evening the Sergeant has been drunk!	
"	27	22	a very good smoking concert. G.T.V. Still ashowing, nothing to report. G.T.V	
"	28	20	Showery weather milder than the last week. The men & the waggon orderly & the men drew their Xmas puddings. Several fatigues. G.T.V All weekly and monthly returns rendered. G.T.V	

WAR DIARY or INTELLIGENCE SUMMARY

Army Form C. 2118.

Place	Date	Hour	Summary of Events and Information	Remarks and references to Appendices
LE PARADIS	1918 June 29	22	Showery weather. In the forenoon I inspected the billet	G.T.V.
"	30	23	Cloudy weather. In the forenoon I inspected all the other teams & tools & party to repair the bad parts of the main road through the village.	G.T.V.
"	31	24	Showery. Owing to the wet & boggy condition of the ground I am made arrangements to move up and immediate made through all the gates. My authority over the army & the late of the drainage.	G.T.V.

G.T. Van Nostrin
Lieut. R.Can.E.
O.C. No 3 Field Co. Canadians

A.D.M.S., 16th Divn. No.S.192/359/1.

AMENDMENT TO 16th DIVISION MEDICAL ARRANGEMENTS
No.S.192/359 dated 29-11-18.

Para.6. for "EAR, NOSE, THROAT & EYE CASES" substitute the following:-

EAR, NOSE, THROAT & EYE CASES

Suitable cases will be sent, on Sundays only, to No.112 Field Ambulance, to arrive not later than 1500 hours.

Army Book 64 and two days rations must be carried.

Cases will be sent to No.6 Casualty Clearing Station by O.C.112 Field Ambulance to arrive by 0900 hours on Mondays.

Officers will be seen by appointment through this office.

FIELD AMBULANCES ACKNOWLEDGE.

W.J.E. Bell
Lt-Colonel, R.A.M.C.,
A/A.D.M.S., 16th Division.

Headquarters.
16th Division.

Copies to all recipients of 16th Divn. Med. Arrangements.

'B'

A.D.M.S.No.S.192/359/2.

AMENDMENT TO 16th DIVISION MEDICAL ARRANGEMENTS DATED 29-11-18.

6th December, 1918.

<u>Para.5.</u> for "DON GROUP" read "ASCQ GROUP".

Headquarters.
16th Division.
Copies to all recipients of 16th.Div.Med.Arrangements.

Lt-Col:RAMC.,
A/A.D.M.S.,16th Division.

'C'

A.D.M.S.16th Div.No.S192/359/1.

AMENDMENT TO 16th.DIVISION MEDICAL ARRANGEMENTS
FORWARDED UNDER A.D.M.S.16th Div.No. as above.
-o-o-o-o-o-o-o-o-o-o-o-o-o-o-o-o-o-o-o-o-o-o-o-o-o-o-o-o-o-o-

EAR,NOSE,THROAT & EYE CASES

Delete para.4 and substitute the following:-

Officers will make appointments through Officer Commanding, 112 Field Ambulance, who will arrange transport.

Headquarters.
16th Division.
10th Dec.1918.

H.S.Frazer, Major
for
A.D.M.S.,16th Division.

Copies to all recipients of 16th Div.Med.Arrangements.

Confidential

War Diary of

113th Field Ambulance.

From 1st January 1919 to 31st January 1919

Volume 36.

WAR DIARY or INTELLIGENCE SUMMARY

Army Form C. 2118.

JANUARY

Place	Date	Hour	Summary of Events and Information	Remarks and references to Appendices
LE PARADIS	1st	22.30	Lt-Col Van der Hoeven M.C. proceeds on leave to United Kingdom	J.S.C.
	2nd	23	Took out executive carrier on as usual. Kept execution first a step to execution	J.S.C.
	3rd	23.30	Capt. P.R. Nicholls proZt) as Anaesthetic Specialist to No.13 C.C.S. Capt. B.S. Boscawen to 5th Royal Scots Fusiliers. Lieut. C.A. Boscawen 11th Hussars	J.S.C.
	4th	19.30	Officers and Buffet Staff Lt. Anderson Strang R.E. These time Weather still inclement — took princess Bicycle stolen from Butler No. 2245 Dr Ross I.N. R.F.A. (P.13.)	J.S.C.
	5th	180	Pte Lawson Wm was accidentally kicked by a horse and having his left arm wounded to CCS There are Battle time Photoph left with for examination	J.S.C.
	6th	20.10	vey far this available map for future	J.S.C.
	7th	22	A.D.M.S. 16th D.W.t No. 61/1173 received. Weather fine. Pte Taylor evacuated to No.13 C.C.S. Horse classified by D.R.V.S. today. Major Palmer Anzaines unit from 112.F.A.	J.S.C.
	8th	22.30	Fine Sunday Day 5 programme as usual	J.S.C.

Army Form C. 2118.

WAR DIARY
or
~~INTELLIGENCE SUMMARY~~
(Erase heading not required.)

Instructions regarding War Diaries and Intelligence Summaries are contained in F.S. Regs., Part II. and the Staff Manual respectively. Title pages will be prepared in manuscript.

Place	Date	Hour	Summary of Events and Information	Remarks and references to Appendices
LE PARADIS	8th	21.20	One Great Coat (proceed) 647 M.V.S. and 10 3 Inch of Strength both (proceed) in Cookhouse. Whitewashing Stables finished	J.G.
"	10th	22.	Pte Whitehead admitted Hospital and Struck off Strength Arrival by Pte A.D.M.S. Corp. Divisional Grant of 7400 Rancs received.	J.G.
"	11th	21.	Four boys, fireplace in Cookhouse finished. 14 O.R. granted days leave to K.H.E.	J.G.
"	12th	21.15	Fine. Church Parade at 10 a.m.	J.G.
"	13th	21.	Started checking Equipment in accordance with Orders from A.D.M.S.	J.G.
"	14th	20.	Pte Normanton left unit today for demobilisation. Work proceeds on rearrivals.	J.G.
"	15th	23.	Ptes Eccles Enoe, Scrutington Irvine, Ford, Baker (proceed) to Concentration Camp Today for demobilisation and are Struck off Strength	J.G.
"	16	23.	A fine day. Rearrivals finished – Latrines moved	J.G.
"	17	24.	Equipment checked and returns	J.G.
"	18	21.15	Pte Dean G. left unit for demobilisation. Major Vernon left unit for temp. duty with 111 F.A. and vacancies	J.G.
"	19	21.0	Pte Mirfield evacuated sick from No.15 C.C.S. and Struck off Strength. Pte Mirfield Sch. 52 Forms. Ca. 16/14	J.G.

Army Form C. 2118.

WAR DIARY
or
INTELLIGENCE SUMMARY.
(Erase heading not required.)

Place	Date	Hour	Summary of Events and Information	Remarks and references to Appendices
LE PARADIS	20	19.	Col. Bowen came today to present Sgt Peacock with D.C.M. and Pte Fairey, Deans, Duncan, Gardner, Wilson L, Sgt Latham L/Cpl Bryan & Pte Brown and Bullock (R.C. att) with divisional parchment certificates. He also presented 1914-15 ribbon to 16 O.R. of the unit. J.6.	
"	21	22	3 returns got down the afternoon of Armson, 4 to have been proved 15 days retention on account of illness. Sgt. G.C.D Barnett, Actg/Sgt H Barrison Cpl. T.S. man were deputised to act dispensed in the morning & was struck off the strength from to-day. ST vanderlyn cant Sgt Evans Franks resisted. One N.C.O. twenty nine men were inspected to the disposed centre for demobilization from this list of the strength from to-day. J.T.V.	
"	22	22		
"	23	23	Heavy frost in the afternoon Ernest an inspector of the sanitary arrangements. J.T.V.	
"	24	23	Still bitterly cold. Pte Wood G.E. having been transferred to no 13 C.C.S on the 13th is struck off the strength from that date. J.T.V.	

WAR DIARY
INTELLIGENCE SUMMARY
(Erase heading not required.)

Army Form C. 2118.

Instructions regarding War Diaries and Intelligence Summaries are contained in F.S. Regs., Part II. and the Staff Manual respectively. Title pages will be prepared in manuscript.

Place	Date	Hour	Summary of Events and Information	Remarks and references to Appendices
LE PARADIS	Jan 1919 25	24	Frosty, but not quite so cold. In the forenoon I inspected the sanitary arrangements, some of the billets. The men had a church parade in the evening. G.T.V.	
"	26	23	Fall of a couple of inches of snow. Church parade in the forenoon. G.T.V.	
"	27	23	Frosty again. Sent the carpenter to make some stands for the private buckets. Received a G.R.O. to the effect that gunners are to be demobilised along with coal miners. G.T.V.	
"	28	23	Lovely sunny day + slight thaw. In the forenoon I inspected all the stable - horses shown. Old James J.W. transferred to no 11 C.C.S. on the 26th and 7 in district by the strength from that date. G.T.V.	
"	29	23	Frosty weather. Sgt. A. Ross proceeded to no. 32 C.C.S. for duty, in struck off the strength from to-day. G.T.V.	
"	30	24	Nothing to report. Outside forms at a stand still, in account of the weather. G.T.V.	
"	31	20	Bitterly cold. Syring + Mackenzie returned off leave from U.K. A.F. B 213/3 rendered according to new establishment. 2 sections. Differences to officers + 47 other ranks. G.T. Vanderlyn Lt Col R.A.M.C.	

No. 113 Field Ambulance

Army Form C. 2118.

WAR DIARY
or
INTELLIGENCE SUMMARY.
(Erase heading not required.)

February 1919

Place	Date	Hour	Summary of Events and Information	Remarks and references to Appendices
LE PARADIS	1	23	Very quiet. In the afternoon the final bouts of the Divisional Boxing Competition took place - Divn Hygiene & our Ambulance won the lightweights. Sgt Johnson having been demobilized whilst on leave to EC U.K. in stead of returning to ES 10/1/1919. G.T.V.	
"	2	24	Slight thaw during the day. Drive to Monaghan for weekend to No. 11 C.C.S. in search of HG strength from WO 1/2/1919. = @ H.K.H. to Brise & walked into TEMPLEUVE in the afternoon. Photos in my Kodak on W-112½ Field Ambulance. Lt Col Weir the officer & Major Cavanagh & 3 men present. To tea by the A.D.M.S. G.T.V.	
"	3	23	Investigate = 2 m. Sgt. Q.M. Sgt. Q.M. Thakenham, Sergt/Sgt Toig, Sgt Gaard Bennett, Newton, Baggley, So/Sgt Hamilton, Cpls Wood, Mann, & Rawnsen have all been confirmed in Chevrons & on the date - made lance cpls have promoted to the corresponding acting rank. G.T.V.	
"	4	23	Inorganic to add - some rain towards evening. We got another large motor truck from the workshop yesterday & now have two large lorries and two motor lorries also. G.T.V.	

Army Form C. 2118.

WAR DIARY
or
INTELLIGENCE SUMMARY.
(Erase heading not required.)

Instructions regarding War Diaries and Intelligence Summaries are contained in F. S. Regs., Part II. and the Staff Manual respectively. Title pages will be prepared in manuscript.

Place	Date	Hour	Summary of Events and Information	Remarks and references to Appendices
LE PARADIS.	5"	24	Pte Monaghan (R.A.S.C. attached) having been discharged from hospital, is taken on the strength again. G.T.V	
"	6	23	Heavy fall of snow during the night. The revised establishment for a Field Ambulance has been approved under authority of War Office letter 121/France /3194 (S.D.2) dated 19th Dec., 1918. As only one officer of the rank of Major is authorised, Major R.J. Vernon reverts to his permanent rank of Captain. - D.R.O no 219 - 1010 dated 5/2/19. Sgt V.C. Godber was evacuated to no 39 Stationary hospital (via No.13 C.C.S) on the 4th Feb 1919, + is struck off the strength from that date. Capt. R.J Vernon reports to the 112 A. Field Ambulance to say "To temporary duty. G.T.V	
"	7	24	Sharp frost. Rate of exchange for February - 5 francs (French) = 3/12 5 " (Belgian) = 3/8 should be According to new Establishment our total strength 3/11, midwifery attached R.A.S.C., but we are deficient of 4 officers + sundries+subordinates (R.A.M.C.) + of 2 R.A.S.C. (H.T.) we have a surplus of 6 drivers. R.T.V.	

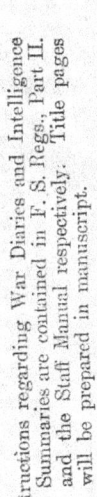

Army Form C. 2118.

WAR DIARY
or
INTELLIGENCE SUMMARY.
(Erase heading not required.)

Instructions regarding War Diaries and Intelligence Summaries are contained in F. S. Regs., Part II. and the Staff Manual respectively. Title pages will be prepared in manuscript.

Place	Date	Hour	Summary of Events and Information	Remarks and references to Appendices
LE PARADIS	8	23	Hard frost. I appointed Capt. T.H. Dempsey RC/Ka/CH until Maj. from LG 7/2/1919. The under mentioned were detailed for duty at No. 57 C.C.S., & have been struck off the strength as from LG 6/2/1919 (A.D.M.S. no 81/48 dated 6/2/19) No. 64122 Lce/Cpl Murdoch T. " 3415 " Pte Clifford G. " H/FVO 25 " Sutorius A.E. " 33098 " Nolan R. " 64360 " Grant G.63.	
"	9	22	Bitterly cold. Major G.63 Cavanagh left for Lille yesterday afternoon, having been granted leave to the U.K. from the 9th to LG 23rd. All ranks left behind bemoaning our return. Return from Rubier rendered. The weekly Tentage & Hutts return have been cancelled.	G.T.V.
"	10	24	Not quite so cold — lovely sunshine. The men played a football match in the afternoon.	G.T.V.
"	11	23	Crisp sunny weather. No. 64129 Pte C. Brummer is struck off the strength from MG 27th Nov. 1918 Reported overhouse man killed in Regimen.	G.T.V.
"	12	24	Lovely weather — clean sky-fresh. Duseilo ambulance photo taken by the band.	G.T.V.

WAR DIARY or INTELLIGENCE SUMMARY

Army Form C. 211

Place	Date	Hour	Summary of Events and Information	Remarks and references to Appendices
LE PARADIS	13	24	Nothing to report. S.T.V	
"	14	23	In the person of myself & the other ranks Cpl. A. Booker, our A.D.M.S. went to my ward type at my hospital in the Montin & hand for him, & gave him a red tie of flannel. Pts Cpl. Ravel W & Barry W.G. were appointed to do head service. The 1st R not yet demobilized. Present strength 2 Lieut & officers + 152 other ranks. 55 other ranks + 1 officer have short in R.O.S.C demura awaiting S.T.V	
"	15	23	2 Serjts Read & Irwin + 1 driver Wilkinson, Pte Beady & Long have been demobilised & have to leave at length from 23/11/1919. L/Cpl T.H. Templer Austell S/12A Such & admin in camp Quincy S.T.V	
"	16	24	Nothing to report. S.T.V	
"	17	23	Clancy & Lanng, Lee Cpl T.H. Temper, having been evacuated to No. 11 C.C.S. in church Sp. the strength from the 15-2-1919. On the 16-2-1919 No.10456 S/Sgt T. Shay was deputed to the Divisional Sanitary Section. S.T.V	

Army Form C. 2118.

WAR DIARY
or
INTELLIGENCE SUMMARY.
(Erase heading not required.)

Instructions regarding War Diaries and Intelligence Summaries are contained in F. S. Regs., Part II. and the Staff Manual respectively. Title pages will be prepared in manuscript.

Place	Date	Hour	Summary of Events and Information	Remarks and references to Appendices
LE PARADIS	Feb 1919 18	23	Misty & damp. Onfas a furosils all staw precautions are being adopted & carried out. — thus 9 motor ambulances, etc.	G.T.V.
"	19	23	Mild, cloudy, windy. Paid a visit from Lt D.A.D.M.S. in the afternoon.	G.T.V.
"	20	24	Hot. It had work on ware. I have been attending 15 – on average about half a dozen patients a day.	G.T.V
"	21	23	Mild windy, showery. The undermentioned, having been detailed for duty to No 1 C.C.S., are struck off the strength from 20/2/1919. No. 400141 Pte Canston W.A. " 40021 " Clarkson W.A. " 17745 " Salmon L.A. " 62268 " Hawkes G. " 9600 " Johnson W. " 65643 " Langton S.C. " 64554 " Paynes T.W. " 40049 " Putnam C.P. " 75736 " Penny J.S. " 46208 " Shipley C. No 20262 Q.G. Cobb & no 82037 Pte Barley S.J. were each taken on 20/2/1919 to Dispersal Centre on demobilisation.	

WAR DIARY or INTELLIGENCE SUMMARY

Army Form C. 2118.

(Erase heading not required.)

Instructions regarding War Diaries and Intelligence Summaries are contained in F. S. Regs., Part II. and the Staff Manual respectively. Title pages will be prepared in manuscript.

Place	Date	Hour	Summary of Events and Information	Remarks and references to Appendices
LE PARADIS	22	23	Total strength of unit week ending 22/2/1919. 4 officers + 137 O.R. Ranks. - 4 R.A.S.C. (M.T.) surplus to Establishment; 170 R.A.M.C. deficient. Vehicles as per "3" section establishment; 2 motor lorries surplus. No. 70666 Pte Clayton F.H. has been granted special leave to U.K. from 2/3/19 to 9/3/19. G.T.V.	
"	23	24	Church parade. In the afternoon transports the cooks house to all the billets. G.T.V.	
"	24	23	Cloudy windy. Again no pneumonia work. G.T.V.	
"	25	24	Marked temperature rather foggy. I am leaving the the unit to hand over command my Cadre. G.T.V.	
"	26	24	Mallet whole weeks. Recent commands my Cadre. Nothing to report. G.T.V.	
"	27	23	Truly 4 servant officer at 14.40 the great a much hoped T/Major L.S. W. Browne returned to take to early the following being N.COs, Miller W, Murphy Jas W, Thomas W, Roques J., Q R.A.S.C. Clarke; F. Kay/Cpl Sampleton T.H., A/c/Cpl Coulmar J., Pte Clark J.M.H, Rowe T., Gould E., Bell W., Macdonald J., Watkins T., Walkins R., Parnell C.J.R, Roberts, G.T.V.	

WAR DIARY
or
INTELLIGENCE SUMMARY.
(Erase heading not required.)

Army Form C. 2118.

Instructions regarding War Diaries and Intelligence Summaries are contained in F. S. Regs., Part II. and the Staff Manual respectively. Title pages will be prepared in manuscript.

Place	Date	Hour	Summary of Events and Information	Remarks and references to Appendices
LE PARADIS	28	24	Cloudy mild. No 161 Sgt Hodson P. rendezvous for UK from the 26-2-19. F 14-3-19 in charge. 7th Dennis T H S Pringle C. was on patrols with approval under the 27-2-19 — re-admitted under A.O. 4, 1918. TOD along R.Q. sent for week ending 28-2-19. 4 Officers & 135 other ranks. To expect re-attachment & re-open 4 Officers & 68 other ranks RAMC, train & R.A.S.C. drivers and has horses — 2 light carts approved & 2 ridden examples. On the morning of the 27th ult. Gue workable & 10 pts., purchases etc. 1.2. Capt Lansbury, TEMPLEUVE, to temporary duty.	

E.T. von der Nym
Lieut R.A.M.C
O.O. 113 & Field Ambulance

WO 38

Confidential

War Diary

From 1st March 1919 To 31st March 1919

113 Field Ambulance

14d/3551

Volume 38

17 JUL 1919
Capt RAMC
Comdg

Army Form C. 2118.

WAR DIARY
or
INTELLIGENCE SUMMARY.
(Erase heading not required.)

Instructions regarding War Diaries and Intelligence Summaries are contained in F. S. Regs., Part II. and the Staff Manual respectively. Title pages will be prepared in manuscript.

Place	Date	Hour	Summary of Events and Information	Remarks and references to Appendices
LE PARADIS	MARCH 1919 1	28	Nothing to report. 9.T.V	
"	2	24	Cloudy, cold. No. 204057 Pte Charles F (62) was admitted to No 39 Stationary Hospital on the 28-2-19 & struck off the strength from that date. No. 3345 Pte Clifford has been taken on Co Strength from 24-2-19 (Auth. D.M.S. M.P.1455 a/22-2-19). 9.T.V	
"	3	24	Dull raining. In the absence of 9 mornings all ale idle. M2/221740 Pte Banbury A.J was granted extension of leave to the 21-1-19 (Auth W.O.a.G. 45-a/13-1-19. 9.T.V	
"	4	23	Showing weather. Eleven O.R. on Y Corps Lorries were despatched to DOUAI to carry Pte demobilisation No. 64236 Pte Roots. S.B. was admitted to the 112 Pt. field Ambulance I and 2 V.D.H. 9.T.V	
"	5	28	Very mild. Pte Jewitt E. has been recalled leave to CALAIS from 5-3-19 to 14-3-19. No. 69167 Pte Tompkin H. No. 3345 Pte Clifford were deputised to the Dispersal centre for demobilization on the 3-3-19. 9.T.V	

WAR DIARY
or
INTELLIGENCE SUMMARY.

(Erase heading not required.)

Army Form C. 2118.

Place	Date	Hour	Summary of Events and Information	Remarks and references to Appendices
LE PARADIS	March 1919 6	24	Showing weather. Further repairs are being made to the men billets. G.T.V.	
"	7	23	Showing. In the forenoon Inspected the cookhouse & wagons. All weekly returns rendered. G.T.V.	
"	8	20	No. 401062 S/Sgt. Lawson R.R. having been demobilised written leave to the U.K. no officer of the strength from this 2-1-19. up to date noted strength 8 offrs + 8 others + 132 other ranks — 4 officers + 74 other ranks. R.A.M.C. agreement, 3 R.A.S.C. (H.T.), strength. Total strength 8 horses ie 2.5 - different. 8.12 draft horses. Made surplus. Rec'd a firm 3 section establishment. G.T.V.	
"	9	23	Showing written. C.R.M. Sergeants have sent U.K. from this 9-3-19. 6-23-3-19 + no 112053 Pte Ham A Special Fr the same honest - auction letter 16/7 Div A A/0-3/593 26/7 23-19. no. 204057 Pt. Clinton M. having been to hospital, is taken on the strength again. G.T.V.	

WAR DIARY or INTELLIGENCE SUMMARY

Army Form C. 2118.

(Erase heading not required.)

Instructions regarding War Diaries and Intelligence Summaries are contained in F.S. Regs., Part II. and the Staff Manual respectively. Title pages will be prepared in manuscript.

Place	Date	Hour	Summary of Events and Information	Remarks and references to Appendices
LE PARADIS	MARCH 1919 10	23	Cloudy mild. Good progress is being made in getting the wagons into good order again, properly tallied etc and thoroughly overhauled. G.T.V	
"	11	24	Windy very mild. On the forenoon 9 inspected all GS Wagons. G.T.V.	
"	12	21	Cloudy day, variable wind, miles. In the forenoon Stores B & C X Limp. knees were sent to HQ 10 B.A. Brigade R.F.A. to succeed G.S. Limbers H.M. was evacuated this a.f.n. 1127 Dvr L.C. Anker was admitted to no. 39 Stationary Hospital, on March 8th. On transfer from 10-3-19. no. 64972 La/Cpl Hodgkinson E.J. is appointed 2/Cpl with pay from 10/2-1-19. Auth A.G. 59/275/19 G.T.V. Lovely weather. In the forenoon 9 inspected the attire wagons, men kits of gunners the men kit & football match G.T.V.	
"	13	23	Cloudy but pleasant weather. Present strength gunners 1 400 & Officers + Rank 123 other ranks. + 2 Gunners - 4 Officers + 82 oth ranks dispatched, 12 horses.	
"	14	23	Ref. complete. Our present animal strength is 10 horses + 2 mules.	

Army Form C. 2118.

WAR DIARY
or
INTELLIGENCE SUMMARY.
(Erase heading not required.)

Instructions regarding War Diaries and Intelligence Summaries are contained in F. S. Regs., Part II. and the Staff Manual respectively. Title pages will be prepared in manuscript.

Place	Date	Hour	Summary of Events and Information	Remarks and references to Appendices
LE PARADIS	March 1919 14	23	The w/m N.C.O's given were despatches to the dispersal centre, 5 a day for demobilisation. No. 441553 Sgt. Munro B.F. " 9423 " Latimer R.C. " 217,15 Pte. Butterworth K.G. " 326.08 " Bush S.W. G.T.V	
"	15	23	Cloudy rain. No. 187/418182 St. Conolly D. R.A.S.C. attached were despatches to concentration camp for demobilisation yesterday. G.T.V	
"	16	23	No. 22245 Dr. Rowe J.W. (R.O.R. attacks) Army been evacuated to No. 11 C.C.S. (No. 112 R.F.A.) on return of the strength from the 15-3-19. On the afternoon of this party of fifteen N.C.O's, men in two motor ambulances to visit our old haunts at BAILLEUL, LOCRE, + KEMMEL. G.T.V	
"	17	24	Nothing to report. G.T.V	
"	18	23	Quite first weather for the summer. Inspected the Nisset wagon. G.T.V	

Army Form C. 2118.

WAR DIARY
or
INTELLIGENCE SUMMARY.
(Erase heading not required.)

Instructions regarding War Diaries and Intelligence Summaries are contained in F. S. Regs., Part II. and the Staff Manual respectively. Title pages will be prepared in manuscript.

Place	Date MARCH 1919	Hour	Summary of Events and Information	Remarks and references to Appendices
LE PARADIS	19	23	Fresh sunny weather. Capt. R.G Vernon has been detailed for Temporary duty at no. 42 C.C.S. No. 105856 Pte Taylor M. having been evacuated to no. 39 Stn. Hospital (via 112 F.A.) on the 18-3-19, is struck off the strength from that date. G.T.V.	
"	20	23	Very cold during the night. Had a fall of snow in the morning. Under instructions from A.D.M.S. our two mules were detailed for dropped down to the Base. G.T.V.	
"	21	22	Cloudy day variable temperature. Received orders from the a/a D.M.S. to send two light draft horses to the 11th Hampshires regiment. Our present strength is 4 officers + 120 other ranks. + 4 officers + 83 other ranks (R Am C) represent according to 2 section establishment Horses - out of the establishment of 34, we now have 2 lgt H + 5 heavy drgt. G.T.V.	
"	22	23	Cloudy very cold. Received orders from the a/A.D.M.S. - have my equipment and gun parked at TEMPLEUVE - near the station. G.T.V.	

Army Form C. 2118.

WAR DIARY
or
INTELLIGENCE SUMMARY.
(Erase heading not required.)

Place	Date	Hour	Summary of Events and Information	Remarks and references to Appendices
LE PARADIS	MARCH 1919 23	23	Lovely sunny weather. Issue the equipment most of the wagons return today to TEMPLEUVE. G.T.V.	
"	24	23	Cloudy pl. sunny. In the evening we have a dance for the Ambulance down at the factory received by the 155 Coy R.E.s. G.T.V.	
"	25	22	Very cold. No. 63688 Pte Vollans T. having been wrenched 6.39 Sty Hospital (no 112 F.A) in 23-3-19 is struck off strength from that date. The u/m N.C.Os & men were despatches to the dispersal centre to-day for demobilisation:-	
			72/5R/0173# Sgt Atkins C. of 144 Coy. R.A. S.C. attacked.	
			75/8398 " McCauley B " " "	
			00 Wilkinson G. Rome.	
			64297 Forrest C.S. " "	
			66780 " Bumbly E. " "	
			76340 " Ayling R. " "	
			58840 " Roberts C. " "	
			69348 " " " G.T.V.	
"	26	23	Pleasant weather. Sgt Reverell has been granted leave to U.K. from 27-3-19 to 10-4-19. Capt R.J. Vernon was deputized to the Dispersal Centre on 25-3-19 for demobilisation. G.T.V.	

Army Form C. 2118.

WAR DIARY
or
INTELLIGENCE SUMMARY.
(Erase heading not required.)

Instructions regarding War Diaries and Intelligence Summaries are contained in F. S. Regs., Part II. and the Staff Manual respectively. Title pages will be prepared in manuscript.

Place	Date	Hour	Summary of Events and Information	Remarks and references to Appendices
LE PARADIS	March 1916 27	18	Cold north wind. Lieut. George returned from leave yesterday afternoon. No. 1611 Sgt. Graham R. detailed for duty with No. 2 C.C.S., in stead of Cpl. Strong R. from this date. G.T.V.	
"	28	23	Cloudy & cold. In accordance with instructions from DG 2/1 D.M.S. proceeded to the HQ Corps Major J.B. Cavanagh M.C. proceeded to the 115 Corps where he is to take on the duties of D.A.D.M.S. to the D.D.M.S. He is struck off strength from to-day 5.T.V.	
"	29	17	Heavy fall of snow in the morning. No. 34349 Pte. Hay alack H. was admitted to the 112 F.A. with V.D.H. & on its return to 2/1 D.M.S. informed me that he was given two errors orders to be demobilised forthwith. G.T.V.	
"	30	23	The w/m N.C.O.'s men two cases at the Convalescent Camp to-day for demobilisation. Cpl. Hawkins J. Pte. Page P. Pte. Parker J. Sgt. Harmon J. "Fawcett T. "Trull W. Pt. "Cornwick a.w. "Phillips J. "Mawdsley F. "Wilson C.W. "Spiers B. "Seymour H.S. G.T.V.	

Army Form C. 2118.

WAR DIARY
or
INTELLIGENCE SUMMARY.
(Erase heading not required.)

Instructions regarding War Diaries and Intelligence Summaries are contained in F. S. Regs., Part II. and the Staff Manual respectively. Title pages will be prepared in manuscript.

Place	Date	Hour	Summary of Events and Information	Remarks and references to Appendices
LE PARADIS	March 14.19 31	12	Unit under, having received orders from LG a/A.D.M.S. to proceed home forthwith to be demobilised, have, on his instruction, handed over the command of the ambulance to Capt. F.W. Damond R.A.M.C. Authority to demobilisation is D.A.Q.M.G. mini M.M 314 (AmD.1) E.T. van der Vyver Lt. Col. R.A.M.C.	

Vol 39

Confidential

War Diary

113th Field Ambulance
140/3550.

From 1st April 1919 To 30th April 1919

Volume 39

17 JUL 1919

Major RAMC
Comdg.

Army Form C. 2118.

WAR DIARY
or
INTELLIGENCE SUMMARY.
(Erase heading not required.)

April

Place	Date	Hour	Summary of Events and Information	Remarks and references to Appendices
Le Pareds	1	9.0.	Fine day with bright sun throughout. Heavy rain commenced by the dusk from 8½. Van der Spuy inspected & inspected new pilots. Also inspected new readings No.s 45 & 48 both of which are claimed fairly serviceable. These are being up and No.s 8 & 3 49 Pts stopped & ceased to 38 Sta. Hos. full.	
"	2		Weather continues fine, slight fog during the morning. Visited station this morning & inspected new hangars & tentage are being built at Selly as field quarters - road for mess Maj. Brice 6 Pts Reinfs. to U.K. from 39/4/19 to [?]. Grated leave to W.O. from 7/4/19 to 14/4/19. A [?] airplane came down by airplane fully. Pilot uninjured. Three cairns used in plates to obtained. Amb. from 112 to Take Pilot back to no. 5 station	
"	3		Fine day - falling [?] weather worked. 12 Pts due after lunch - (Football match today 12/8 ofters - Jame Vft. Saw all [?] arms [?]. Funeral opened door to be [?] 64&3 Pts	

Army Form C. 2118.

WAR DIARY
or
INTELLIGENCE SUMMARY.
(Erase heading not required.)

Instructions regarding War Diaries and Intelligence
Summaries are contained in F. S. Regs., Part II.
and the Staff Manual respectively. Title pages
will be prepared in manuscript.

Place	Date	Hour	Summary of Events and Information	Remarks and references to Appendices
Le Havre	4	21.00	D.R.O. stated 3/4/19 — Men allowed to wear badges of rank as stated against name. Major J.W. Beaumont — Auth: C.B.S. 304 - Authority also rcvd affect pmnt rate of pay & Allowances. Very fine day. Dated Pass at Station this morning granted 11.2 J. Amts this afternoon him thirty scripts granted to (repair)	
"	5	"	first day.	
"	6	21.00	U.K. 14/4/19 to 8-3/19 728. 4 es 5'3 Pte Lear O.C. Reas.H.T granted leave to to ordinary Anne for Relief.	
"	7	21.00	No appointed no M.O Pr 9/4. Off. one - pete Tempture - waited previous Camp to wagon park. usual duties - Dated T. of ww. & wagon park affd	
"	8	21.00	" 5'9233 Pte Bond H. granted leave to U.K. 8/4 — 22 3/19 " 7/616156 Dr Thomas T Reas H.T granted leave to U.K. pvd from 9/4/19 to 2 3/4/19.	
"	9 10	21.00	Nothing to report.	

Army Form C. 2118.

WAR DIARY
or
INTELLIGENCE SUMMARY.
(Erase heading not required.)

1/4/19

Place	Date	Hour	Summary of Events and Information	Remarks and references to Appendices
St Paul's	11	21:00	Cpl Davis having returned from Corps med. Inspection fell into action. Assumes roledy N.C.O. for week.	
St Paul's	12		No. 64463 Pte Lewis G.E. granted leave to U.K from 12-4-19 to 26/4/19. Nothing to report, usual duties - every P.O. useful, carry & wagon park.	
"	13		M/2/63235. Pte Jacobs J.B. granted leave 14/4/19 at H.Q. front.	
"	14		No 68111 Pte Whitaker J.W. & 180036 Pte Wright J. transferred to 11.2 Infy Bde ambce & 1137 Lab ambc nch Myr. O.R.S 16 Dir Emy from dates 1.4.4.19.	
"	15		M/2 101431 Pte Roly L. M.T.C. & M/2 049720 Shurrock J. having returned to 16 Div M.T.C. on strength from 4/4/19 and April 5-5-19 respectively.	
"	16		No. M/2/193011 Pte Brown W.C granted leave to U.K 17/4/19 - 1/5/19.	
"	17		The fom. have been detailed to act as Cmtee Commtee Cpl Wood F. Pte McDonald J. Pte Hunter J.	

April

Army Form C. 2118.

WAR DIARY
or
INTELLIGENCE SUMMARY.
(Erase heading not required.)

Instructions regarding War Diaries and Intelligence Summaries are contained in F. S. Regs., Part II. and the Staff Manual respectively. Title pages will be prepared in manuscript.

Place	Date	Hour	Summary of Events and Information	Remarks and references to Appendices
Le Sombre	18	21.10	M.O. Company H.Q. having been dismissed whilst on leave to U.K. to which Coys strength as from 7.12.18 full. Past the unit at 14.00 hours.	
"	19	"	No. 41137 Pte Sulgrave I granted leave to U.K. from fund. 20.4.19 to 4.5.19. No. 16690 Pte Harding I admitted to 112 F.A. with gastr- enteritis. Pte S Battye G.C. degraded to R.A.S.C. training centre 14960 Ellechot & struck off strength as from 19.40 auth. S.A.J. W.M.C. 2110 9/1-4-19. Firstly all O.R. holding from now debited to time of leaving dates in army orderly Lists 253.	
"	20	9.00	nothing to report - full	
"	21	"		
"	22	21.11	The undermentioned were despatched to concentration camp Ypres for dispt - 41935 P.M. Sgt Thirlwin O.A. Reml. f/ 0.13.10.3 ML/ Perram A. Coss 417 f/ 0.35.5.19 " Walker 7 "	
"	23	"	Pte Thirland so struck off strength having been accepted for	

D. D. & L. London, E.C. Wt. W1771/M2031 750, C3 5/17 Sch 52 Forms/C2118/14
(A7091)

Army Form C. 2118.

WAR DIARY
or
INTELLIGENCE SUMMARY.
(Erase heading not required.)

Instructions regarding War Diaries and Intelligence Summaries are contained in F.S. Regs., Part II. and the Staff Manual respectively. Title pages will be prepared in manuscript.

April

Place	Date	Hour	Summary of Events and Information	Remarks and references to Appendices
Le Havre	24	2 pm	Fine weather - visited P. of war camp. Sent Dr McKeown to see Pace and Pte Oswald. Ordered me transferred to 1st Aust Gen Hos 46 Coy R.G.A. Dr Pace C.E att 46 Coy R.G.A. Pte Arthur granted leave to U.K 25th - 10th April	
"	25	"	Visited wages park -	
"	26	"	Visited wages park & P. of war camp - Handycraft cold & wet.	
"	27	"	wet & stormy - nothing to report	
"	28	"	weather still stormy - cold & wet - 5½°. Dr Ball G. granted leave U.K 29th - 13¾ ". Pte Chappell G. returning from 159 Aust Horse Cs & letter re strength of the unit. Pte Ashley struck off strength of this unit having been admitted to No 2 Central Gen Hos 2/4/18 Whilst on leave in U.K. Auth: & to Cmds 23/4/18 9 ⅛	
"	29	"	Very miserable day - rainy continually. Sgt Cyphus B. proceed to 14.7 Roylcen Fort Tilbury 1/5 for a further course of two not expected to Conv. Camp Fr Genesthalgen Dr Pochaine A. C.	

D.D. & L. London, E.C. Wt. W17711/M2031 750,000 5/17 Sch 32 Forms C2.-0/14
(A2001)

Army Form C. 2118.

WAR DIARY
or
INTELLIGENCE SUMMARY.
(Erase heading not required.)

April

Instructions regarding War Diaries and Intelligence Summaries are contained in F. S. Regs., Part II. and the Staff Manual respectively. Title pages will be prepared in manuscript.

Place	Date	Hour	Summary of Events and Information	Remarks and references to Appendices
Le Pradro	30	9¹⁵	Cold & wet, clearing towards evening - find usual routine - visited O.g. of war comp.	

J.W. Drummond
Major ?—
113 f. ant—

www.ingramcontent.com/pod-product-compliance
Lightning Source LLC
Chambersburg PA
CBHW080916230426
43668CB00014B/2140